Naked in Oh! Calcutta! and Other Stories

A MEMOIR

Samantha Harper Macy

(P)

PORTAL BOOKS

Library of Congress Cataloging-in-Publication Data

Names: Macy, Samantha Harper, author.
Title: Naked in Oh! Calcutta! and other stories : a memoir /
Samantha Harper Macy.
Description: First Edition. | Beverly Hills: Portal Books, 2021.
Identifiers: LCCN: 2021917984 | ISBN: 978-0-578-95621-3
Subjects: LCSH: Macy, Samantha Harper. | Actors and
actresses—United States—Biography. | Theater—United States—
History. | Motion picture industry—United States—History. |
BISAC BIOGRAPHY & AUTOBIOGRAPHY / Entertainment
& Performing Arts | BIOGRAPHY & AUTOBIOGRAPHY /
Personal Memoirs | BIOGRAPHY & AUTOBIOGRAPHY /
Rich & Famous
Classification: LCC PN2287.M188 N35 2021 | DDC
792/.028/092—dc23

Editing by CJ Schepers
Book design by Jennifer Mola

To all the boys I've ever loved

and

to my husband, Bill Macy, who put up
with me all these years with his wisdom,
humor, and appreciation for who I was,
who I am, and who I am becoming.

Contents

PART I

HARRIET

Daddy's Little Girl and All Her Boyfriends

PART II

SAMANTHA

The Rebel and the Rebellion

PART III

SAMANTHA AND BILL

Getting Down to It

PART IV

LA LA LAND

New Birth, New Life

CHAPTER 53

Foreword

I first met Samantha in 1971 during the production of the film *Oh! Calcutta!*

It was the theatrical pay-per-view, shot-on-videotape version of the scandalous off-Broadway review featuring nudity in short, bawdy erotic scenes, skits, songs, and dances. The pieces were written by a stunning array of slumming writers: playwrights, screenwriters—Pulitzer, Oscar, and Nobel prize winners—even a Beatle.

Samantha was part of the cast of five men and five women. I got a job as a production assistant, a gofer, through someone else in the cast, Bill Macy, an old friend of my father. I was seventeen, a sheltered, innocent high school student in Brooklyn with an interest in movies.

Billy Garber, as Macy was known in East Flatbush, had known of my interests and was kind enough to get me this gig. For no money but meals and a professional screen credit. My duties were wide and varied. Everything from finding, purchasing, and picking up one hundred corned beef sandwiches at 3 a.m. to pushing a raft across a pond while on top, Samantha and a guy, both naked, leisurely necked. All the while hiding my head below the side of the floating platform as I sank into the muck.

Samantha in her first big show was super professional, sweet, and fun. And Billy being the oldest, most experienced, and least inhibited cast member, was the defender and rabble-rouser of the troupe against producer injustices and cheapness. Soon thereafter, Samantha and Billy became a couple and then married.

In all the years I've known Sam I knew of her history generally, broadly. But until reading her memoir I didn't know all the amazing events, details, and insights she experienced. Her story is really quite remarkable. She seems to have been a part of so many seminal social and cultural events, like a Forrest Gump or a Zelig. Her memoir offers her unique POV of key zeitgeist moments.

A small-town country girl makes her way to the big city. She finds ways to overcome the obstacles that such a journey usually entails. Samantha's story is specific and universal, of its time and timeless. A metamorphosis from a small-town Southern girl to a mature woman on the large stages of New York and Hollywood, including a long marriage to a wild (in the best sense) and extroverted (to put it mildly) Brooklyn Jew.

Paying her dues. Learning her craft. Bravely taking the plunge and risking all to appear nude in *Oh! Calcutta!* But her down-home smarts and innocence protects her. She embraced the naturalness and honesty of performing in the altogether.

After writing a novel about powerful, supernatural women, Samantha has turned her attention to the men in her life—family, friends, and lovers and how they influenced her and she them. What an interesting cast of characters…

Pablo Ferro—the innovative, unorthodox designer who became a creative partner to some of the great filmmakers: Kubrick, Ashby, Jewison, and Demme.

Hal Ashby—whose humanist films ranged from comedies to dramas: *Harold and Maude, The Last Detail, Shampoo, Coming Home.* Samantha was in his Woody Guthrie biopic *Bound for Glory* and his gambler romp *Lookin' to Get Out.*

Norman Lear—who revolutionized TV, casting Samantha as a regular on *Mary Hartman, Mary Hartman,* the groundbreaking, surreal late-night soap opera.

Jon Voight—an accomplished star, who realized he could still learn something from Samantha's acting classes.

And the many fascinating non-celebrities she encounters in her life. For the most part, all very nice people. But more than a lucky coincidence as Samantha seems to bring out the goodness in others. A supportive cheerleader to her friends and colleagues, always encouraging and excited by their accomplishments.

I wasn't aware of all the struggles, illnesses, and difficulties Samantha went through. She kept them to herself but reveals them here. She doesn't complain about the hard times and doesn't gloat over her triumphs. Through it all Samantha maintains her kindness, curiosity, and generosity. As she told me recently, every day is a battle to achieve an open, loving spirit.

A fearless, hardworking seeker, Samantha has written an open, honest, tell-all (and then some). Racy and juicy, yet tender and sweet. Hedonistic, yet innocent. What a journey. What an adventure. I hope you enjoy *Naked in Oh! Calcutta!* as much as I did.

—Barry Strugatz, award-winning filmmaker, director, and screenwriter of comedy film hits, *Married to the Mob* and *She-Devil*

Preface

Samantha Harper Macy (*ne´* Harriet Lloyd Harper) was raised in the small town of Batesville, Mississippi, where she lived an enchanted childhood isolated from most of the larger world. Her vision of life changed at nineteen, when she was a sophomore present during riots at the University of Mississippi in 1962, sparked after James Meredith became the first black student to enroll there, allowing her to witness firsthand a key moment in civil rights history and the birth pains of momentous change in the Deep South.

After receiving a master of arts in Speech and Theater at the University of Illinois in 1964, she traveled to New York City, arriving in The Big Apple, a virginal young woman of twenty-one. Within seven years, she found herself on the vanguard of the sexual revolution, performing nude in stage and film versions of *Oh! Calcutta!* She watched the rise of the antiwar/hippie movement sparked by the Vietnam and Cambodia wars, the ravages of the Kent State massacre against unarmed students, and the downfall of Richard Nixon, meeting along her way an eclectic group of artists and innovators who'd influence the rest of her life. Her marriage to actor Bill Macy brought her to Los Angeles and the chance to chase her girlhood dream: to go to Hollywood and kiss all the movie stars.

Prologue

I entered my dressing room and stripped down to naked, put on a robe, and started gluing on eyelashes and painting my face. Red lips smiled back from the mirror and I laughed. Soon I would be dancing a slow striptease from the apron of the stage, staring into the darkness of a packed house. It would be a thrill, as always, a super-charged high with no alcohol or drugs, just pure adrenaline. An enchanted moment to be lived again and again for another year on Broadway.

"How did I get here? Me, this woman with a straight and narrow, innocent and conservative past?"

I'll tell you, if you like, first by flashing forward into a future that will come from this joyous, bareass-naked romp, then double back and earnestly tell my story from the start.

The year was 1988. We were at the beach. Actually, we were in the home of Hal Ashby, director of a decade of mega hits, including *Harold and Maude, Shampoo, The Last Detail, Coming Home, Bound for Glory, Being There, Lookin' to Get Out, The Rolling Stones: Let's Spend the Night Together,* and *The Slugger's Wife.* His was a two-story home on the Malibu Colony's one-mile stretch of beach property. The exclusive guard-gated community housed the wealthy, including a lot of artists and celebrities. Producers, directors, and movie stars lived and frolicked all around, thriving in the privacy and capacity to plan films, conceive music, and/or make megadeals, all while lying on their sundecks, roofs, or in beachfront parlors, the nearby ocean singing and dancing its various moods.

Hal's house was the oldest in the colony. A wood-frame house that made you feel like you were in a boat when you slept upstairs, with its steep-sloped ceiling of dark wood held up by hand-carved beams, as the sounds of waves lapped the ever-shrinking beach outside.

This particular afternoon, I was sitting beside Hal, who lay on a couch in his downstairs sunroom. I was holding his hand. Behind me there was a little kitchen, with a counter facing the beach.

From time to time, various others would come in to make tea, put something in, or take something out of the fridge, or just sit nearby. Usually, there would be another friend or two holding his other hand and/or a foot, instinctively knowing that when someone is dealing with a serious illness, human touch is the most comforting thing in the world. But now it was only me.

As we sat, I marveled at the number of incredible actors, directors, producers, musicians, cinematographers, and other film artists who were among his visitors or who had come and gone in the two or so months since Hal's escape from Johns Hopkins Hospital in Baltimore, Maryland, when he and Grif—who had a boy's name but was most definitely a girl—had made a run for it. Theirs was a great love, a ten-year romance that had deepened and become more precious with each day.

The doctors at Hopkins wanted him to stay and undergo experimental procedures, but Hal had wanted to come home. So Griffie brought him back to Malibu, opened up his Rolodex and called all his contacts, inviting everyone who wanted time with Hal to come, and soon.

And come they did. By the droves.

As we sat in the sunroom that afternoon, I marveled again at the deep feelings that all these people had for Hal, and at their creativity in relating to him, through their wit, their music, and the depth of their love, something you could feel when you passed through the doorway.

These were his lifelong friends and collaborators, many of them, and the newer ones, like me, had an instant rapport with him.

I'd played small roles in two of Hal's movies, but I was there primarily for Grif. We were very close—two young actresses from Alabama and Mississippi who had met in LA and fallen head over heels into each other's lives.

I loved her and I loved Hal. I was right where I wanted to be.

I leaned into him, "You are surrounded with the most amazing people. They are all such individuals. Incredible people and artists."

"You are one too, Samantha," he said. "You just don't know it."

He was right. I didn't.

But now as I think back on my life, what had brought me to that moment with Hal and what has led me to the present, I'm finally beginning to understand.

Fate, fortune, and my lucky star gave me a life that's been fascinating, both in the events that I've been allowed to witness, and in the paradoxes and contradictions of my nature and my times.

With your permission, I'd like to tell you my story, with its adventure, its comedy, and a bit of its tragedy.

It's the story of my life as seen through my loving experiences with men, with an homage to women who have offered a different perspective into love's magic.

But mostly, it's about the budding desire for and eventual fulfillment of intense, sensual, mysterious, sexual love…with all the fun and with all due respect to love's lessons that are carved into my soul.

And, it's about love that happens among artists—the undertow of attraction as we labor together to give birth to something new. Something significant.

Something beautiful.

PART I

Harriet

Daddy's Little Girl and
All Her Boyfriends

CHAPTER 1

MY DAD, MON PÈRE

I was a World War II baby, born on October 5, 1943, in Greenwood, Mississippi, and named Harriet Lloyd Harper for both of my grandmothers. My father was stationed at the Army Air Force base there. He was a flight instructor who taught pilots advanced flying skills needed for the raging war against Germany. He was the first love of my life. What can I say? We just dug each other from the start.

When my mom first set eyes on me, she let out a scream. "Oh no! She's too big! Her ears are floppy! And she's covered with a red rash!"

My dad took one look and said, "She's perfect."

He was an optometrist by trade and a healer by nature, able to pull almost anyone out of depression, fear, or defensiveness into good humor, courage, and self-acceptance. This he did by just being present, looking people in the eye, listening to them without judgment, and mirroring the intrinsic goodness he saw in them. It has struck me that his profession as an eye doctor was a cosmic witticism, a metaphor so plain that it would be missed by most people. He helped people with their vision, both physically and spiritually. He was also a teacher.

Dad taught me what he knew about love: that it was about the actions you take for the benefit of others, and the feelings of happiness and affection you feel in their presence. He taught me that to love was to see the good in people, even if they were out of touch with it in themselves. Also, that love involved granting freedom. To love truly, he said, meant I had to allow others the freedom to make their own choices without my interference or manipulation.

That last lesson of Dad's was the hardest for me. Most of what he taught me about love was nonverbal, but as for the freedom issue, he used words. Once, during my high school years when I was sad because a boy I liked was out with another girl, Dad said, "If you really love him and think he is having a good time, you'll be happy for him."

At the moment, I couldn't really take that in. But in the years that followed I began to see the value in his words. Not that I didn't suffer from jealousy now and again, but his bit of wisdom allowed me to create more love in my life than I could've ever imagined.

One day, we were on a long drive and hadn't spoken to each other for a while. We liked it that way, not feeling the need to entertain each other, liking the quiet. Out of the blue, he said, "If you hold out your hand and a little bird lands on it, don't close your fingers and trap him. That will only make him want to fly away. Instead, leave your hand open, and he'll always love coming to see you, knowing that he is free to choose."

This was a radical teaching for a young Southern *girl* in training to become a Southern *lady*, and it served as a counterbalance to all that society was teaching me about love: of being wary, of needing to be possessive and controlling, of competitiveness, and of the moral imperative to somehow own our mates and, in turn, be owned by them.

Not to say that precautions weren't in order. It's true that adolescents, male or female, aren't well equipped to handle sexual love. It's a force that's destroyed many young lives, so boundaries are definitely in order.

Yet, sometimes caution causes more pain than remedy. Men and women often fear each other more than they can love one another. My father's gift to me was the ability to create love, to make love, and to experience its transformative power throughout my entire life.

As I look back on my childhood, I see the budding and unfolding of my own feminine power as I began to discover this most mysterious force of nature. And, I'm still to this day, knocked out by the class of the boys I came to love—their spirit, grace, humor, and daring.

But most of all, their willingness to care for me.

This book began as a series of poems to all the boys I've ever loved. In the chapters ahead, some of my poems are included; they tell you not only the true stories of my life, but also the flavors of those times.

CHAPTER 2

BABY LOVE

When I was four or five years old, we lived across the street from a little towheaded boy named Duck Oldham. (For those who didn't grow up in the South, "towheaded" means having very fair blond hair, almost white.) I'm ashamed to say I'm not sure of the proper spelling of his last name. But in my defense, that's not something a four- or even a five-year-old girl was likely to know.

I remember we talked on the phone sometimes. Our parents would make the calls for us and let us visit that way. Or, we'd have adventures out in the world together, sometimes with my little brother, Sterling. I have a snapshot somewhere of the three of us: cute kids bundled up for cold weather, Duck in a cap with ear flaps and Sterling looking chubbier than he was, all wrapped in thick wool sweaters and a coat, his eyes flashing and that devilish smile beaming beneath his knitted cap.

Much to the consternation of my mother, my father had chosen to set up his optometry practice in her hometown of Batesville, a tiny, undistinguished place located on the first hill northeast of the Mississippi Delta. She'd hoped to move closer to his people down in Laurel, where his father, Dr. William Sterling Harper, Sr., was a Vienna-trained eye, ear, nose, and throat specialist who ran two hospitals, in addition to his own private practice. His home with my grandmother, Harriet, for whom I was named, sat comfortably on a street lined with gracious two-story wood-framed houses—most with screened-in front porches—and across from a park that was actually a small forest of dogwood and white pine trees.

She'd ring a tiny silver bell at mealtime and be served dinner, with her family when we were visiting, by her cook (who wore a black uniform with a white apron), all of us listening to Granddaddy's telling of the same gentle stories and jokes that he told every night. She called him "Dr. Harper" to his face and referred to him by that name in all conversations about him. She glowed in his presence and doted on his every word, utterly charmed by him.

But my daddy, Billy, had loved Batesville, and felt right at home in that small, sweet, unthreatening town. Our first home, across the street from Duck, was a small two-bedroom house that Daddy had rented from Momma's older half brother, Tom, who lived with his wife Sadie in the big house on the corner, facing away from our little rental in his backyard.

Almost all of Momma's family lived in Batesville and its surroundings: her two half sisters, Louise and Sadie Bell (not to be confused with Sadie Tom (Tom's wife), Momma's half brother, Penson, who wasn't quite right in the head, and her parents, Alma and William Peter LeMaster, who lived on a farm six miles out of town in an area known as McKiver, just over the Tallahatchie River and beyond Red Hill.

Only Miriam, my mother's younger and only full-blooded sister had managed to escape Batesville. She'd married Joe Saia, an Italian (an exotic choice in those days, especially since he was a head shorter than she was at six foot two in her stocking feet), and they moved to Wiggins in South Mississippi, an even smaller town than Batesville.

There, they opened a dry-cleaning store and started raising sons. Their nearest neighbors and closest friends were Dizzy Dean, the colorful, nationally renowned baseball announcer and his wife, Patricia. Both families left their doors unlocked so they could go in and out of each other's houses at will. South Mississippi was looser than Batesville and sounded exciting. But it was a five-hour trip away, so we didn't get to see Miriam and Joe except when they brought their boys home for Christmas.

Every Sunday my family would go out to McKiver to visit my grandmother, Alma and "Mr. Will," as they called my grandfather, out on their farm. Granddaddy wouldn't socialize much, but sometimes he'd sneak up from behind, poke me and whisper, "Hold out your hand." Then he'd drop a ripe fig that he'd just picked from a tree in his orchard into my palm.

He had a hard pain in his past. His first wife, Miss Sadie, had died giving birth to their fourth child. They'd been warned by their doctor that if she ever tried to have another child, she would lose her life. So, he carried a great burden as he faced her loss. He'd made a home for his children and the two daughters born to his second wife, Alma, but he couldn't handle a lot of noise, or music, or life. He spent most of his days out in the fields and pastures. He was present for meals when we sat down at my grandmother's round table, however, and always blessed our food with the same prayer, "We thank thee for these and all our many blessings. Amen."

Mammy, as we called my grandmother, was the social one. She held the family together with her humor, love, wit, good cooking, magic, and charm. All through my adolescence, whenever I was hurt or confused, I wanted to be at Mammy's house. I'd go spend a couple of days with her, catching the school bus into town. Those mornings, she'd run across the road waving a white scarf to flag it down for me. I'd ride my old plough horse, George, chase her chickens, pet the hound dogs and feed them bites of cornbread, and then lie in the grass in her front yard, sometimes watching the rain fall out of the sky (as long as it was warm and there were no signs of lightning or a distant rumble of thunder).

But when I was five, we didn't go to Mammy's house except on Sundays, though once in a while, I'd spend a night with her during the week. Most of my childhood was lived in that tiny house in town, where Sterling and I came home one morning after staying a few nights at Aunt Sadie's house to greet Daddy and Momma as they returned from the Memphis hospital (sixty miles away, and better equipped than the small Batesville clinic) where she'd given birth the night before. In her arms was our little brother, Peter.

In those days, Duck was my best friend and playmate. My hero, secret confidant, and pal. We even got away with playing "doctor" once in a while in a tiny tent behind our house—until we finally got caught and had to put an end to that.

I don't remember many of the times that Duck and I had, only that we had them. It was special every time Momma called me to the phone and quietly announced, "Harriet, it's for you," then whispered, "it's Duck!" It was a particular thrill to skip across the street to play marbles with him in his backyard, or to look out a window and watch him set the kickstand on his bike near the side of his daddy's garage, then leap over a little ditch to reach our narrow street, cross it, and stroll to our house.

When he died some years ago, I sent this poem about him to his widow, and she wrote back saying how much it had touched her and that she was glad to have it.

"Baby Love"

"I'll show you how to ride my bike!
You stand on the second step. Up here! By my back door.
I'll hold onto the handlebars,
Ready now, get set, GO!"
And, when I didn't move, he yelled "HOP ON!"
And I leapt, finding my feet, pedaling into the wind,
rising, like a kite,
Flying! My heart so light it sailed both me and that bike
For three whole seconds, maybe four
And the child in me did glide through
Heaven's gate on her first ride.

The bully came from out of sight,
kicking dogs and cats and tykes.
And Duck would grab his trusty bike and
ride to me and yell,
"HOP ON!"
And we'd make our great escape, holding tight
as our hearts raced.
I knew Duck would keep me safe.
He was so sweet, his manner mild.
He was the first true love of my child.

CHAPTER 3

ADOLESCENT MAGICIAN

At age seven, I began to discover dreaming, and what it takes to make dreams come true. It was a dawn of understanding that there *is* magic in our freedom to soar with imagination, and to feel with intensity our heart's desires. As you'll see, I still had problems with my timing (i.e., of turning my dreams into actual realities). This is a poem about my love life in the first grade of elementary school and the eight years that followed, crazy for a little redheaded boy named Larry:

"Young Love"

"I like you!"

"Go away!"

"But, I like you," I would say.

"Well, I don't like YOU!" he would bray,
laughing as he ran away.

"Keep your secrets," Mom implored.
"Don't let that boy get so sure!"
But my heart, so wild and pure,
could not wait to tell him more.
"I LOVE YOU!" Oh, for pity's sake!
He never did give me a break.

Three thousand days I longed for him,
and watched him court his sweet girlfriends.
At night, I dreamed and talked to the stars and healed his
wounds in phantom wars and cried for what could never
be and rocked his soul inside of me.
Eight whirling times around the sun, a nightly web of
dreams I spun and raged and wept and called the wind
and envied all his neat girlfriends.
Until we all turned sweet fifteen.

Girl-child passions a power brew, so faeries laughed
as dreams came true, and duckling down turned snowy
white and fireflies danced in soft twilight.
How odd that when he finally saw, his need,
his fire, his love so raw,

I bruised his heart, and saw it break.

Was it just for old times' sake?

Yes, I stole his heart and made it break

though I really didn't mean to.

Was it Father Timing's trick?

Or a faerie unbinding her spell in the very nick?

Waving her wand, scattering light,

catching a dreamer in her flight,

Whispering a truth that I already knew:

Some dreams really aren't meant to come true.

Or was God in His heaven tending his child,

Keeping her free to grow and play?

The boy and I were saved, anyway.

My heart had finally moved along

to others it would lean to.

My soul was singing siren songs

to new loves it had seen to.

The Batesville Elementary School building sat just off town square, like something out of an old faerie tale. Two stories high with a basement used for music classes, it was constructed of old red brick, warm to the eye, with a circular paved turnout in front, and white cement trim around the massive double-door entrance.

Its most favored feature was a large tubular slide from a second-story window that served as a fire escape. As preteen girls, we weren't allowed to wear our hot, new wire-rimmed hoop skirts to school for fear they'd reveal more skin and underwear than was acceptable in those days (you know, in case there ever *was* a fire). On fire-drill mornings, we loved sliding through that long, steep funnel on our way to safety, but we sure missed getting to show off our latest and greatest fashionable attire.

There were playgrounds on all sides of the building. The one for the little kids was out front, between our institute of learning and the town square's five-and-dime store.

That's where, at seven years old, I fell in love with Larry Robison. He was a head shorter than me, a scrambler who got into fights on the playground. I'd march out and fight anybody who was beating him up. He hated that. It's probably the reason it took me so long to win his heart.

Even though I won at least part of his heart, then bruised and broke it for a while, we repaired most of the damage done between us, and remained good friends and running buddies, dating on and off throughout high school.

CHAPTER 4

RANDY ON THE BAND BUS

Randy was cool. His mother was a high school English teacher. I had a mad crush on him throughout my sophomore, junior, and senior years. He never asked me out, but he played trombone in the Batesville High School band, marching in the front row behind me and the rest of the majorettes. I was new, having just made it through tryouts, trading my long wool pants and old band uniform for a short little satin and sequined outfit, strutting my stuff and twirling a baton instead of playing my flute back in the rank and files. On band trips, we gravitated toward each other, snuggled together on the bus in the dark, and made out like bandits. I guess that's what we were: bandits. Stealing kisses and cuddling and having a great old time.

The only dates I ever had with him were on Sadie Hawkins Day, where it was the tradition for girls to ask boys out that one night of the year. I'd ask him to go to a movie and have refreshments afterward and pick him up at his house in whatever car my family had at the time, while his mother and father stood in the living room and watched us, pretending to protect him with hidden smiles (enjoying the reversal of roles with parents of girls) out the front door.

Once for a joke, I sneaked his handkerchief out of his pocket while we were making out at a drive-in movie, then smeared it with red lipstick when I went to the concession stand to buy us Cokes and popcorn. Later, at his front door, I slipped it back into his jacket while we kissed goodnight.

The next day, he brought it back to me and said his mother told him to make me wash and iron it. She was witty with a dry sense of humor. I did as I was told and got a kick out of it.

In the end, Randy was the fish that got away. But that was okay, as I was discovering, there were lots of fish in the sea.

"Randy on the Band Bus"

It's getting dark, the night is sweet

It smells of fall and white boots polished

on marching feet and uniforms.

The snare of drums. The sax that hums,

then squeaks, then shrieks.

I grab a seat by the window, down the aisle

on the yellow school bus for the long, sweet ride,

far into the Mississippi Delta.

I see my boy there, hide my smile,

and hope he'll come and sit awhile.

When it's dark tonight we'll pleat up time and tuck our-

selves down deep inside, where a piece of us will always

ride, receiving timely shelter.

When it's dark tonight, we'll sail the tide that's drowned

the moon down deep inside the sacred pools of gentle

bliss, the warmness of his softest kiss.

And all I was before tonight is shouting,

"Helter Skelter!"*

As I'm diving with him into life, heading for the Delta.

*This was long before the murderous Charlie Manson, in the days when "Helter Skelter" meant utter chaos.

CHAPTER 5

HE LOOKED JUST
LIKE JOHN WAYNE

Johnny looked like John Wayne, though a lot skinnier, and he drove a panel truck for work and pleasure, long before anyone had heard of an SUV, though it served as one for us. It was a small delivery truck with a fully enclosed body, no rear windows, and a multi-purposed cargo area behind the driver's seat. Johnny used it on his farm and in town for recreation. He had a wicked but good-natured wit and a sharp mind, and he loved to laugh more than almost anything.

At our forty-something class reunion which I attended alone, he and his wife, Margaret, took me to dinner before the dance that Saturday night. We were being ever so proper; after all, I *was* an old girlfriend. We went to the Sizzler, parked, entered, and ate. He paid the check and escorted us to his car, opened the back door and settled me in, tucked his wife into her front seat, then walked around to sit behind the wheel. As he put the key in and tried to turn it, he stopped, dumbfounded. Then solemnly said, "This is not my car."

The car parked next to us was identical to the one where we sat, and was, in fact, his. The hilarity of the situation—us trying to be so cool and do everything just right—and the absurdity of us all settled into someone else's car hit us hard. We started laughing and couldn't stop. The next day, Margaret told me they had to sleep in separate bedrooms that night because every time one of them started to fall asleep, the other one had another fit of laughter.

Back to his infamous panel truck and our teenage years. Johnny lived on a farm and used the truck during the week to haul dry cow manure. On weekends, he swept it clean and used it for dating. Sometimes he'd put lawn chairs in the back so he and his date could double with other couples or just take a bunch of classmates and have one big party. Whenever we went out, we'd do tomboyish things, like go climb the fire tower and then get French fries and Cokes at a truck stop near the intersection of two state highways that edged our town. We hunted and collected bugs for biology glass and cut down a Christmas tree from who-knows-whose land, dragged it from the woods, put it in his truck and somehow got it to my house. We picked wild muscadines hanging in grape-like clusters and offering an intoxicating, exotic flavor, reaching the vines by standing on ladders that leaned against tall trees—the fruit hot and ripe, dripping in the sun. We'd squeeze their thick skins and shoot the pulp right into our mouths and still come home with enough fruit for Momma to make a jar or two of jelly.

I dated a lot of boys in high school. My parents' strategy was to keep me moving and get me into college still unmarried, and it worked because of two rules Daddy set down for me:

#1. I could never date the same boy two times in a row. I had to go out with at least one other boy before I could see the first one again.

#2. I had to make straight A's, or I couldn't go out on school nights.

As a result, I hauled ass and studied hard and was attracted to smart boys who liked school and did their homework. We'd study together, lured by the prospect of straight A's and more playtime. While we studied, sometimes the boys would tease, placing a hand on an "off limits" zone. I'd stab at them with my pencils (or a compass if we were doing math). At one of our later class reunions, several men showed me their scars, lead marks in their palms, still visible after all those years.

Johnny's panel truck saw a lot of action, including picnics and joy rides. We'd go cruising around town and look for buddies in other cars parked with their casual dates or more serious girl-friends. A bunch of us took a trip in that truck to the Mid-South Fair, sailing up US Highway 51 to Memphis, headed for the fairgrounds. We somehow got caught up in a presidential parade, a bevy of motorcycle cops behind us with Richard Nixon's limousine following them. We opened the rear door and waved at all of them. Closer to home, we liked to ride that truck around the picnic grounds at Sardis Dam in Panola County, Mississippi, and run over the limber saplings that were growing in the shadow of the big levy, just so we could see them spring back and forth.

Johnny once picked up my mother walking home from town and seated her in a lawn chair in the rear of his panel truck. But instead of dropping her off at our house, he sped past it and drove to the baseball field, still muddy and wet from that day's rain. He drove in circles, skidding around the field, laughing at Momma's screams as she slid around in the lawn chair in the back of his truck. She was only half-angry though and secretly loved the joke.

My senior year, Johnny asked me to our biggest class party, but I already had a date. It would've been a lot of fun to go with him. The next year, I left to start school at Ole Miss (University of Mississippi), while he joined the US Merchant Marines and became an engineer in that service. The Merchant Marines have ranks like military men, and great discipline and training. Many of them, like Johnny, became naval officers, lived a good part of their lives at sea, and travelled the world over. (The function of the Merchant Marines is of merchant shipping and the financing and manning of ships, a discipline particularly valuable to our country during war times.)

Years later when I moved to New York City, I stumbled one night into a bar in my neighborhood, depressed because I'd spent too much money on a dress. I was sitting having a martini at the bar when the door opened, and two men walked in: Johnny, who I hadn't seen since high school, and a pal of his. As soon as he saw me, without batting an eye, he turned to his friend, "I told you we were too close to home to do anything!" He'd just gotten back from sea duty and ended up convincing me to go change into that new dress for which I'd paid thirty-five whole dollars (a big sum back then, if you were making your living as a waitress). Then he took me out for a night on the town.

There were other nights in New York when he'd come to the Big Apple to advance his knowledge so he could qualify for a higher position in the Merchant Marines. He'd stay at their academy in Kings Point, Long Island, for a few days to study and endure a barrage of tests. One late night he called to invite me out to see him. I was waitressing at the celebrated Palm Court at The Plaza Hotel and didn't get off till 1 a.m. We'd had a big snowstorm, and I had to talk a cabby into taking me on that chilly and slippery, deserted twelve-mile ride. There was always a long line of cabs at the service entrance to The Plaza, because waitresses and other tip earners were notoriously good tippers themselves. By 4 a.m., I'd finally made it to Johnny's snug little quarters at the academy.

After catching up and celebrating with a few beers we suddenly got tired and stretched out on two single beds in his room. In the lightening of dawn, he said, "Come on over here and lay down with me. Hell, we've known each other for twenty-two years. You know I'm not going to do anything out of line." So, of course, I moved over next to him and let him put his arms around me. "Harriet Harper (my name at the time), I've been setting you up for this for twenty-two years!" His laugh was delicious and so was he. Johnny could always make my heart sing, though we didn't do the deed then or ever, as by then I was in love with someone else. And, so was he.

So, for you Johnny, I offer these sparse two lines:

"This free verse has <u>gone on</u>...
Some guys just can't be contained in a poem."

CHAPTER 6

"KILLER" AND HIS DADDY'S ICEHOUSE

His real name was Robert, and my mother said if I'd call him that, he'd appreciate it. So, I did.

And he did.

But everybody else called him "Killer" or "Kill Kill." It was an irresistible nickname for a fairly short, slim boy with braces on his teeth who'd run over a cow one foggy night in his daddy's car on the road to Sardis Dam. Whether or not the cow had actually died was always in question, and somehow, his father never learned the truth about how his Buick got bent the hell out of shape. Of course, everyone in school knew—and they never let Killer forget it.

He had soft brown eyes, and like all the boys that I liked, he was funny. Walked with a swagger. Planted begonias in his front yard. And his daddy owned an icehouse just off the town's public square.

That icehouse played a big part in why Robert and I lasted as long as we did.

He was older than me by two years, and that made my parents nervous. On several occasions, my dad tried to make me stop seeing Robert, but somehow, he stayed in the picture; that is, until one day he almost lost me for good and for all. There was a girl in town known for sleeping with any boy who wanted her, and a story was going around about the night she crawled out of her window and sped away in Robert's car to park on a dark country road. They were spotted and interrupted, and from what I came to understand, Robert's reaction was both irate and comical. The story was funny enough to get a lot of play, and I heard it being told all over school.

My puritan adolescent self was incensed, and when he came to my house to try to see me, I let him have it, "How dare you! Get lost, goodbye! I never want see you again," or something rather dramatic like that—filled with the full force of my rage.

A few nights later, he showed up again at my house and said, "If you want to break up, okay. But let me just show you one thing first." He pleaded and I gave in, driving off with him and not even knowing where he was headed. It turned out to be the big dirt parking lot in front of the icehouse, which now sat in darkness away from the street. He got out and asked me to follow him and we walked to the large, insulated door of the ice locker, where water gets poured into forms and freezes. Then the forms are removed and the ice is stored as tall blocks, ready to be cut and crushed for customers ordering ice by the pound.

As he unlocked the door and opened it, it suddenly occurred to me that he could lock me in there and leave me to freeze to death till morning. But curiosity won out and I entered the huge dark room with him. Then Robert snapped on the lights.

My heart stood still. The room was filled with color. He had put food coloring in the vats of freezing water, and the blocks of ice standing all around made a rainbow of yellows, greens, blues, reds, and violets. I stood there breathing the cold air, stunned and amazed at his inventiveness and nerve. Whether he realized it or not, I knew (though I couldn't verbalize it at the time) that this was the act of an artist. He was sharing something of himself. No apologies. Just a demonstration of who he was. I was also instantly aware of what the stunt would cost him with his father.

I think we went out for a Coke after that. I didn't mention leaving him again but broke up with him about a year later. I don't know why, but I think my father won the last round and persuaded me to not let myself get tied down too early.

It was a bittersweet end to a small romance that was not without its magic.

So…a few words of not quite verse to an old, old soul.

"Robert"

My darling Robert, Killer, too.
Tragic-comic dancer that you were,
You hid a pain I could not name.
I loved the touch of you.
Your mystery, too.
And your braces never got in our way.

CHAPTER 7

THE OUT-OF-TOWN BOY

Nothing's as exciting to a young girl as an out-of-town boy driving a good distance just to date her. Especially if the boy's handsome and from an exotic place like Itta Bena, a tiny plantation town deep in the Mississippi Delta. Many years later, the legendary B.B. King named his blues club in Memphis, The Itta Bena Restaurant, for the town where he was born and to celebrate the richness of the spot. Even though B.B. King was pointing mostly to the black community, Jimmy Duncan who was white, also did his trombone playing time with ease, hard work, and a sense of fun. Often players from both sides shared their tricks of the trade and grew together from making music. In those days, there was a friendly crossover between black and white musicians, when music was music—a space that touched no other place.

Jimmy was thrilling in all the musical magic I've mentioned. He was also tall, blond, cool, and strikingly handsome with an off-beat athletic vibe. And, ahh! Oh yes! We met in the coolest way imaginable.

Mississippi has had for over half a century an award-winning all-state band sponsored by the Lion's Club, the largest service club centered in cities around the planet. It's now comprised of 1.4 million people working to improve the world through helping those in need. One of their focuses has been excellence in music. For most of the years since its inception, the Mississippi Lion's band has won top international honors, both in concert and marching. Every year, the band is rebuilt from scratch and auditions are held to fill new positions. So the competition among musicians, drum majors, and majorettes for those coveted spots has always been fierce.

Players, of which Jimmy Duncan was destined to become, must be proficient in sight-reading, scales, arpeggios (productions of tones in a chord, in succession and not simultaneously), concert playing, and marching. Drum majors must conduct complex musical compositions as well as lead and inspire. Majorettes, of which I was destined to become in my own right, must be proficient in dancing, twirling, and strutting, and must perform with unbounded enthusiasm, joy, and stamina.

Back home in Batesville, we were in full-out competitive mode, and as it were, landed more than our share of majorettes. Sue Evans marched in the band twice, both in 1959 and 1961, her sophomore and senior years. Bonnie Ferguson, Peggy O'Neal, and I were picked in 1960, our junior year (amazing, three girls from one small town in that humongous interstate competition).

The entire band, once formed, rehearsed at Ole Miss, twenty-three miles from my home. The players convened in a concert hall to prepare for an indoor competition before being taken outside to practice their playing while marching. Meanwhile, we majorettes were taught our routines in an indoor studio and then joined the rest of the band on a field near the boys' dorms to prepare for our upcoming parade in Chicago—the "Great American City!" A dreamland.

Behind the drum major and a few dashing twirling majorettes was a lineup of eleven girls, each carrying a large wooden letter that spelled out "Mississippi." Being the tallest in the bunch, I hoisted the middle "S." We heaved our letters this way and that, up and down and all around, while behind us, the band played "Grandioso," a well-known parade march composed in 1901 by Roland F. Seitz. Powerful horns, stirring percussion, and a delicate, delicious solo piccolo countermelody surrounded and embraced us.

Back then, Jimmy played trombone in the front row right behind me, but it took a while for us to find each other. My first memory of him was our trip to Chicago, long after our rehearsals at Ole Miss. The "Windy City" was abundantly rich in culture and thrilling for our 150-some Mississippi teenagers.

After we'd gotten settled at our hotel, the adults chaperoning us organized a little evening trek for the whole band. Not knowing the city, we naturally followed their lead, taking a raised train out to the Aragon Ballroom, which was designed in a Moorish style with an interior reminiscent of a Spanish village. The huge dancehall, named for a region in Spain and within close proximity to the

Chicago "L" (elevated railway) made it a popular Chicago attraction for decades, often with crowds in excess of eighteen thousand during each six-day business week. Secret tunnels under the nearby Green Mill Bar, an old-time hangout of Al Capone, led to the Aragon's basement.

The place was five miles Uptown from the Downtown happening city. It was dark and had images of luminescent clouds floating back and forth across its ceiling. It didn't take long, however, for some of us teenagers to tire of that. So Jimmy's date, Nan McGahey, and I asked the chaperones if the four of us (including my date, whose name and face I don't remember) and another couple could take public transportation back into town.

Permission granted, we all went to hear Jack Teagarden, a famous trombonist and singer, perform in a restaurant jazz club that sat beside a river which opened onto Lake Michigan. After the show we boarded a boat that was docked near the front entrance for a moonlit ride on the Great Lake. The rest of the trip is kind of a blur. We were in town for less than a week and had both a concert and parade to perform, so there wasn't much free time. Some of us did make it over to the Second City comedy club to watch actors improv suggested skits that the audience shouted out to them. They were outrageously good.

The trip was a walk on the moon and the parade its highpoint. Marching, strutting, and dancing in windy sunshine with rich sounds of music swirling around us…well, it was a teenage high for the ages.

As we boarded the bus for the all-night ride back to Mississippi, Jimmy and I managed to swap seatmates and ride together. (I'm beginning to see that I had a thing for dark buses and handsome boys.) The night gave us semi-privacy as the bus traded flickering lights of the big city for the dimness of the interstate highway, and I nestled into his arms happy to stay there till morning. We even dozed off some, my head on his shoulder. When the bus arrived in Oxford, home of Ole Miss, all our parents eagerly awaited their offspring. I saw my mother, grabbed Jimmy's hand and walked him over to her, saying, "Mother, I'd like you to meet the boy I slept with last night."

Now, Jimmy and I email each other from time to time, and he recently reminded me of that moment. He joked that he almost had heart failure when those words tumbled out of my mouth, but then suddenly my mother was laughing, and he knew in that instant what a terrific relationship I had with her.

That experience of Jimmy's was a great reminder of the exceptional times I'd spent with my mom. The last two decades of her life were awful for her and for me. She suffered and was a monster at times, seducing me with her sweetness one moment and breaking my heart in the next with her malice and ire. I didn't blame her though. She was in a lot of pain, and pain in itself is a monster.

When Jimmy reminded me of that transcendent moment, celebratory, joyous, humorous, and fine, he gave me back a piece of my mom. Memories that I'd buried for a while came alive again.

I treasure these memories, much as I treasure the long miles that Jimmy drove to see me and our walks on the beach at Sardis Lake. He was a year older than me and getting ready to start college at the University of Mississippi. He took me to a pre-rush frat party in Jackson for the Ole Miss Chapter of Delta Kappa Epsilon (DKE), and a few months later, stopped by to see me on his way from Itta Bena to Oxford for precollege enrollment.

The next year I became a freshman at the same school, and Jimmy took me to the Pi Kappa Alpha Roman Ball, where the boys dressed in togas (I don't remember what the girls wore) and we all danced till we were drenched with sweat and high as the moon on beer drawn from kegs on the front lawn and hot music on the dance floor. A few months later, I took him as my escort to our sorority date night, all gala and balloons at the Kappa Delta House.

Then he disappeared from my life. I'm not sure how or why it happened. We were all drinking and partying many a long weekend and working hard as students. As almost a joke, another boy I was dating gave me his frat letters to wear on a chain around my neck. And, I believe around that time, Jimmy met his future wife, Elizabeth. For whatever reasons Jimmy and I drifted apart. More than fifty years went by before I heard from him again. Out of the blue, he emailed me, saying his grandson had asked if he'd ever had a girlfriend before his grandmother. He told the boy yes, several, but only a few had touched his heart. In thinking over that conversation, he realized—one of them was me. I smiled to remember how he'd touched my own heart. Sometimes life is just plain sweet.

After years of teaching and coaching, Jimmy was recruited into "corporate America"; he'd had a long business career, capped off by the dream job as director of the Memphis Botanic Garden. It's stunning to see pictures of the place and note the beauty he's brought to that spot. He recently sent me a photo of him at Lake Louise in the Canadian Rockies taken by his wife on their ten-day vacation. They've been happily married since 1965, and have a terrific life, complete with children and grandchildren. The whole nine yards.

I remember him as a boy who loved long drives, walking on the beach, and playing trombone. And that moonlight ride around Lake Michigan after hearing the legendary Jack Teagarden playing his jazz trombone into the night is, well, a hard memory to beat.

Jimmy was a class act.

A Southern gentleman who played a mean horn. And, who gave me along the way, not only beautiful memories that stretch way back, but also a priceless reminder of how wonderful Momma really was.

CHAPTER 8

MY MOM, MA MÈRE

I started this book with words about my father, what he taught me about love, especially about loving men, but also about being a lover of people, of life itself and its magic. But my mother also had a part in that.

It really does take two to tango.

Her tango with my father was full of affection, laughter, sensuality, and goodwill. They were a great team, and now, after many years of remembering only how tough she could be and how hard the end of her life was (on her and on me), I'm flooded with memories of her brilliance and fun. She set the stage for my rambunctious adolescent years and for a wide range of attitudes—from strait-laced puritan to wild, outrageous free spirit—about love and sex that I still embrace and sometimes wrestle with in my own, ongoing tango with love.

Boys were always welcome at our house, especially wild packs of Mom's students (she taught English at Batesville High for years, quitting when I reached fifteen and entered school there, so as not to cramp my style). I remember a horde of high school seniors sitting around the kitchen table, eating apples from her wooden bowl—they ate so many that she ended up buying plastic fruit. They'd be talking or joking around, seeming to enjoy her company whenever I passed through. She loved good fun, and our house was a magnet for pranks.

One Halloween, after rolling our yard with toilet paper, a bunch of drunken boys wrapped a chain around the oak tree that stood at the front end of our lot, next to the driveway. They had the other end of the chain tied to the rear bumper of their car. They yelled and threatened to pull down our tree, then sped away into the night, tearing their bumper right off and leaving it in the middle of the street. Howls of "damn you, Mrs. Harper," echoed up to our house. Of course, we knew they didn't really mean it.

My mother's advice when I got old enough to date was, "Enjoy the boys, but don't let things get too heavy. Keep the mood light." Eroticism was something never mentioned, or thought of, for that matter. When glimmers of fantasies came to me, I squelched them before they could even get started.

I've often said that if you put William Faulkner, Tennessee Williams, and Pat Conroy in a room with a case or two of good bourbon, they'd probably write a story with a lead character like my mother. To understand her, you'd have to know blistering heat. Mississippi heat. Her childhood simmered and boiled in it, and in the intense heat of loneliness for her father, William Peter LeMaster.

Her mother had seen him once take a horse-whip to his second son, a mentally unstable teen-ager, the child of his first wife, who'd died while giving birth to their fourth child. This made my grandmother overly protective of her own children, and she kept them away from her husband, William, as much as she could. For Mom, to be cut off from this markedly accomplished, yet remote and taciturn man, felt like rejection. For years, she suffered quietly and deeply from it until she went off to college where she met and married my father, whom she adored.

Together they set out optimistically, yet with different goals. His was to become a quiet country optometrist, connecting with people one-on-one, bringing his gentle humor and willingness to listen to their stories, their lives with an open heart. He loved creating a world of peace, happiness, joy, and healing.

Hers was to reach for the finer things in life. To seek the beauty in music, theatre, literature, and art—and deeply experience it. To recreate it in her own life as best as she could. And, of course, to love and worship my dad, her hero and salvation.

Her lighter side was playful. She was a fine and popular teacher, adoring great literature and sharing her passion for it with her students while keeping her sense of humor and love of good fun always in the foreground.

She was my champion, my confidant, my good friend. That's why it was all the harder whenever her darker side appeared, throwing her into violent rages that were sometimes short-lived, but frightening nevertheless—leaving me feeling unworthy of her love. Between fears of displeasing her, and trying to live up to my dad's image of me as *perfect*, I was pretty boxed in.

I stayed that way not only through high school, but through three years and three summers at Ole Miss, nine months of grad school at the University of Illinois, and two-thirds of my first year living in NYC.

There was, however, merit in this initiation of my life with all its pleasures and pain. My parents' good cop/bad cop method of controlling me instilled a measure of safety. Interlaced with her moments of tough, emotional bruising, there were also amazing adventures, intimate conversations, and the sharing of her innate wisdom about much of life. Times of closeness that, indeed happened, but with less frequency in her later years—when she was deeply shaken by tragedy.

There is much more to tell of those times, and of her, and much more to tell of her beauty before her fall.

She'd led a full life before a roadblock put a screeching halt to her wondrous path. But I'm getting ahead of myself. There is more to unfold.

A story worth telling, in its own time.

CHAPTER 9

SHADOWS AMONG THE CHURCH BELLS

Until l left for college, I'd lived in a small, semi-rural, largely segregated town. When I say "largely," I speak of a paradox of race relations in Batesville and the surrounding areas. In many ways, the whites were closer to the black communities in Batesville and other small North Mississippi towns than metropolitan areas like New York City and Chicago. Even though there were social barriers, and in some cases, hostilities founded on bigotry, I'd witnessed very little of that in my early years. The predominant energy I experienced with the black people in my life was love. So, I mistakenly assumed that treating all races with respect, as my family had, was the norm.

Yet, there was an undertow. A silent danger, an established unfairness that I sensed and felt but couldn't understand or hope to address, much less solve. In my younger years it didn't surface often, but I do remember two instances worth telling.

Both involved Eloise Gates, the most beloved of all our nannies (or "nursies" as we called them). There were others I remember, but no one that could touch her. She was with us through all our junior high and high school years, and my brothers, Sterling and Peter, and I adored her. Pretty, sweet, and deeply kind, Eloise was in her thirties when Mother hired her. She cooked and did a little cleaning (though that wasn't her strong suit), played with us, and covered our tracks when we were bad or had forgotten to do our chores, or make our beds. She fried the best chicken and sizzle-baked luscious cornbread, setting the iron pan with the breadstick molds into the hot oven till the lard in each tray melted and bubbled, then dropped in batter from a spoon where it splashed and crackled as she closed the oven door. She'd boil our butter beans and field peas with slabs of salt pork, cook our okra with butter, and made the best skillet corn and turnip greens I ever ate.

She was unmarried but had a lot of children at home. She gave birth to two of them while working for us. When she was pregnant with her last child, my brothers fiercely competed for her attention. Sterling would start by saying, "Name it for ME," then Peter would chime in "No! Name it for ME!" and the two would start chanting it over and over, literally begging till Momma or Daddy made them stop. When Eloise had her baby, she named him William Sterling Peter after Dad and my two brothers. She called the child Sterling, and he grew up to be a nark reporting drug infractions to the local police, and later a good chef at the local country club. He also cooked for the best restaurant in town out on Highway 51. But that's another story.

Author Kathryn Stockett wrote *The Help* some years ago, a novel-turned-movie that portrayed a class of white people in Jackson, Mississippi, who wouldn't allow their black "help" to use the bathrooms in their fancy houses. I was outraged to hear that. Eloise was welcome to use all the rooms and every facility in our house and so were the maids of every family I knew. We thought of her as a second mother, a part of our extended family, and she loved us back with loyalty and pride.

That's why I was also shocked one night when Eloise ran into trouble at the town square after witnessing some kind of brawl or street fight. The police were called and turned their attention to *her*. Questioning quickly turned into accusations and intimidation, and possible violence, until an uncle and a cousin of mine stepped out of the crowd to protect her.

Dad was white as a sheet when he came in and told us what had happened and how lucky it was that Bubba and Tom had been there right at that moment. I'd never thought of Eloise as being vulnerable or unsafe in our town, and had no clue that black people, without white friends to defend them, could encounter real danger just going about and living their lives. I know this sounds naïve today, but I was a preteen living in the 1950s, and much of what was going on around me was hidden.

On another occasion, after Eloise had moved into town from across the Tallahatchie River (which bordered Batesville and had been its center before the railroad came through), she managed to buy a small house on a street behind the public library and the Methodist church, when tragedy struck, and she lost her new home to a fire. At that point, my father loaned her the money to rebuild and when she was ready to paint her house, inside and out, I wanted to go over and help. My mother took me aside and said, "Harriet, you can't do it. If you go to her house and some nut doesn't like it, he might just take it out on Eloise or her children. If that happened, it would be your fault. You cannot risk their safety, no matter how much you want to do this with her."

It seemed to me that there must be an under-culture lurking, out of sight from most of the people I knew. There was almost no clear evidence of it, yet there were hints and clues, now and then. It was a shadow slithering beneath our golden, wholesome world. I could never have imagined the monster that would rise from that slimy subterranean pool less than a decade later.

But I'm getting ahead of myself. Just take this as a preamble to the story I'm about to tell you regarding my life at Ole Miss and the momentous beginnings of change that I was to witness in my future.

CHAPTER 10

WINDS OF CHANGE

I spent three years, including unforgettable summers, at the University of Mississippi. It was a time of monumental upheaval, transition, and chaos. As a young woman, I witnessed changes so profound that they were paving the way for a new South, while at the same time, being a normal college student, I adhered to the longstanding reputation of Ole Miss as primarily a party school. It was also a school of scholarly achievement and academic merit, but we played that down as best we could.

My first year there was relatively calm, filled with all the feelings of a girl who'd once been a big fish in a small pond and now found herself a minnow surfing waves in a sea of academics, theatrical productions, and an emerging social life. But at the beginning of my sophomore year, my perception of my world changed, dramatically. Ole Miss was taken by surprise and shaken, as was the whole South, in a violent, shattering eruption of opposing forces in our culture.

On October 1, 1962, having won a major Supreme Court battle, James Meredith, a US Air Force veteran, became the first black student ever to attend Ole Miss. The rest of the student body had arrived in September and were settling in. There was a mix of great fanfare and massive tension on Friday, September 28, when Governor Ross Barnett (one of a number of state officials openly against Meredith's enrollment), had to escort James into the Lyceum Building so he could register there as a student. I was in The Grove, a park that faced the Lyceum, ideal to watch the men that exited their black vehicles surrounded by guards, ascended the stairs, and passed through glass doors. As the Governor turned to acknowledge the onlooking crowd, I noted his grim look and the snap in his eyes, hinting that this peaceful day might not last into the night.

The Grove on the old campus is graced with more than thirty kinds of trees, among them oak, ash, elm, holly, pine, sycamore, walnut, sweet gum, flowering dogwood, and magnolia. It's flanked by

Fulton Chapel, an Ole Miss landmark that was converted into a 650-seat theatre, and several other Georgian-style buildings, as well as the aforementioned more modern Lyceum Building.

Truth be told, although most of the gathering crowd was curious and there to see history in the making, my main goal (and that of most girls at The Grove that day) was to find boys who'd be our dates for the upcoming football games. Back then, coeds didn't go to ballgames unescorted, and any sorority sister who found herself dateless at game time pretty much had to hide under her bed till the night was over, to save her reputation. I remember one weekend when I had no date till just minutes before game time. An older sorority sister ran in breathless to say she'd found someone to take me. When I asked if he was cute, she hesitated, then said, "Well, he'll do in a pinch—and this is definitely a pinch."

That early fall day at The Grove, the light shifting through changing leaves in a warm, lazy, almost sultry breeze, we all waited to catch a glimpse of James Meredith. I sat on the shoulders of some big guy (can't remember his face or name), my eyes on the car that carried James as it pulled up to the front steps of the Lyceum. A reporter stood beside me with a press pass (real or not, I'll never know) that said *Chicago Tribune*. As soon as James stepped out of the car, the "reporter" took off his press pass, tucked it in his pocket, and started loudly chanting, "Get that nigger!" hoping to start a riot. None of us joined him, however, and he found himself shouting alone. Eventually, he melded back into the crowd and clipped his press pass back to his outside pocket.

In the weeks prior, Governor Barnett had ordered the highway patrol to surround the campus for our protection. Newspaper articles from neighboring states urged people as far away as Louisiana to come make a last stand for "states' rights." There were some real thugs hanging around the highways and byways of Oxford, and later that night, through a mysterious executive order, the highway patrol was ordered to stand down, and our campus was soon riddled with violence. Cars were burned, a French reporter was shot dead, and tear gas hung in the air, clung to buildings and tress, and found a permanent home in low-lying sidewalks and pathways.

My parents drove twenty-three miles from home to rescue me. But from the time they got me in the car till we'd reached the Batesville city limits, I wept, screamed and begged them to take me back to campus, asking who'd be left in charge if all the peace lovers ran home?! I guess I made my point, because they suddenly gave in, turned around, drove back to Oxford, and dropped me off at the rear entrance to my dorm—probably glad to get some peace and quiet.

My roommate Carol MacKewen and I quickly established a phone network with some of the dorm boys, plus sorority and frat house students. We were in the thick of *everything*. The reporter who was shot fell right outside our window. We were on the first floor, and Carol risked her life to go outside, wrap him in my blanket and then hold his feet up, thinking he'd had a heart attack. He'd been taken away (we didn't know whether he was dead or alive) by the time I rushed back from my quick trip to Batesville.

Guys from the boys' dorm told us that the highway patrol had returned, and were shooting tear gas *into* the boys' dorms, forcing them out and into the dangerous riots. Finally, Saturday morning came, and with it, President Kennedy's orders to activate the Mississippi national guard and to call in Army troops from Memphis, Tennessee. As I recall, a paratroopers' division was also present, along with military tanks and trucks. All in all, thirty-one thousand army troops, national guardsmen, and marshals descended onto the campus. Injuries were in the hundreds. A second man was shot dead in the night, a white jukebox repairman. No one knew why. In the weeks to follow, as we made our way to classes, our eyes continued to burn from leftover tear gas. The mood was grim. Depression and shock affected everyone. But the heaviness eventually faded. You can't keep wide-eyed, optimistic Ole Miss coeds down for long, at least not forever.

We broke the ice with the US Army and national guardsmen and even made friends with them over time. My part in that happened this way: military men set up checkpoints across campus and stopped cars indiscriminately to search for weapons or any other signs of danger. Even though I still lived in the dorm, I was also a Kappa Delta and took my meals at the sorority house. Every Thursday, the cook made chicken potpies, which we hated (we liked our chicken fried and didn't care for English peas, potatoes, and starchy gravy with a crust on top), so there were always mountains of them left over. Among us was a particularly beautiful, buxom blonde named Jan Harris. We persuaded her to climb into the trunk of one of our cars holding a silver platter stacked high with chicken potpies, then drove around through various checkpoints till we got stopped. When the soldiers ordered us to open the trunk, Jan popped up holding the tray and said in her sweetest Southern voice, "Hi! Are ya'll hungry?"

Soldiers streamed out from the nearby woods; rifles drawn. They converged on our open trunk and were instantly stunned by Jan's beautiful face, grace, and style. Her sexy little skirt, sweater, and knee-socks didn't hurt either.

Everything was better after that. The military guys relaxed a bit, seeing that most of us weren't only nonthreatening, but also friendly and playful. The campus settled down. James made it through his first year and the rest of his time there without serious incident, partly I'm sure because he was under 24-hour federal protection.

After watching interview after interview on TV with the most uncouth ragamuffins the press could find as examples of typical Ole Miss students (most of them had little or no education, were dirt poor, and unkempt), I learned a valuable lesson about the media's quest for sensationalism over the truth. I also learned about the complexity of truth—it doesn't ever fit neatly into boxes—and no group can ever speak for all of society.

Even now as I look at articles about the Ole Miss riots of 1962, I wonder how much of history has been slanted. Troops topping thirty-one thousand seems excessive, knowing that our student body was only five thousand. But these facts have been uniformly reported, and I believe them to be true. Some historians say the integration of Ole Miss was the last battle of the Civil War. Even standing in the thick of violence that night, I hadn't realized the extent of what was happening.

Rumors were flying about who was responsible for removing roadblock stops and other barriers going onto the Ole Miss campus. I believed, and still believe, that the initial protector force was the Mississippi Highway Patrol. Articles talk only of US Federal men in charge of the scene. But Federal Marshalls wouldn't have motive to shoot tear gas into boys' dorms.

Some reported that Ross Barnett gave the order for the highway patrol to stand down. Others blamed Senator George Yarbrough for that atrocity. NPR and NCPR report that while Ross Barnett publically promised to block James Meredith from campus in Oxford, privately he was on the phone with John Kennedy trying to strike a compromise. Whether it was Barnett or Yarbrough who called the patrol down, those officers failed us. Federal Marshalls were then deployed, fighting against (at least some of) the state highway patrollers who were dumping tear gas into the boys' dorms to escalate the riot. That part of history is a little murky and very messy. I do know with clarity my experience of the student body of Ole Miss, and I want to report that here.

At the time and in all the years that followed, I never heard one person—not a frat brother, sorority sister, a fellow student, a staff member, or any theatre major among my friends—ever utter a disparaging word about James Meredith. I never heard anyone express hatred against him or threaten violence.

That said, there certainly was an underground bigoted element among us, and we saw evidence of it when a student in the Speech and Theatre Department had her room vandalized after she'd hung out with James at the Student Union Building. That was *chilling*. Even with the white-robed pointed-hat boogey men in the dark of our figurative basement, bigotry on campus was never approved of or condoned by teachers, staff, or the student body as a whole. For most of us, James's presence was not an issue. Making good grades, earning scholarships, and exploring extracurricular and social activities (including boys looking to start careers and girls looking for their MRS degrees) were foremost on our minds.

We were naïve and selfish not to realize how traumatic those years must've been for James himself.

Like the legendary American baseball player, Jackie Robinson, James Meredith was in a league of his own.

Mostly, we were still kids. Life and Ole Miss held potentials for us that were irresistible. I got my first taste of freedom, my first break from home, and a heap of adventures, especially after I joined forces with another wild-girl virgin like myself. We honed the art of partying with the boys without giving away more of ourselves than we wanted to. Raw and green as we undoubtedly were, we did love playing with the young men of Ole Miss.

And, we loved loving them—even if it was just a little bit.

CHAPTER 11

ME AND THE OTHER WILD VIRGIN

I had absolutely no serious relationships with men while I was at Ole Miss, though there were momentous times partying with extraordinary, unforgettable guys. I believe my reluctance to "settle down" and my attraction to boys who didn't want to was because of a dream I was holding in my heart. It had begun in secret much earlier and had gathered so much momentum—that by the time I reached college—it couldn't be stopped.

Better said, it had taken hold of me, and I didn't want to stop it. Dreams have power, at least the ones we keep alive. When we imagine something we want, feel our desire for it over and over again, picture how it would look and feel to have it, dreams that begin as mere fantasies can become real possibilities. And if we come to believe in them, give ourselves to them, live inside them as if they were real (at least for part of our days and nights), they continue to grow in power, eventually triggering actions and events to support them.

In other words, dreams can come true.

My "power dreams" began to emerge when I was a teenager hiding my bruises from the world. Like every kid on Earth, I sometimes felt left out, got my feelings hurt, longed to belong, and didn't always feel that I did. I ached for the adoration (yes, I admit it) of talented, beautiful girlfriends who sometimes snubbed me and for admiration from boys who chased after them but seemed not to like me at all. Feeling lost and abandoned often, what with my mother's moods and the unpredictability of my girlfriends jockeying for position within our crowd, and me with no steady boyfriend, wanting instead to play with "all the boys," I needed something from a mysterious future that would make me feel safe. Make me know that I was going to be all right. Better than all right. I was going to be terrific. Someday, I'd be ravishing, an exotic beauty, and all of them would see me and care for me. I'd belong.

So, I dreamed of going to Hollywood and becoming a movie star, and fed that big dream for hours, days, weeks, months, years. And all the baton twirling, strutting, flute playing, tap dancing, talent shows, and beauty pageants that filled my nights and days fueled my desire to see that dream realized.

I dreamed of having the allure, mystery, and beauty of Marilyn Monroe, Jane Russell, Ginger Rogers, Bette Davis, Myrna Loy, Barbara Stanwyck, Lee Remick, Joan Crawford, Lauren Bacall, Katharine Hepburn, Elizabeth Taylor, Carol Lombard, and Natalie Wood to name a few (and believe me, there were plenty of others) of the goddesses who ruled the Silver Screen in my day.

Even more, I longed for intimate encounters with rugged, handsome, sensitive, creative, charismatic male actors—the film gods who played opposite those magnificent women and ignited our passions in dark theatres on Saturday nights. Actors and actresses enjoyed intimacies in their work that weren't publicly sanctioned anywhere on Earth, certainly not in the South. I'd brag to our crowd that someday I'd go to Hollywood and kiss all the movie stars. That felt like the ultimate freedom—like that of wind, rain, and fire.

When I told my mom of my plans, she immediately amended them. "You don't mean Hollywood, Harriet, you mean New York. You want to go to New York and become a stage actress."

"Okay," I said. If that dream made her more comfortable, I could go for it. Besides, New York was appealing in its own right. My dreams shifted their locale, but not their intensity.

By the time I got to Ole Miss, reveling in my virginity, which I wore like a halo, the acting dream became my ticket out of the Deep South. As it drew me on, I got cast in college productions and discovered, I really *liked* acting. And my passion grew up even as it grew wider and deeper. So, unlike most of my peers, I didn't pursue an MRS degree from Ole Miss or a business career in Mississippi. Instead, I cashed in my ticket to ride out of the South and into a much larger world filled with possibility, adventure, freedom, mystery, and as it turned out, magic.

But the fact that I didn't really "get it on" with men in college didn't stop me from developing one of the deepest friendships of my young life—with that other proud virgin I mentioned before—Kaffie Mallette.

Of all my beautiful roommates and sorority sisters, she's the one I loved most. We first roomed together in summer school after my sophomore year, and she taught me how to belly up to the bar and drink beer with the boys, to challenge myself and them, to see and believe in myself as being on equal footing with the best of them. All hard liquor was illegal in Mississippi, but each county voted on whether or not to allow sales of beer and wine (i.e., to be "wet" or "dry"). Oxford, home of Ole Miss was in a dry county, so getting legal alcohol meant driving thirty or forty miles to a road-stop dive beyond the county line—a little dump of a place that served pickled eggs and crackers along with tall, cold pints of beer. Liquor laws in Mississippi were screwy and dangerous. They almost buried me, could've caused a crash that put me under once and for all. But I'm getting ahead of myself.

During that summer with Kaffie there wasn't a problem in the world that could bring us down. She helped me bust me out of my parents' self-imposed rules (they'd stopped drinking by the time I reached college and never introduced me to alcohol or taught me how to handle it). Kaffie had zero hang-ups about downing booze. She did it with zest, humor, flare, and enthusiasm. She passed her style onto me, and we boogied many a night double-dating with boys we liked at the county line (girls never went to drinking holes unescorted), always managing to walk a straight line into our dorm before curfew. Most importantly, she taught me how to behave the morning after I'd made a fool of myself getting drunk and throwing up on the side of some highway on the way back to school, saying, "OH NO! Don't be embarrassed. This is the fun part! Just put on your sunglasses when you see the boys and say, 'Oh, GOD, can you BELIEVE last night?!'"

We trolled for dates at the Ole Miss Annual staff office, drinking rum and Cokes in the dark room with photographers and writers. We took road trips to the Gulf Coast and Vicksburg, hocking our possessions to pay for gas, sleeping on floors, staying up all night in a club in Gulfport (on the Gulf of Mexico) to watch our buddies play and sing in a folk band, then getting them to buy us breakfast in the morning.

Someone once asked me how we could've remained virgins while partying so hard with red-blooded young men. It must be said that in those days, college men were, for the most part, gentlemen. Southern gentlemen, at that. Kaffie and I had a nose for those who weren't and never put up with anyone who tried to push us to places we didn't want to go. In the 1960s Deep South, NO meant NO. Boys planned to live where they'd been raised with future careers to think of and future wives who'd expect them to behave as honorable men. Boys who had sex on their minds as a top priority usually found girls who were willing and got married early, many under the gun, as there was zero access to birth control for unmarried girls.

Today, according to the 2015 documentary *The Hunting Ground,* which I saw at an early screening, one in every four college coeds is raped on campus. This happens in even the most elite Ivy League colleges and state universities. Rape was unheard of at Ole Miss back in the 1960s. Fierce chaperones and housemothers protected their girls. Boys (our guys, anyway) were also our champions and protectors. As I mentioned before, Kaffie and I knew we could trust the men we dated. We had a nose for the good guys, and never were attracted by any others. It was a different time. Beautiful in its own way.

On campus, Kaffie lived on hamburgers with mayonnaise and sweet pickles, and Cokes. She'd put out her cigarettes by standing them on their filters across her windowsill, little soldiers all in a row. She had a gorgeous face with killer dimples and a beguiling sense of humor. And, she loved and accepted me at first sight, without reservation. We'd raid the halls of our dorm for leftover fried chicken and French fries thrown out by other girls. She stood by while I crammed for tests late at night, burning the candle at both ends so I could make my grades, and earn a fellowship to grad school (as my parents had sworn me to do). They'd wanted me to major in Education, thinking it would ensure me a teaching job. I promised them that I'd win a fellowship and earn my master's degree, making me eligible to teach in college, if they'd let me study Speech and Theater.

Before big tests, we'd take Dexedrine (better known in those days as "speed") to study, but I was the only real student in sight. She'd get high and start cleaning our room or sharpening her pencils. Whatever activity she was doing once the drug kicked in, she'd do *all* night. Kaffie got engaged to a great guy that summer. I made straight A's as I'd promised my parents.

Eventually, our summer together was over.

There was a legend at Ole Miss about the statue of a Confederate soldier that stood in The

Grove. Graduating classes filed past him on the way to receive their diplomas. It was said that if a virgin ever passed by him wearing her cap and gown, he'd tip his hat to her. Kaffie and I swore that if he didn't tip for us, we'd blow his friggin' head off. Fortunately, for us and for him, we graduated after summer school the following year and our diplomas were mailed. We'll never know if he would've tipped. I'm sure somewhere, a ghost of a soldier is glad.

Another highlight of my time at Ole Miss was the kiss that the legendary Johnny Cash gave me at the end of his campus concert, rushing off stage and into the audience to grab me and plant a big one on my lips. I heard he'd whispered afterward to one of the frat brothers taking care of him, "I didn't kiss the campus whore, did I?" They laughed and told him no, he was safe on that front.

Another splendid memory: staying up at the DKE House watching Julie London, the sultry singer and actress, play poker after her show, and, oh yeah, the not-so-splendid memory of almost getting kicked out of school after someone reported me to the Dean of Women for drinking beer.

This was a campus where kegs were tapped on fraternity lawns and bottles of beer packed in washtubs were there for the taking. Now and then, one person got arbitrarily punished, made an example of just to keep the law alive. That's what happens when laws are blatantly unenforced, seldom enforced, or randomly enforced.

Hard alcohol was illegal in Mississippi in the 1960s. Various counties had voted wet for beer and wine, but you couldn't *legally* buy hard liquor anywhere in the state. Yet, the two cities on the Mississippi Gulf Coast (Gulfport and Biloxi) were dripping wet and wide open. Flashing neon signs depicting people sipping rum drinks with little umbrellas toppling out of cocktail glasses lit up bars along the beach fronts.

Liquor laws were the doing of teetotalling Baptists and greedy bootleggers, strange bedfellows for sure, but together, a powerful coalition. For the most part, the laws were a joke. But the liquor laws had a darker side, too—they were used to keep racial and ethnic minorities "in their place" and the socially unpopular, powerless and separate. Why I was targeted, I'll never know. I must have really pissed somebody off along the way.

Whoever ratted on me for drinking beer also said that I'd entered a boys' dorm on a campus north of Ole Miss, which was true. Earlier that year, we'd made a rest stop at a Tennessee college on the way home from our concert singers tour of the World's Fair in NYC. I'd sleepily stepped off the tour bus to use the dorm's bathroom and returned just minutes later.

I'd been on a roll for three years and three summers at Ole Miss without a sign of trouble. Now I was a scapegoat—and in *big* trouble.

At my hearing before the Dean of Women, looking at the student council females that flanked her, I noted that every one of those girls had been drunk with me, numerous times.

I gave a fine piece of acting at that hearing, half of me knowing that I was on trial for my life, and the other half watching me perform. I drew a few tears from my fellow students telling them how hard my parents would take my expulsion from school. And, I learned that trying not to cry is a good deal more powerful than a cascade of water sliding down my cheeks.

The fact that I was in every honorary society on campus and had been offered fellowships from the University of Illinois and Yale, in the end, held some sway. They put me on probation for six weeks, and all ended rather reasonably. We were in my final semester, and within a few months I was released from Mississippi and on my way to the adventure of a lifetime.

The Big Apple—where the good times rolled. But for Kaffie and me, it was never goodbye. She stuck with me through my wildest times, then and throughout my life. And bless her, she was my champion in Mississippi after I'd let New York City and its enticements influence me more than I, or anyone else I knew, could've ever predicted.

CHAPTER 12

THE BOY FROM CHICAGO

How can I possibly jump into my NYC years without telling you about the outrageous nine months I'd spent at the University of Illinois earning my master of arts, and about Jay, the boy who shared some spectacularly classy times with me?

Jay was a tall, good-looking, smart (VERY smart) guy working on his master of science on his way to a PhD in physics. We met in the fall and dated during the two semesters I'd spent there, and also partied with a group of his super-intelligent, cosmos-tripping mates who became my friends, too.

They stood by me through a chaotic, threatening time.

Ole Miss had barely escaped being demonized after the riots of 1962 when James Meredith became the university's first black student, and in spite of this storm at my alma mater, by a stroke of good fortune, I'd received a full fellowship to study performing arts at the University of Illinois.

Mississippi had recently produced two Miss Americas in consecutive years—Mary Ann Mobley and Lynda Lee Mead—and was enjoying a reputation for gracious Southern living, generous hospitality, and beautiful women. That ended in a swift, thudding crash in June 1964 due to the horrific murders of three young civil rights workers: James Chaney, Andrew Goodman, and Michael Schwerner in Neshoba County, near Philadelphia, Mississippi.

By the time I'd arrived on the campus in Champaign, Illinois, in the fall of that year, the faculty members who'd voted to grant my fellowship had some serious changes of heart. They questioned the choice of me as a fellow, decried my Southern speech, and refused to consider casting me in their productions.

"Well, she can't be in my Shakespeare!"

"Or, my Chaucer!"

"Certainly not my Molière!"

Anonymous people slipped horrible photographs of young black men who'd been lynched under my dorm room door. Coming from Mississippi, I was instantly regarded as a bigot and a redneck by many who'd never even met me.

Strange as it may seem, I wasn't bothered by the slurs against me. Whether or not they were meant to frighten, intimidate, or punish, I didn't know. I did know who I was and what I had stood for in Mississippi—and that I had no need to prove myself. I found these biased perceptions of me odd, ironic, and kind of funny.

I *had* been utterly intimidated by the thought of performing on the big stages of the U of I campus and extremely nervous about auditioning and being accepted as an actress. Now, all that trepidation and stress was behind me. I'd never be considered for casting by any of the faculty members, period. It was an odd relief. As a native Mississippian, I'd been branded and sidelined, and that was that. But there was a plus side to all this. I was suddenly on course to receive my master of arts in record time. In nine months, in fact, if I minded my "P's and Q's," I'd be done and free of school. Having met my part of the bargain with my parents, I could choose to either go home and teach in a Mississippi college *or* fling myself into NYC and try to make it in legitimate theatre. I could go for the real deal and dream—a career in show business.

My college advisor gave me a key to the library stacks, where I worked many days and nights. My one acting assignment was in a small and undemanding production of Sartre's *No Exit* (directed by a graduate student), leaving me ample time to explore the musty library shelves for material on ancient theatre history. I spent nine months doing research on the lives and styles of long-dead actors and for my quasi-thesis, wrote a paper on the nineteenth-century British Shakespearean actor Edmund Kean, a turbulent genius noted for his portrayal of Richard III.

Meanwhile, I had to undergo a regimen of classes.

One of them was a directing class taught by Miss Clara Behringer, an overly eccentric teacher. She asked us to select a scene from classical theatre, cast it, rehearse the actors, and perform it in her class—all the scenes in just one afternoon. I chose Shakespeare's "Mechanicals' Scene" from *A Midsummer Night's Dream*.

But I had a problem: I didn't know anyone in the theatre department, so I had no actors to cast.

As luck would have it, soon after, Jay took me to a party one Saturday night with some of his friends from the Physics Department. I asked if they'd act in a scene for me, and they all said yes. Bless their hearts, they were willing, eager, in fact, to jump in, even though none of them had ever set foot on a stage before. They came to rehearsals happily and on time and were fabulous sports about putting in the long hours. I, being very inexperienced (having never directed anything before), spent much rehearsal time trying to make them look and perform like actors. I coaxed Jay into taming his gentle stutter. I pounded away on one stone-faced young man who looked like he was in a constant state of shock and taught him how to limber up with facial exercises. I tried to make the shy ones bolder, the brash ones gentler. In short, I attempted to neaten them all up and make them as presentable as possible.

When my troupe arrived in class the afternoon of the performances, they fortunately, forgot everything I'd tried to teach them. Jay stuttered louder and harder and more frequently than ever before. Stone Face locked in his expression and stared wildly into the lights, and all the rest of my actors reverted to their individual eccentricities—brashness, bashfulness, and the stumbling awkwardness of being in an unfamiliar setting. They were themselves, warts and all—and they brought down the house. The students in the audience laughed till they cried. The scene was the hit of the afternoon and, at the time, the greatest success for me at that school. When it was over, Miss Behringer stood up and faced my fellow students who were still wiping tears from their eyes, and said, "Well, that scene is pretty much foolproof."

She was right, of course. I couldn't take credit for that little miracle. It was a gift. I'll never forget those daring "lost boys" acting so earnestly, giving themselves to the imaginary circumstances, putting on their small play for the king. They were bold, brave, and beautiful. And, they were a riot.

Jay and I had lots of fun together. He took me to meet his parents in their gracious home in Winnetka, Illinois (just outside of Chicago), during an ice storm of astounding beauty. We had some fabulous nights on the town in that frosty, windy city. I took him home to Batesville to meet my parents, and they loved him. We talked about getting married but decided not to. He confessed that what he needed in a wife was someone to keep him grounded and take care of his social life, while his mind was off soaring through the galaxies or plunging into subatomic particles.

I told him that if I didn't go to NYC and reach for my dreams, I'd never forgive myself (or him) for talking me out of it. So, we let each other go.

We were ships on separate courses. But there was moonlight on the waves beneath us and occasional flashes of phosphorous from the ocean to mirror the stars. Wherever he is, I hope he smiles, remembering.

I know I do.

And now, finally, and at last, I can take you to NYC with me. Hang on to your hats—and prepare to ride!

CHAPTER 13

LEPRECHAUNS

When I arrived at NYC's legendary Barbizon Hotel (exclusively for young career-seeking women) on the dusky evening of September 16, 1965, I was met by two angels...or faeries...or perhaps they were leprechauns. They may have been ordinary men, but in light of how events unfolded from that peculiar night, I have come to quite seriously doubt it. They were, I like to think, guardians or counselors perhaps, from one of the many alternate universes to our own. Whoever they were, they sure made one grand welcoming committee.

My plane had traveled through rain and fog, and the woman sitting next to me kept saying how brave I was to move to New York, knowing not a single soul there. Fortunately, she was blind and couldn't see the tears streaming down my face during much of the flight. In my purse, I had a check for $600, borrowed from The Batesville Security Bank with my master of arts degree as collateral (my promise to the bank was that if my career in NYC tanked, I'd come home and secure a job in Mississippi to repay them). That money was all I had to start my acting career—that and a reservation for a week's stay at the Barbizon—an expensive but safe, upscale space that a stranger had recommended on my train ride home after finishing grad school.

To add to the drama of my arrival in NYC, the bus from the airport passed cemetery after cemetery, miles and miles of miniature skyscraper-like tombstones in the shadows of the big city looming ahead.

I'd promised my parents that I wouldn't go out after dark (can you imagine that?), so when I got to the Barbizon, I hurried to check in at the front desk and stash my luggage in my room, then scurried out in the dimming light to buy a newspaper at a sidewalk newsstand. I needed that paper to search the want ads for a job and was lucky to get it: it turned out to be one of the last to be delivered citywide before a huge newspaper strike commenced the following morning.

When I came back in and was getting settled, I realized my room had no phone, so I went down to the lobby to call my parents from a payphone. After letting them know I'd arrived safely, I hung up and turned around to see two small, ethnic-looking men watching me. They asked if I was new in town and said it would be their honor to show me around my first night in the city. Of course, I said no. I couldn't leave the hotel after sundown and certainly not with strangers. They said, then how about having coffee in the shop right there in the hotel? It was just off the lobby, and I thought, *Oh, what the hell!* Over coffee, they put me at ease. Charmed me, I guess you might say. Whatever it was, I felt totally safe with them. They somehow convinced me to go upstairs and change into my best clothes while they waited in the lobby and made calls for last-minute reservations all over town.

When I came down in my little black dress and string of pearls, they escorted me to a big, dark car and drove us downtown to Lüchow's, a German restaurant on East 14th Street at Irving Place near Union Square (in the East Village). It was exquisite. The dining room was big and grand, and the food was out of this world, though I don't remember what we ate.

Afterward, they took me uptown to The Plaza Hotel on Fifth Avenue and 59th to hear Jane Morgan sing in the chic nightclub called the Persian Room. She was a glamorous, classy songstress and put on a fine show. Then we went for dessert to a small cafe on the Upper East Side where members of the press gathered to talk about the upcoming strike. In the wee morning hours, my kind escorts returned me to the hotel, happy and safe and, dare I say, mesmerized by the city—but only after a quick stop at the landmarked skyscraper Seagram Building on Park Avenue, where they photographed me in front of a fountain lit beautifully in the night. On the way back to the Barbizon, we drove down Madison and up Fifth Avenue where they pointed out spectacular places of worship in the city—St. Patrick's Cathedral, the Fifth Avenue Presbyterian, and the St. Thomas Episcopalian churches, as I'd expressed a desire to find a spiritual home in the Big Apple.

My memory over time was that I didn't hear from them again for exactly one year, but according to letters that I wrote to a friend, which she returned to me decades later, I'd reported that they called me every day for a week to see how I was doing.

On the one-year anniversary of my arrival in New York City, I'd just started working at The Plaza Hotel—the very same hotel where we'd gone that night to hear the singer, Jane Morgan. I was a waitress in The Palm Court, just steps away from the famous Persian Room where we'd seen her that night. I loved that job for many reasons, but especially because the friendly maître d's would let us waitresses take turns sneaking into the Persian Room to watch top performers do their nightclub acts. One of my favorite maître d's, Harry, was on duty that night. I wandered up to him and told him the story of my first night in NYC, then asked for permission to go into the hallway in the side lobby to make a phone call. While I was putting my dime in the payphone and turning to my left, a man next to me was inserting his dime and turned to his right. As we faced each other, my jaw dropped. He'd been one of my two out-of-nowhere escorts my first night on the town! He excitedly told me that he'd just invented a plastic horseshoe for racehorses and was going to make a million dollars. He almost clicked his heels as he turned and headed out the door.

Yep, I think he was a leprechaun, and his buddy, too. That's the best explanation I've been able to give myself throughout the years. Though guardian angels definitely come to mind, and counselors, guides, and faeries do, too, that lucky horseshoe of leprechaun lore might be the deciding clue. In the end, it doesn't really matter the worlds from which they came, or even if they were part of humankind. That night, for me, they hailed from inexplicable realms of mystery and the Great Unknown—a place of benevolent generosity and the magic of pure, gracious love.

That evening launched a series of events that allowed me to stay in NYC in style and to pursue my dream with unprecedented ease. I'll tell you all the ins and outs, with the somersaults and surprising tumbling turns, though it'll take some "twisting of the rope," as they say in Ireland (a Celtic metaphor for the fortunes of love).

CHAPTER 14

THE BEST THING YOU CAN DO IS FALL IN LOVE

When a city opens its heart to you, there's no mistaking it. The morning after my first night in (and on) the town with those two quirky, oddly mysterious fellows, I saw a want ad in my *New York Times*—the one I'd snatched from the shadow of the looming paper strike the night before, and it was now more precious to me than gold. An employment agency was searching for a five-foot-ten model with some ridiculous numbers of 35½ x 28 x 39, certainly not the standard for models. But the sight of those measurements in print jolted me awake like a bolt of lightning. They were my exact measurements.

When I arrived at the employment agency, I was met by a petite blonde woman in a smart business suit, high heels, chic haircut, and tasteful jewelry. After screening me and noting that I fit her ad's description to a T, she sent me off to The Tall Girls shop downtown for an interview, but also instructed me to come back and see her afterward, whether I got the job or not. When I returned still jobless, she asked point blank, "I see you are staying at the Barbizon. Can you afford that?"

"Not for long," I smiled.

Then she told me her story. She was only temping at the agency. Her name was Peggy Simmons, and she and her husband, Bill, had until recently worked as highly paid executives in a large corporation with offices in the city. The month before, while the two of them were on vacation, "a coup," as she put it, happened in the company. They returned to discover that their jobs were gone, taken by others in a swift power play. So, Peggy and Bill were stranded and desperate to hold onto their midtown Manhattan apartment. She invited me to come meet her husband and see their place, perhaps to rent a room and bath from them to help cover their costs.

Their apartment was on the twelfth floor at the corner of Second Avenue and 52nd Street. Beautiful trees planted at intervals adorned the well-kept street. The apartment had two bedrooms, two baths, and a spacious living room with parquet floors. Tucked in a corner was a small kitchen equipped to serve gourmet meals. A dining area with a long table of dark wood looked out through a sliding glass door to a wraparound balcony open to the sky, complete with patio furniture and a view of the five-star Waldorf Astoria Hotel on Madison Avenue. A grand piano graced a corner of their living room. Their furniture was comfortable and tasteful. To top it off, they owned a rambunctious and fluffy, black Standard French poodle named Hillary.

I rented a room with my own private bath for one hundred dollars a month. Meals were included as part of the deal, which I think they came to immediately regret, as I almost ate them out of house and home. Bill cooked beautiful meals. He served us martinis or manhattans and *hors d'oeuvres* before dinner every night. I, being an overgrown teenager, could never get enough to eat in those days. I cleaned them out of breakfast cereals and leftovers. Luckily, they were terrific sports about it all.

Most important to me, Peggy and Bill had been actors in their younger days and knew the ropes. They taught me to start buying *Back Stage* and *Show Business*, the two most important weekly publications with updated lists of acting, modeling, and advertising agencies, as well as open auditions. They advised me to take an acting class and had me sign up with a teacher they knew and trusted. They also told me to find employment in the restaurant business, saying that the hours wouldn't interfere with my fledging career. After one day waitressing at the eatery called Schrafft's (which I never could pronounce correctly), I landed a job as a hostess at Patricia Murphy's 49th Street Candlelight Restaurant. It was just off Fifth Avenue across from Saks and in sight of the Rockefeller Center, with its magnificent towers sheltering the iconic ice-skating rink in its lower plaza.

Patricia Murphy's provided me with food, work clothes (hostesses wore green velvet dresses), a social life, and a feeling of family. I had a wonderful boss named Greg Camillucci who went on to become the *maître d'* at the grand Russian Tea Room where celebrities from Mel Brooks and Woody Allen to Anne Bancroft and Barbra Streisand enjoyed delicacies, the most popular being caviar, blintzes, and vodka. Greg was featured playing himself in three movies shot there, the most famous of them, *Tootsie*.

I also met a part-time waiter at Patricia Murphy's, a soldier stationed in a nearby borough working for extra money and for fun. We struck up a conversation when a gang from the restaurant had beers in a local bar one night after work. He was smart. Sharp. Warm. A man of few words but of deep feelings and close-to-the-vest dry wit. He stirred something in me that I hadn't felt before. I couldn't get enough of him.

NYC had wrapped me in her arms. I was enchanted, I was in love.

I was home.

ME, ELOISE, AND THE PLAZA HOTEL

Just up Fifth Avenue, a mere ten blocks north of Patricia Murphy's 49th Street Candlelight Restaurant, with its blue-haired ladies pouring out of tour busses and filling the two-story building to lunch on shrimp cocktails, sliced London broil, popover rolls, dessert, and coffee for just under ten dollars, sat a gorgeous edifice that would play a strong part in my future.

The Plaza Hotel, towering in Old World splendor just off the corner of Fifth Avenue and Central Park South, its entrance hidden behind a circular fountain made famous by Zelda Fitzgerald's notorious splash and its twenty stories of luxury hotel suites and apartments, had been an icon of New

York City since it first opened in 1907. I sensed both its history and its mystery my first night in the city with those two otherworldly men I mentioned earlier (my gentlemen leprechauns), being wined and entertained in the lavish Persian Room, one of several nightclubs housed there.

That night, little did I dream that within a year, I'd come to work there and, in many ways, consider it home. Indeed, The Plaza Hotel hired and rehired me off and on for a number of years, giving me a chance to tour with theatrical productions and then return whenever I needed work.

My adventures at The Plaza began with a man. Actually, *the* man in my life at the time, the soldier and part-time waiter working at Pat Murphy's. I was already in love with him, and he was smitten with me, too. One day, an ex-girlfriend Carol Hasse, who'd waitressed with him at Pat Murphy's Florida branch some months before, showed up to see him; he spoke to her briefly and shooed her away, then rushed to tell me her news. She'd just been hired as a Palm Court waitress at The Plaza Hotel—and there was another opening waiting to be filled. "You should go get that job!" he said, probably thinking I'd never do it.

But I did. I immediately got an interview with management, and we hit it off from the start. The Plaza didn't usually hire American girls as Palm Court waitresses. European women were typically hired instead to match the European flavor of the room. But Carol and I were exceptions. Funny enough, since we were both from the Deep South, they didn't really see us as Americans. We were more laid-back than average young women, more enjoying of giving fine service, and had a kind of gentility that the top brass liked. I got the job. And much to my true love's dismay, Carol and I became good friends.

On my first night, I showed up at the waitresses' locker room in the subbasement of the hotel, where I met the other girls. One each from Greece, France, and Switzerland, two from Germany, and of course, Carol. We slipped into our uniforms, modeled off those of English upper-class servants: knee-length white dresses with thin black vertical stripes and pretty white cotton pinafores to go over them. On our heads, we wore white pleated cotton doilies with black velvet bows on top. Our shoes were up to us. Later when my legs would hurt from standing too long, Maria, my German partner would say, "Harriet! Your feets is connected to your

legs! Your feets is connected to your legs. Get good shoes—strong shoes! Strong shoes, Harriet!!!"

Once we were all dressed and had freshened our makeup, we headed through the bowels of the subbasement to the dining hall to be served our supper before starting work at eight sharp. We'd work straight through with only a short break until one in the morning, so we needed a substantial meal to keep us going.

The Plaza subbasement was populated mostly by Puerto Rican and other Hispanic workers who knew little or no English. They were just off the boat, so to speak, and had the down-to-the-dregs kind of work, the poorest paid jobs that the place had to offer. As we passed by, they started to whistle and mutter phrases under their breaths, and occasionally called out something in Spanish that none of us understood. I was last in line as we traveled single file through the stacked cartons of merchandise, food, utensils, etc., supplying the kitchens.

As the men made their moaning calls at our parade of young women, all the girls ahead of me lifted their noses in the air and marched on with angry resolve.

I don't know what got into me, but I reacted differently. On impulse, I climbed up onto a carton and started curtsying, taking bows, clasping my hands together over one shoulder then the other in the classic victor's celebration. The more I played with the men, the louder and more enthusiastic the calls became. And the tone of them changed from slightly off-color perhaps, to cheers, applause, and shouts of "Arriba! Arriba!"

The girls were appalled.

"Get down, Harriet!" they wailed. "You don't know what those men are saying!"

But I didn't get down. I kept carrying on until I'd had enough, then took a last bow and clambered down to go to the dining hall with my now disgusted new friends.

We all sat at a large round table. The other girls were each served a sandwich of their choice and iced tea or coffee. I was served hot pheasant under glass, grapes on ice, and various small dishes of shellfish (lobster, shrimp, oysters, the works).

Those subbasement guys didn't speak a word of English, but they did communicate with other Spanish-speaking people at the hotel. They had access to cooks from all the dining rooms as well as the nightclubs upstairs, and boy, did they make use of it. I never felt more welcomed in my life.

From that day on, I knew if I were ever in trouble, ever had someone chasing me, I'd head to the subbasement of The Plaza Hotel, where my boys would protect me. And, that if I were ever on a diet, I'd have to sneak in, hopefully unnoticed, for my evening meal.

I have great stories about the swanky Palm Court, where our regular violinist, Gunnar Hansen, played Viennese waltzes with his accompanist Stanley, whose last name I have forgotten, on the piano. Such characters. The fights they had, chasing each other through the kitchen and screaming disagreements about tempo and who was leading who.

Then there were the roach stampedes in the kitchen when a well-intentioned substitute bartender used bug spray on the shelves behind the bar, forcing out bugs everywhere, including the ice bin. All evening, guests were discreetly calling over waitresses and handing one of us a glass, whispering, "I'm sorry, but this seems to have attracted a little friend."

And, the *maître d's* and their ongoing dramas mixed in with the array of fascinating patrons we served. There was the night when a taxi strike started while we were at work, and The Plaza Hotel let all of the Palm Court waitresses sleep over in one of the rooms of Natalie Wood's hotel suite. It had its own entrance into the hall, so we never saw her or even knew if she was in residence at the time. I recall one wealthy gentleman *of a certain age* who asked The Plaza management for permission to take me out on occasional dinners in Manhattan. Actually, he'd done so for years with my German partner, Maria, who was older than me, happily married, and motherly in her ways, but was now retiring.

He was legally blind and married to an ex-Las Vegas showgirl in her late fifties or early sixties. She had big hair that was dark, long, teased, and sprayed, and wore sequined gowns and furs when he brought her with him to the Palm Court. She often took out her compact to apply lipstick at their table before leaving him to go to the powder room for more serious primping, or to the telephone banks out in the lobby, or who knows where. She was obviously not interested in him.

He and his two brothers owned a fleet of ships that laid transcontinental communication cables on the floor of the Atlantic Ocean, linking Europe to North America. They each were millionaires many times over, and classy from what I gathered. I never met the brothers, but my friend was kind, gentle, and vulnerable. I was very fond of him.

The Plaza agreed to his request and I was summoned to the office where they informed me that he was a gentleman, that I could trust him to be honorable, and that I had their consent to our evenings out together. I found out later that Maria had gone to the office and told the brass that I was a lady, honorable, and that they could trust me to not take advantage of him. And so it was that every few weeks, he'd fetch me in a chauffeured limousine and take me out to very nice restaurants where we dined elegantly and danced, while he shared memories of fishing in a little boat with his dad off the shores of Southern Italy when he was a boy.

Because he couldn't see well, he kept his folding money of different denominations in separate pockets. Twenties, fives, singles, and hundreds all had specially designated compartments in his jacket. He'd assess the kind of service we'd received and slip his hand into the appropriate pocket to offer a bill to a *maître d'*, server, or footman. I once saw him reach for a twenty for a footman hailing our limo coming out of the Waldorf Hotel. When the man was careless and rude to us, Ted (that was his name) took his hand out of the twenties' pocket and reached for a five. The footman never knew what he'd missed.

I was blessed that several times he gave me hundred-dollar tips whenever I served him at the Palm Court. But he was just as likely to slip me a piece of hard candy in a cellophane wrapper, too. He was a very playful, endearing man.

He also had beautiful, quite large porterhouse steaks delivered to my door every few weeks. I shared them with my neighbors, Julian Barry and his wife, Pat. One steak fed their whole family.

When I landed my first dinner theatre job, Ted took me out to celebrate, wining and dining me. It had snowed that night. He tried to gift me a hundred-dollar bill as we sat in the back of the limo on the way home, but it didn't seem right to take it, so I said no, repeatedly. This hurt him deeply, and he made the driver stop and let him out to stagger in the snow with tears in his eyes. I was dumbfounded, so confused. I was just trying to be gracious, but then he cried out, "What good do all my millions do, if I can't share some of it with you?" and kept on walking. The driver took me home and I never saw my friend, Ted, again. But I did write to him from North Carolina, sending the letter to Harry, my favorite *maître d'* of the Palm Court. He read it to Ted while his wife was in the powder room and said that it moved him. Unfortunately, he died before I returned to NYC, but I was glad that my letter had reached and touched him. He was a very special man.

I could also tell you about all the television and movie stars we served, and performers in the hotel clubs, the cooks, busboys, and coat checkers, too. And, of course, the other Palm Court waitresses. What women they were. What lives they lived. There's a whole other book in me about that place.

For now, suffice it to say, that I loved The Plaza Hotel and was charmed by it from the ground up.

I was especially taken with Eloise, the fictitious little girl from the *Eloise at The Plaza* children's book series who lived on the top floor, had all kinds of adventures with the staff, and who reportedly knew everybody's business in New York City. Her portrait hung on a wall opposite the Palm Court. Looking at it, one could easily imagine her calling up room service and ordering one raisin and seven spoons, as she did in one of the books about her.

For me, that portrait reflected the soul of the place, the style, grace, humor, and love of tradition that combined to serve as its trademark in those most remarkable of days.

In 1998, The Plaza Hotel was sold to Donald Trump, who made his wife Ivana its president. They overspent remodeling, then led it into bankruptcy. Corporations too numerous and complex to mention here have subsequently gobbled it up.

It's glitzier now. A different resonance.

All things change. The old dies and the new is born. Sometimes we're happy with that, and other times, not so much. I admit to some ambivalence about The Plaza's new face.

But returning there after many years and talking to workers I knew back then; I could still feel the love. Could see a glow in their eyes and feel it in mine—and sense the power of our memories of what once was.

Lopez, one of the few males working as waiters in the Palm Court back in the day, and our union man, was still there after twenty-some-odd years, serving my husband and me at our table among the potted palms that gave the room its name. After taking our orders, he leaned down to my ear. Glancing at Bill he said, "I hope he a nice man. You a very nice girl!"

I asked him if the money was still good. He said yes. "If I need to, can I come back?" I whispered.

His face beamed and he nodded with a secret smile, then strutted off to get our food and drink.

The real stuff of life doesn't die easily.

CHAPTER 16

GOODBYE HARRIET

I can't say the real name of the part-time waiter I met at Patricia Murphy's 49th Street Candlelight Restaurant, the soldier finishing out his time in the army, stationed in a neighboring borough. He's a private person, conservative in his own way, and I honor this. There is, in fact, much about our time together that I can't tell and don't want to, because intimacy requires privacy. Intimacy between two people is powerful. I still honor the intimacy that we once had and, indeed, may have again, as we move into a life of ever-deepening friendship.

But I *can* tell you this: translated from Hebrew, his name means "beloved." At least, that's what he told me. But then he also told me he was Jewish, and that was a bit of fiction meant to get me off his back about coming to church with me. As you've probably guessed from the fact that I still remember all of that, I was head over heels in love with him.

We played out our romance in the tradition of the times, of the society and customs as depicted in the movie *The Apartment*, that 1960 American comedy-drama cowritten and directed by Billy Wilder and starring Jack Lemmon, Shirley MacLaine, and Fred MacMurray. In 1960's NYC, the war between the sexes was full blown. Men lied and cheated, dangled promises they would not keep, and single women tried to barter sexual pleasures for security and a home that they hoped to wrestle away from the current wives of powerful men.

Meanwhile, virgins like me tried to seduce the men we loved into commitment and marriage, while our wished-for intendeds often struggled to remain free and unattached, trying to figure out what they wanted to do with their lives—besides just earning money to support a family.

So, my love and I played out our own drama, much of it comedic with tremendous highs and lows, intense love and hurt on both sides. In the long run, we managed to salvage the love that was there, is still there, and will be always. That's a minor miracle, an accomplishment that's significant to me, and for which I'm grateful.

The good times were very good. He gifted my life in so many ways, dragging me to bookstores exclaiming, "What do you mean you've never read William Faulkner? You're from Mississippi, aren't you? What did they teach you in school?" He told me about Lee Strasberg, a premier teacher famous for introducing to America a more sensual, realistic style of acting called "method acting," which had already distinguished the works of Marlon Brando, James Dean, Paul Newman, Joanne Woodward, Shelly Winters, Marilyn Monroe, and others. Lee ran the famous Actors Studio, where already established artists could come and improve their work through scene study with Lee. I wrote to him at my new love's prodding and was accepted into his acting classes.

My guy and I also visited museums across the city, had dinners in nice restaurants, saw *Funny Girl* and *The Odd Couple* on Broadway with their original casts. We romanced while watching the skaters at Rockefeller Center, and even had our own Christmas tree in the service stairwell between the upstairs and downstairs dining areas at Patricia

Murphy's. We'd meet on the landing between our two floors during breaks. We had dinner and heard Tony Bennett sing at the Copacabana nightclub, a memory to savor; there's no magic nor music like Tony Bennett's. We courted and dated for nine months, playing out our hands. Mine, the virgin party girl. His, the I'll-never-get-married single guy. We drank pitchers of beer at an Irish pub with sawdust on the floor where we knew the bartenders' names and every Irish tune on the jukebox, then made out like bandits on the couch in the dark living room of Peggy and Bill Simon's sumptuous apartment, where I was renting a room.

But then everything changed on Palm Sunday of 1966, when in a burst of overconfidence (after I'd finally talked him into going to church and had two martinis afterward to celebrate), I abandoned my long-held plan to be a virgin bride. I'd like to say I did it after careful consideration, but I didn't. I was impulsive. But I knew that time was running out. He was ending his stint in the army and would leave soon. I wanted to make love with him, and in that moment, was willing to pay a price if ever there was one. And, of course, there was. How could there not be, given how rigidly we'd held onto our beliefs about sex and how much we'd invested those beliefs into our self-images at the time?

Overnight, the dynamics in our relationship changed. Like Sampson, who lost his strength once his hair was shorn, I lost power in the relationship when I gave up my virginity. I know now that I didn't have to do that. But suddenly, my world was upside down. Whereas I'd been the one he sought, I became the one waiting by the phone or looking over my shoulder for the sight of his face as he appeared, and disappeared from my life, again and again. Our dance was sometimes to the tune of Dolly Parton's joyous *Here You Come Again* (and here I go), but increasingly it was more often to the strains of Ricky Nelson's sadder song *Stood Up* (brokenhearted, again). We were on a yo-yo ride, a push-pull of seeking and retreating, embracing and rejecting, two souls torn. Lost.

The most valiant thing we ever did was break up. After two years of an on-again off-again romance, when he stepped over the line of what I could handle, we let go of each other, and did so with the grace of our two natures: a bit of our real selves, and I might add, a bit of our old style. I met him in a seedy bar a few blocks from my home, but we were much too much emotional to handle it then and there. We decided to see each other one more time, the following morning.

When he met me at my place, we made a deal. I asked him to leave NYC and not let me know where he was going and to not register himself in any phonebook in the country, that is, to disappear and give me a chance to get my life back on track. I needed New York. He didn't. I told him I was in danger of losing my respect for him and I didn't want to—didn't want to lose the love I felt. I asked for two years, in the name of all that we held most dear. He complied. I know, because there came a night when I called every city in every state I could name, searching for him. Bless him. He wasn't to be found.

Two years later, almost to the day, I was standing at 59th Street and Sixth Avenue. I'd toured in two dinner theatre productions through four Southern states and was working as a singing waitress wearing Roaring Twenties' satin and velvet outfits trimmed with rhinestone and pearls, fishnet stockings, and high heels at the Gaslight nightclub. Along the way, I'd met a lot of men and was enjoying my freedom. As I stood on that corner feeling the sunshine on my face in that late summer afternoon, my mind wandered to him. I wished to see him again, to tell him I understood so much more about him than before. I'd recently joined the Screen Actors Guild and had changed my name to comply with its rules, but *he* had always called me by my given name. In the catch of a breath, I heard him say it then. "Harriet Harper." I turned, and there he was—standing right behind me.

Maybe because of the shock of the moment, all memory of what happened next is lost to me. I do know that we were both very happy to see each other, overjoyed, in fact. Where we went to catch up is a total mystery to me, maybe the Russian Tea Room across the street. Or, maybe not.

But we did catch up that day, saw each other from time to time, and talked on the phone, too, me sharing my adventures at the Gaslight and him making me laugh with his wry takes on my stories. We even met off chance at an Irish bar on the East Side and hung out once, maybe twice.

And then, almost with no notice, life separated us again. Magic was afoot, and through a series of small and large miracles, I was cast in the West Coast production of *Oh! Calcutta!*, a notorious, raucous, and in some scenes completely nude off-Broadway NYC play, then opening on the northern

Pacific coast. I left NYC singing, "If you're going to San Francisco, be sure to wear some flowers in your hair...." I was getting naked for all the world to see. Becoming a new person, a phoenix rising out of the ashes of the dying Harriet.

Born new. Born free.

And, for a time at least, born to be wild.

A few months later, my beloved first lover flew to San Francisco to see me in the play. I still have a picture of us in Golden Gate Park, me sitting on the grass peering down at his face, him with his head in my lap, eyes closed.

It must've been a lot for him to take in. I was now a working actress, and even though the show was scandalous, it was also a hit, and I was a hit in it. I was bringing down the house every night and twice on matinee days. My hair had grown long, it fell down below my shoulder blades, and I was in better shape than ever before from the intense workouts the choreographer put us through before each show.

Nine months later, after I left the show and came back to NYC, I moved in with him. We had a few fun months of summertime highs, affectionate and off-the-wall times of comings and goings in his apartment, until it became clear that we couldn't go back to what we once had.

The feelings were still there, and as I said, I suspect always will be. In the few times we've spoken in recent years, I have to catch my breath and restart my heart at the sound of his voice (a conditioned response to hearing him say my birth name, Harriet Harper).

During those few 1970 summertime months, he met his future wife, another long-legged brunette from Mississippi, gorgeous and a natural wit. And that summer, I had adventures with lots of men, some who became major players in my life, and also some whose names I don't recall, but who were still a blast at the time. I was playing hard and didn't want to look back at what was now my past.

So, what on earth were the events that led this virgin queen to sing risqué songs, act in raunchy stage scenes, and strip off her clothes to dance naked on the West Coast and then in NYC, both off and on Broadway, and in the movie version of the same show?

I've promised to tell you how that came about. But I have to set the scene first. To add to all the casual loves of that summer, my next-door neighbor Julian Barry, a screenwriter (among his many professions), and his two great artist collaborators, Pablo Ferro who directed me, and Don Calfa who acted opposite me filming Julian's screenplay *The Inflatable Doll*, all helped launch my small but cherished film career. They had tremendous impact on my life, both personally and professionally.

They were the ones who made it okay to have loved so deeply and to have lost.

They inspired me to excited dreams.

They made me glad to be alive.

PART II

Samantha

The Rebel and the Rebellion

CHAPTER 17

JULIAN, PABLO, AND DON

This is a rap about three guys who changed my life. They each played a private part, unique as a jazz solo: cool, hot, lively, seductive. As disarming as passion and as powerful as innocence, which was at its core. Together, they worked as a force, an inspiring trio in my psyche; to hang out with them was like wading into a deep and ever-widening river of mindful, soulful, rhythmic pleasure. To make a movie with them was absolute, get-down-to it fun. They're a big part of the girl I am today.

The girl? Really?

The woman? Yes.

The girl that I'll always be, and the woman I became and am still becoming. Each man had impact that was unique with singular style. But they were alike in wit, resourcefulness, creativity, and courage. Great and loyal friends to each other and to me, these three from my 1960s. Originals all. Ingenious and utterly wild.

I like to tell the tale of strolling down NYC's Upper West Side one day, near Broadway, when the heavens opened up and God said, "Harriet Harper, you have been so good for so long that I'm going to introduce you to a few of my boys." These three were God's boys, His men in my life. A couple of them were "my boys," in a stunning adventure into free love. Meeting them was the "break" that every actress needs, my first connection to the artistic world. But I wasn't destined to be only an actress... meeting them was a break in my life. For my spirit. And for my soul.

I learned from them to throw out rules that others had made up for themselves and to restructure my character on principles of my own. Not that I didn't pay for it later, but only because I thought I had to. (It takes a lot of thought and exploration into our subconscious and unconscious minds to make such radical changes. It took me years to sort out the mega transformation of my belief system that, at the time, I so blithely and naively thought I'd mastered.)

So, who's on first? Well, I suppose Julian was first, but Pablo was "on first." And I'm still ahead of myself, telling the story backwards and sideways, the way I like it I guess, with all the juice.

Yes, Julian was first. A jazzman, actor, stage manager, director of theatre companies and plays, a man of letters, movie and television scripts, of histories and librettos—working by his wit—his greatest talent, a way with the words. Hip and magnetized to all things hip, drawing situations to himself by the sheer force of his talent, passion, desire, intensity, dark humor, and ultimate humanity. A good provider for his family, a daring man, a hedonist, a man with a trumpet, a man with good friends, a man who smoked pot before people knew much about it, before they were sure it was cool. A brave man who was known on occasion to get stoned and then paranoid, and then hyperventilate and be sure he was dying. Those were the days before you could trust your "connection," the guy who supplied your weed and before you could know for sure what was in it. Maybe for that reason, Julian wrote *The Inflatable Doll*, about a drug connection who claimed not to be one but who was. It was my first movie, directed by Pablo and where I met Don, its leading star, at the first read-through.

But here I am, out in front again.

Back to Julian. Julian Barry, who later wrote *Lenny* about the life of the over-the-edge hip comic Lenny Bruce, both the Broadway play and the screenplay for the 1974 grand slam of nominations for Oscars, five in total including Julian for screenplay and director Bob Fosse. Julian was darkly funny, upbeat, witty. A cool cocksman. My neighbor and friend who did me the ultimate favor, past all dimensions of fortune and fate, when he introduced me to Pablo.

Pablo Ferro, *Pablito,* who coaxed me out of my chrysalis, gave me a space to dry my wings, and let me fly with him through a universe of music, love, sex, and good conversation.

The first time we went out, after dinner and up to his infamous pad, Led Zeppelin or the Rolling Stones or some other rock band blasted from his stereo, a connected light machine flashing rhythmic, vibrant, colorful patterns synced with the sounds—the psychedelic effect way too much for me in this alien place with giant hanging portraits of Coney Island circus freaks and rows and rows of love beads hanging from his walls and mirrors absolutely everywhere, most notably above his bed.

He noticed I was uneasy and said, "What kind of music would you like?"

"Do you have any Johnny Mathis?" I said shyly, then shuffled into an adjacent room and perched on an elevated chair across from his bed.

"Uh. I don't know." Then he proceeded downstairs, opened a closet door, and started spilling albums into the hall. It took him some time, but finally he returned, a record in his hand. "Will Frank Sinatra do?" As soon as he put it on, Frank's music slowed the light machine which began to eke out weak, tame, and rather lame pastels.

Pablo. All grace and generosity, the perfect host, looking like he just stepped off of a nickel… with his Aztec nose and flowing mane.

From time to time, his various girlfriends took it upon themselves to brush and untangle his thick, glorious hair. There was a lot of it, and it took two women working together to do it right. I saw days of watching them play with him a long time after our first meeting, and I loved those moments (granted, I was entertained by others who partied upstairs, down in the kitchen, and in various rooms on both floors), but no more than I loved being one-on-one with Pablo alone, as lover and friend, enjoying his off-beat wisdom, and profiting from his advice whenever I asked for it. Easy and adventurous, we played like children exploring the far side of the moon.

I once asked him, "Pablo, how do you get work? I have trouble understanding you when you talk and I'm *dating* you." (Yes, I used the word "dating" in those days.) He was co-creating with directors and stars from two continents: Stanley Kubrick, Norman Jewison, Steve McQueen, Jonathan Demme, and Hal Ashby, to name a few. He did over a hundred title sequences and trailers for the best movies made, constantly inventing and innovating, and seemingly relaxed with it all. He answered me, in his inimitable Cuban accent, "If I have a meeting on a film, I go in and help them with their picture. If they want more, they have to pay me." I didn't realize that he already had a body of work that got his foot in the door. He was unassuming and didn't need to impress anybody. He never mentioned that he was a star in his field. To me, he was just a man from another planet, or maybe another world.

But his greatest gift to me was spiritual, and it was through his actions, not his words.

When he caught a bullet (intended for another) in his neck, in the late '60s (and at the height of his career), he was wheeled into the hospital and given last rites. Well, almost given last rites, because he refused them. When the priest asked him to repeat, "Forgive me, Father, for I have sinned," Pablo said, "No. I can't say that." The priest asked him why. "Because," Pablo answered, "I have never sinned."

What more can you say about an innocent soul, full of wonder and creativity, and living as he had always lived: free.

And that brings me to Don.

Pablo once described himself to me as a two-girl guy. With the rare exception, I was never all that interested in having another woman around when the two of us were hanging out, but I found that given the opportunity, I immensely enjoyed being a two-guy gal. Particularly, if the two guys were Pablo and Don, as I discovered at the table read of *The Inflatable Doll*.

Pablo had seen me act in San Francisco and asked me to do a little movie he was directing. I said only if it didn't require having sex on-camera. He said, no, come on down. And there was Don, Don Calfa himself (with a future that held movies, including *Return of the Living Dead*, *Weekend at Bernie's*, and *10*, directed by Blake Edwards, and a TV career including two episodes of *Kojak*, three episodes of *Hill Street Blues*, and seven episodes of *Barney Miller*), reading at the table with stringy hair and unkempt mustache, working on a limp for the part. *Freaky*, I thought. But he had a soft light in his eyes and was as eager, enthusiastic, and affectionate as any young wild man I'd ever seen. He was (as my character in *The Inflatable Doll* put it) fascinating.

I remember running into him on a long block between Fifth and Sixth Avenues (maybe 55th Street) a month or so after the end of shooting. We danced at the sight of each other and raced to grab and hold on and laugh and celebrate and laugh some more. Then we turned and continued in our opposite directions, waving goodbye with big happy smiles. That was a metaphor for Don and me. We loved like puppies in the same litter, basking in the wonder of just how good life can be.

We'd made the movie and fell in love with it, along with Pablo and Julian and each other, then and now—and for all time. That's the thing about art and love. Both connect you to eternity.

My favorite times with Don stretched out over decades but in the '80s, our most precious moments involved binoculars to gaze at the full moon rising and twin sets of earphones hooked up to Supertramp. Or was it The Motels?

He turned out to be an awesome connection for me, too, at a most opportune time. New to California in 1973, I went seeking representation with a fairly good agent who sent me on a "look-see" to famed casting agent Lynn Stalmaster, who looked, saw, and heard my country voice and sent me over to meet Hal. The Hal that I'd heard about from Pablo for years. *Hal Ashby* who was doing a movie about Woody Guthrie's early drifter days (*Bound for Glory*)! I drove over, parked my car, walked into the building and rang for the elevator. When it opened, Don stepped out.

"Oh, my God," he blurted out, "what are you doing here?"

And when I said, "Seeing Hal!" Don hopped back in and rode up with me. He knocked and swung open Hal's door and loudly announced, "Hal, it's Samantha! From The Doll!"

The rest, as they say, is history.

The best of it untold.

As fate would have it, I ended up doing a small part in Hal's movie *Bound for Glory* on its last day of shooting. I played a casting agent at the renowned Coconut Grove nightclub who was auditioning Woody Guthrie (David Carradine) for a singing part in a stage show for the club. Hal had originally told Lynn Stalmaster that he was considering me for the much larger part of Woody's wife. Lynn passed that information along to the agent who'd sent me to him, and she signed me. For the first time, I had professional representation in the movie business!

Hal, I think, was one of God's boys, too.

CHAPTER 18

A FEW MORE WORDS ABOUT PABLO

Iwant to tell you a little more about Pablo Ferro, as he weaves in and out through the pages of this book and the story of my life.

The night we met, my neighbor Julian Barry and his wife, Pat, were throwing a party in their apartment next door. A gaggle of show business people crowded into their small first-floor flat and a downstairs bedroom reached by a staircase (which they'd built unknown to their landlord), leading to the basement of an adjoining building that Julian had converted into an office for turning out his writing—including an episode for the hit TV series *Mission Impossible*.

The building where we lived on East 88th Street between First and York Avenues had been poorly renovated some years before I moved in and shared three small rooms with my former roommate from grad school, Susan Haber. She worked days in a pharmaceutical firm, and I worked five nights a week waitressing at The Plaza Hotel, and five days hostessing at Patricia Murphy's 49th Street Restaurant. So we managed not to trip over each other in our tiny quarters. She slept in the bedroom in back, I on a foldout couch in the living room.

The walls separating the apartments were so thin that every word could be heard through them. In the mornings, Julian and Pat would get up and sit at their table adjacent to our living room wall where I slept. Pat wouldn't have to raise her voice whenever she said, "Good morning, Harriet. You want a cup of coffee?"

"Thanks! Love it!" I'd answer, as if there were no wall between us. Then I'd head on over. We often kept our doors unlocked and slightly ajar and walked in and out of each other's places at will. They also had two great kids, Sally Ann and Michael, who I knew and loved and sometimes babysat.

On this particular night, I'd gotten home from my day job and was enjoying the roar of the good times coming from next door.

Then, suddenly, things got very quiet. I sensed whispering. Then their door creaked opened and I heard a soft knocking at mine.

When I opened it, a small, dark man with long hair, love beads, a headband, ruffled tuxedo shirt, bell-bottomed pants, boots, and a full-length black cape, stood there, holding an empty cup in his hand. "Can I borrow a cup of sugar?" He had a soft Cuban accent.

I slammed the door in his face.

A roar of laughter came from next door and Julian yelled above it, "It's okay, Harriet. He's with us!"

I sheepishly opened the door again and peered out at the gentle man. He smiled. "You want to go to dinner?" he asked.

"Sure," I said, grabbing my purse and jacket, as we headed out.

We drove in his big car downtown and ate at Lüchow's, the same restaurant where a year ago, I'd eaten with the two leprechauns my first night in the city. Afterward, he took me to his apartment on Second Avenue near St. Mark's Place, a popular street in the East Village. Coney Island tent flaps adorned with paintings of "Lola, the Monkey Woman" and "Jojo, the Armless Carpenter"—she with a beard and he hammering a nail into wood using only his feet—hung on the walls of a downstairs extra room.

We passed the doorway to that room and through a sizable kitchen with a high ceiling, then climbed up a flight of stairs on the far side to his bedroom suite, visible from the floor below, as there was no wall in-between. In fact, it was a loft, filled with a large bed and two hammocks, one hanging over the bed and a second one directly across in front of a mirrored wall. Rows of love beads hung on hooks beside his bed, and a board of artistic lightbulbs that glowed with tiny filaments of metal flower arrangements. The bulbs were arranged to spell the word "LOVE." Topping all of that, music dazzled and danced with the light machine connected to his stereo.

As I mentioned before, mirrors were *everywhere*. A ceiling mirror reflected both his bed and the hammock hanging over it. Around a corner, a mirrored ball rotated on the ceiling, flashing fractured light in all directions. Below it, a raised lounge-like chair sat alone. I thought it might be a dentist chair and only discovered years later that it had been designed for another purpose: gynecology.

I dropped my purse on Pablo's bed and fled to that seemingly safe, suspended chair, where I perched, both terrified and intrigued, and where I stayed while he went downstairs to find music more in my comfort zone (Frank Sinatra that ended up substituting for Johnny Mathis).

I don't know how long we listened to Frank, but suddenly I rose off my chair. He saw I was ready to leave and stood near his bed while I retrieved my purse.

Whatever came over me in that moment is still a mystery, but instead of heading for the door, I turned, pushed him down on his bed, stripped off his clothes and, as the saying goes, had my way with him. I made love to him in every way I could imagine, which I admit, was limited at the time. He just lay there, surrendering and watching. When it was over, I sat next to him while we pulled on our clothes and said, "I must apologize. I am so sorry. I was afraid I was going to run out of here and never get to know you."

"That's okay," he smiled, "you're harmless."

That was the start of our relationship, or better said, our friendship. Pablo was an artist first, but beyond that, his friendships were highly valued. When he loved you, whether sex was involved or not, it was forever. He'd call me every few weeks and we'd spend a night together or maybe a weekend.

Sex with Pablo was an adventure. He was creative and innovative, always stretching his imagination and mine. I remember one night while we were in the midst of it all, I felt him moving oddly and opened my eyes to see him maneuvering a camera on the edge of his bed with his foot. "What are you doing?" I rolled my head, straining to see.

"Making a movie."

"Well, cut it out!" I said. And he did.

I knew he had no plans to show the film of us to others. He was just being Pablo, in love with moviemaking.

He brought me sex toys, introducing them at just the right moments, all warm from being hidden beneath his body during the preliminaries. And he gave me sex-enhancing drugs. I'd smoked a little marijuana in those days, but Pablo's weed was like no other. And the "poppers," as we called these little capsules of amyl nitrite, which he would break and press between our noses as we got lost in the rising tide of music and sensation and each other, produced wave after wave of erotic pleasure. One of his girlfriends in a recent documentary about his life said she was sure in those days that she'd die of pleasure. She feared that the headlines would read, "Eighteen-year-old dies of orgasms." Those orgasms could go on and on for quite some time, a ride up a mountain and out to the stars. It was something to write home about, not that I would've dared.

You might think these were the actions of a womanizing man. Far from it, though, at first, I encountered doubts and fears. On one occasion, while stoned and lost in sexual acrobatics, I heard my mother's voice and that of my puritan adolescent self along with other protesters screaming, "This is wrong. This is terrible. Stop it right now. He just wants you to be lewd and vulgar to satisfy his weird, warped appetites!" I opened my eyes and observed this man, so invested in the moment. So eager to please me, to give pleasure, to satisfy my every desire. I made a choice, then and there. I told the voices, "Oh yeah? You think that's vulgar? You think that's lewd? Well, get a load of this!" I dropped all efforts to be ladylike and went for the gold, discovering a part of me that I hadn't known existed. A powerful, raunchy, and oddly respectable part, that I learned in that moment to honor and adore.

The drugs, the lights, Pablo's mind, the incredible music of the times, the feeling of being accepted and loved for who I was, created a world of eroticism that I could live inside for days at time.

And when it was time to stop playing, we went back to work, doing what we did as money-makers and artists.

Through it all, neither of us was possessive of the other. He never talked much about other women, but he didn't hide the fact that he loved women and they loved him. I had other men in my life, too. It was all easy. Fun. Intelligent.

One night we were sitting and talking. "Pablo, sometimes when we're making love it's like a whole universe is floating above me, with planets and moons and orbits all different from mine. What's that all about?"

"That's fucking," he said.

Conversations with him were a riot.

Ten years later after he moved to LA, we lingered and chatted at a sushi bar one night. "My

God, Pablo! I'd forgotten how much I loved talking to you."

"Oh, yeah," he smiled. "The talking was always great."

There's more to our story, and it will be told.

CHAPTER 19

TWO MORE OF
GOD'S BOYS

In 1966 and 1967, after I'd moved into the apartment on East 88th Street next door to Julian Barry, his wife, Pat, and their two children, Sally Ann and Michael, I went on the road touring in a couple of dinner theatre productions across four Southern states. Julian, a theatre man himself, liked to tell a story about returning home from one of *his* tours...a road company of a hit musical, with an orchestra and a huge cast and crew that, having been together for six or eight months, had begun to form couples and enter into personal relationships. As the train carrying everyone crested the final hill to reveal the NYC skyline shining brightly in the night, Julian stood up and loudly announced:

"All romances are hereby *cancelled*!" A rye piece of wit, and taken that way, by all.

Our little productions were much more modest. They were nonunion, and the actors actually lived above the dining areas of the theaters and worked as waiters downstairs before the shows. After serving the main courses and directing our audiences to the dessert tables, we'd run upstairs to our rooms and change into our costumes, then dash out onto the stage, which was in the center of our living area, ready to be lowered to the floor below at showtime. There were six of these theatres in all, three in North Carolina, one in Atlanta, Georgia, one in Roanoke, Virginia, and the last and most fancy, in Nashville, Tennessee (the same one featured in Robert Altman's 1975 movie, *Nashville,* which the American Film Institute ranked as one of the greatest movies of all time). They were called The Barn Dinner Theatres and ingeniously designed.

As I mentioned, stages were lowered hydraulically from the second stories with out-of-breath actors frozen in tableaux, ready to move when the stage came to rest amid three tiers of tables on all sides packed with diners finishing their coffee. We lived on our small salaries and any tips from our customers. It was a gentile version of "the Borscht

Belt," those once-thriving summer resorts in the Catskills where Jewish families flocked to vacation and enjoy live theatre.

Our productions weren't mighty, that's for sure. But the intrigues among the cast could've rivaled that of Julian's big musicals. They were outrageous, brazen, daring, and often hilarious. How else were we to get our much-needed R and R? We were the only entertainment in those smaller towns. When our show went dark every night, so did the whole county, except for the occasional truck stop.

The first of my shows was a production of an old warhorse of a play renamed by our director, Ken Eulo, as *Ladies' Night in a Turkish Bath*. The cast had three men and six women. We rehearsed in New York, then traveled south in a dilapidated, made-over school bus with a functioning potbellied stove heater at its center. We dubbed it the "Wolf-mobile," after the tour's producer.

So, on a cold night leaving the city, I found myself sitting on the Wolf-mobile with Jim, the leading man. We made out all the way to Charlotte, North Carolina. As I've said, I have a thing for handsome men on dark busses. But Jim was too uptight to be all that playful. He was appalled at the condition of the bus and thinking only of whether this show could actually launch his career. My sense of adventure and happiness that I had a job in the profession of my dreams was much more on my mind. Anyway, as Cyndi Lauper says, "girls just wanna have fun."

When we got to our first stop, something extraordinary happened, akin to the magic of my first night in NYC, when those two odd, little "leprechaun" men showed me all about town, uptown and down.

Now two years later, as I staggered off the bus in Charlotte and into the theatre where we were to perform and be housed, another leprechaun was waiting there to greet me, and this one was undeniably Irish. He was tall and thin with brown hair and a likeable face, holding a welcoming sign with my name on it, singing loudly and laughing the words, "Harriet Harper, I love you!" I swear on my life, this is true.

The trouble was, I didn't know him from a hole in my sock, had never heard of him, couldn't imagine where I'd met him, and was convinced I never had. But he embraced me and held me to his heart. He pointed to the welcome signs he'd pasted all around the theatre. He explained that he had seen my name in ads for our upcoming production and patted me on my back, laughed and hugged me again and said he was my greatest fan. Bear in mind, I'd never worked before as a professional actor. To this day, he has never explained how he knew of me (or at least, thought he did). I finally let it go and gave into the comfort of his welcoming arms.

His name was Charlie Murphy, the lead actor in the production that preceded ours on tour, a recently imported British comedy called *The Knack and How to Get It*. I found out later that he'd been a protégé of Ann Jackson and Eli Wallach (one of the best-known acting couples ever) and had lived with them in their apartment on the luxurious Central Park West for a time.

Our entire company saw Charlie's show that night. He was mercurial, all arms and legs and pratfalls. Elfin, winsome, vulnerable, enchanting. Our cast was knocked out, touched by his humor and sweetness. We'd meet up each month whenever our shows overlapped a few days. By the third month, he proposed and I said yes.

Yes?

What else was I to do? *I was supposed to get married, wasn't I? Women were expected to do that, weren't they?* At this point, I hadn't yet met Pablo or Don, or had any of those wild experiences I was just telling you about. In fact, at that point, I'd only slept with two men in my life: my first love (whose name I have never said, and will never say), and Larry, a kind and gentle unemployed actor who worked as the service elevator operator at The Plaza Hotel—and that was just a one- or two-night stand. Charlie and I were two babes in the woods, but I didn't know it then.

When his tour finished, he went back to New York, and I stayed on to greet the new leading man in my show, there to replace the still disgusted Jim who'd quit, setting his sights on something a little higher than The Barn Dinner Theatre circuit.

This new guy was a different kind of creature from any I'd ever met. Paul Cavonis was handsome with dark eyes, curly brown hair, an athletic body, and a spirit like Zorba the Greek's. And Greek he was—fully embracing his culture, cooking Greek food for a party he threw for our entire production when his mother and sister visited. He loved to dance and romp and get into it with women. Basically, he was an out-and-out hedonist, a bad boy, and just plain fun. I couldn't resist. I put my engagement to Charlie on hold and played house with Paul until the end of our tour.

If you want to know the nitty-gritty about me and Paul, it can be summed up in this little story. My husband, Bill and I, taped a cartoon from *The New Yorker* to our refrigerator. It's old and yellowed and curled and shows a woman in a black cocktail dress with a wine glass in hand. She's introducing a lightly bearded man in an unfitted jacket to her husband, who's standing in a conservative suit beside her. The caption says, "Honey, this is Jack. He's the one who taught me how to do that thing you like."

Paul was that guy in my life, my first romantic tutor as it were. He was only the fourth man I'd ever slept with and, as I mentioned, very different from the others. He was a street guy raised in New York's Hell's Kitchen, red-blooded, with good-natured animal instincts, a cheerful disposition, and a feel for women. His father had been a laborer who worked as a waiter, and drank and gambled, paying no attention to his family except to beat his wife now and then and give her two dollars a day, one for each child, as her total income from him. Growing up, Paul would steal money to pay their rent from beneath his father's pillow while he slept.

His mother was a hard-hitting woman who cleaned up Broadway theatres after the crowds had left. She expressed her rage and fought to keep her son away from bad company and unfriendly police by beating him daily within an inch of his life with a stick or a pipe—especially if she heard he'd been fighting in the streets. Part artist, part con man, Paul was a mad mix of energies.

At his first rehearsal with us, when we were on a break, he strutted over and sat down beside me. "I've been looking over the women in the company, and you're the one I want," he announced easily, glancing around so as not to be overheard.

I laughed and politely excused myself, running upstairs to fetch something from my room, I forget what, that one of the cast members needed for rehearsal. I rushed in and was turning to head back downstairs when Paul came sailing through my door and closed it behind him. I was so caught off guard, so stunned by the surprise of his boldness that I didn't resist him at all; I just let him lay me down and roll me over, as the college drinking song goes. He managed to pull off a quickie with very little participation from me *and* with both of us almost fully clothed. Then we leapt to our feet and sped back downstairs to continue rehearsal.

"You'll never do that again," I said to him as we flew down the hall leading to the stage.

"Next time, I'll do it right," he laughed. And he did, again and again in the following weeks. I became hooked on the heat of it, the wildness, the boldness.

Charlie had been affectionate and effusive, but almost asexual. Paul was unashamedly animal. Sex to him was a celebration, a romp, a party. I was amazed at his prowess. He taught me all the ways that I could please him and rewarded me with moves I hadn't experienced before, teaching me how to receive new dimensions of pleasure. He had the keys to my engine, revved it up, and took me for spins every now and again. But I had to wait in line. There was a steady stream of women in and out of his room. Women he met in the towns where we stayed. It was fun to watch him operate, but more fun when he went to work on me. More importantly, he was the first man to ever be truthful with me—about himself and his intentions.

When our company was getting ready to move from North Carolina to Atlanta, Georgia, he sat me down. "We're going into a big town now with a lot of nightlife. I know a bartender in a cool place and

I'm going to hang with him and meet some chicks. I'm going to fuck a lot of them. But I'd love it if you were in my bed when I got home."

I thought about it and was amazed that he'd told me the truth and gave me a choice. This was in the days before AIDS, so there was no fear of life-threatening sexually transmitted diseases. The only issues between men and women were personal. I said, "Sure. Why not!" Sometimes, you just have to take life's gifts as they come. No promises were broken between us, because none were ever made.

When I returned to New York City, Charlie and I decided to sublet Paul's place on 24th Street between First and Second Avenues, while Paul went back on the road. My time of living with Charlie didn't go well. He'd party every night at a local pub, then bring home all his drinking buddies to sing and tell jokes till dawn. I'd get up early and leave the want-ads section open on the dining table, while I went to work modeling girdles in a showroom in the garment district for $250 a week, a fortune back then.

He still had amazing powers to charm, evidenced by the fact that he got us permission to get married in the neo-gothic grandeur of NYC's St.

Patrick's Cathedral, though he was from Scranton, Pennsylvania and I was not Catholic. His best friend, Jason Miller (Pulitzer prize-winning playwright of *That Championship Season* and an actor best known for his role as the tortured priest in *The Exorcist*), promised that if we got married, he'd stand in front of the church with a sign that read, "The part of the groom today will be played by Charlie Murphy."

When he took me home to meet his family and party endlessly for a week, I talked privately to his priest who told me that the only place in the world Charlie could ever be responsible was on stage. He said that during his whole ministry, he'd tried to get him to "extend the footlights," and become a responsible adult. It was, however, a losing battle. My boy had grown up in a house where his huge Irish family hid behind doors when the bill collectors came calling.

In the end, I came to my senses. One day, when we'd gone to St. Patrick's for mass, I pictured my tiny wedding party from Mississippi in that massive cathedral and knew that there wasn't enough between him and me to make a marriage. I knelt down and prayed, "Dear God, please get me out of this."

And of course, He did.

One night, thirty-five years later, when I was acting in a play which my husband, Bill Macy, had produced for me in LA, Charlie showed up unannounced in the audience. I was having difficulty with the opening scene. He took me aside and gave me wonderful notes—the keys, as it turned out—to playing that scene with the humor and heart it required. This was a gift of a sweet-loving man, whom I'll always hold dear.

I haven't seen him since.

Back in the days when Charlie and I had sublet Paul's place, Paul had left a lock on his armoire and instructed me not to open it. He'd never met Charlie and trusted me to relay the message to him as well. Unbeknownst to me, Charlie had snuck into the back of that armoire while I was out modeling girdles and found a full pound of marijuana, and he and his buddies proceeded to smoke it all. When Paul's tour was over and he was on his way back to the city, Charlie and I were moving out. I cleaned the apartment before we left, even shampooed the rug, and thought everything was shipshape. The thank you I expected didn't come. Instead, Paul called me, irate. He'd discovered the theft and swore that one day, he'd make Charlie pay.

Fast-forward to Los Angeles thirty years later: a Greek man and an Irish man strike up a friendly conversation in the old Joe Allen's Bar on West Third Street. The Greek is now an associate producer in a company run by eminent actors (and married couple), Tyne Daly and Georg Sanford Brown. The Irishman is a witty, out-of-work actor. At the end of the evening, they introduce themselves to each other.

"Hi, I'm Charlie Murphy," extending his hand, expectantly.

And Paul bellows, *"Charlie fucking Murphy! You've got to be kidding me!"* and drags him bodily to the nearest ATM and makes him cough up the price of a pound of stolen grass from way back when.

Me (far left) and the cast of *Ladies' Night in a Turkish Bath*, including actors in the bottom row, John Rude, Jach Shearer, Paul Cavonis, and Barbara Crossland

Stage time for Barbara Crossland, myself, and Paul Cavonis in *Ladies' Night in a Turkish Bath*

A wonderful moment for me from *Ladies' Night in a Turkish Bath*

CHAPTER 20

THE PREACHER
FROM SCARSDALE

Just to back up a bit, let me tell one last tale before taking you on the road that led me to *Oh! Calcutta!* (and all the adventures since).

In the summer of '69, sometime after I'd first met Pablo and a few months before I was cast in the West Coast production of *Oh! Calcutta!*, I met a thoughtful and liberal young "man of the cloth."

I'd moved out of my apartment next to Julian and Pat Barry and their kids after my roommate stumbled out of bed one night to find me asleep on my foldout couch...with an actor I'd just met on my second Barn Dinner Theatre tour. I couldn't blame her for being upset. I wasn't the same girl she'd known in grad school. So I relocated to the

Longacre House for women on the Upper West Side and was living, as happy as a clam, in my new, private world.

A few blocks west of the Longacre, was an Episcopal church. Very informal and funky. Perfect for hippies and out-of-work actors who didn't have the means or inclination to get dressed up to go to services. Actually, I think it was once an old theatre space, as the aisles slanted downward through rows of folding chairs. I don't remember how I found it, but I liked going to church there.

One Sunday morning as I sat in the aisle about a third of the way down, singing a hymn or reading aloud the written responses in my program, I sensed powerful, gorgeous man vibes behind me, to my right. As I listened to the sermon, the vibes persisted.

When it came time to take communion, I left my seat and went to the front to kneel for sacrament. The man vibes followed me, as did the man. He knelt close to me. I had my eyes closed but could feel him.

When the service ended, I walked outside, and he hurried to catch up with me. "What are you doing this afternoon?" he asked. "I'd love you to drive with me up to Scarsdale. There's going to be a garden party given by some terrific people; I think you'd like them."

"I have a date," I turned to him and smiled. "Would you like to come with me while I break it?"

He walked me back to my Longacre hotel lobby and stood nearby while I made the call. "Hey Pablo, I met a man in church who wants me to go to Scarsdale with him."

"Terrific," Pablo answered, meaning it. "Catch you later." I thanked him and turned to my new acquaintance, who was a bit taller than me, with light brown hair, and a nice build, slim and muscular.

On our hour or so drive up, he told me that he was an assistant minister in an Episcopal church in the parish where we were headed. We arrived at a beautiful home with tables set on the back lawn and finely dressed men and women all abuzz with talk of how to end the war in Vietnam. A liberal bunch for sure, and well-heeled. The food was lovely and the guests intelligent. Moving through the tables, I heard whispers and snatches of conversations about coming protest marches. As the party died down, I sat with a group of about ten hangers-on and we spoke more intimately. They clearly admired my date, who was very at home with them. It was getting dark as we left.

"I have an apartment in the attic above our church," he said easily. "Would you like to go there with me now?"

"Sure," I said, climbing into his car.

When we got to the elegant, old church, he was surprised to find the front door locked, as all the other doors. Undaunted, he headed into the church rectory and found a long stepladder, then secured it beneath a window on the second floor of the church house.

"Let's go," he smiled, and started to climb, me right behind him. When we reached the top, he stepped into his place and helped me in. He had a great stereo system and a nice size bed. I don't remember what else. Soft lighting. Candles, I think. We made love all night to music by the Beatles and the Rolling Stones. The next morning, he drove me back to town.

I think I saw him a couple more times that summer. I was still seeing Pablo once every few weeks and the Greek, Paul Cavonis, about the same amount of time. I remember noting that I had four guys in my life now, one for each weekend a month.

Whether I was counting him back then as well, I do not recall.

In the fall, I left for San Francisco and stayed there for nine months performing in *Oh! Calcutta!* We must've kept in touch, because when I got back to New York, he called and came to see me.

He was a very different man when he showed up to meet me on the Upper West Side, our old stomping grounds. More serious. Introspective. There was a sense of volatility about him, though I don't recall him raising his voice. He easily lost patience with our conversation.

A few months before, on May 4, 1970, he'd been one of the protestors against the bombing of Cambodia at Kent State University and got swept up in the violence that ended in the shooting deaths of four unarmed students and the wounding of nine others by the Ohio National Guard. Bloody pictures of the dead had been published in all the national newspapers. The incident sparked a nationwide student strike and forced hundreds of colleges and universities to close. H. R. Haldeman said in his coauthored book, *The Ends of Power,* that the massacre at Kent State led directly to the Watergate scandal and the fall of Richard Nixon. It was a more complicated situation than was reported at the time, but the energy and outrage arising from the incident had shattered the political landscape and polarized the nation.

As for my lover from the church attic in Scarsdale, it was clear he couldn't look at me in the same light as before. I was just an actress, focused on my career and celebrating good times—enchanted by the magic of creating the life of my dreams and high from my first success in show business. He was disillusioned, angry, and frustrated. We never saw each other again.

After all this time, I'm embarrassed and deeply regret that I do not remember his name. In my stories about him all these years I've simply referred to him as the preacher from Scarsdale. I wish I could go to Wikipedia for the answer.

"Who was the assistant Episcopal minister I slept with in the Scarsdale church belfry in 1969?"

Who indeed.

Siri, do you know his name?

I wonder if he remembers mine.

CHAPTER 21

ROAD TO
OH! CALCUTTA!
ACT 1

I always felt that if I ever gave up my virginity to anyone other than my husband on my wedding night, I'd probably bed a lot of men before I was done. Once the rule was broken, what was to stop me?

As you can probably surmise from the last several chapters, that proved to be "right on," as we said in the '60s. Once I got over the two years of the on-again/off-again ride with my first beloved—through all his withholding of sex (for my own good, I presumed)—and all the hopes and heartbreaks, once I got free and on my own, it suddenly dawned on me.

I don't have to be horny and lonely all the time. All I have to do is to stop saying, "No!"

So I did.

The only rule I made for myself was that I'd never fuck anybody I didn't like. Pardon my French (one of the few times that I'll use the F word), but that's the only way to honestly convey how I talked to myself at the time.

I was in full rebellion. The world around me was embarking on a cultural revolution unlike anything seen in human history, with New York City on its vanguard, waving flags and saluting.

Shortly after leaving my first love (or more correctly, asking him to leave me), I went on the road in a play called *Ladies' Night in a Turkish Bath* and then another right on its heels, *Guys and Dolls*. When I returned to New York after those two Barn Dinner Theatre tours, the city had undergone a transformation.

Hippies lined the streets uptown and down, wearing cool, colorful ragged clothes, no underwear, headbands, love beads, and scruffy sandals. These kids were everywhere...in Central Park, in all the parks, smoking grass on the street while they lined up to see futuristic movies like *2001* on balmy summer nights. By day, they sat on the sidewalks and played guitars or just hung out.

Seeing them so carefree, I wanted to apologize for my existence, as I was still working for a living, wearing makeup and dressing straight. I wanted to walk up to them and say, "Pardon me. I wish I understood what you are doing. I don't, but I think you are totally cool."

This was a unique and awesome time in history, never to be repeated, a time of absolute freedom created by two factors: easy access to birth control and the absence of deadly health threats from sexually transmitted diseases. There was no AIDS. No nothing that penicillin couldn't cure.

Women were starting to take their pleasure where they could find it, and I, more than most, was eager to finally engage in love that was truly free.

I'd broken all the rules of Church. Not only was I having sex I was also completely unrepentant. I would not, could not, say I was sorry. A little guilty maybe, but I buried that deep.

Meanwhile, I was discovering metaphysics. Books about it were big in the '60s, teaching us that we humans had an active part in creating our realities. I'd lived through many years believing that everything was happening for my good—a tenet of the Presbyterian faith in which I was raised—and as a result, had watched miracles unfold around me. I didn't want to give up that magic or the charm of love at the core of my spirituality. But now I had to find something more universally true. Something that anyone could use, not just unmarried virgins and believers in old-time religion.

And I found it! In three books.

The first was *The Magic of Believing* by Claude M. Bristol, given to me on a Barn Dinner Theatre tour of *Guys and Dolls* by a skinny and wild, blue-eyed actress with a dirty-blonde, pixie haircut named DeeDee Winner. She'd been cast in another play which preceded ours on the circuit, *The Owl and the Pussycat,* but had disliked her part and herself in it. On a layover with our two companies, DeeDee had managed to convince a chorus girl in our show to swap places with her, letting the young "doll" sink her claws into that big, juicy *Pussycat* role while DeeDee joined our cast to beat the drum in our Salvation Army band.

After every nightly performance, we'd play poker and blackjack with the guys, and DeeDee would whisper card-playing strategies into my ear. It was a funny sight, me still dolled up in my Adelaide makeup, DeeDee with her Salvation Army coat slung over the back of her chair, and five gangster types sitting around a table. She taught me how to draw cards to myself, to see the card I needed, picture it falling in front of me on the table, *to want it intensely,* then let it go and watch it fall. We took their money more often than not.

All the actors lived in the Barn Dinner Theatres' upstairs quarters, which were identical along the whole circuit. In one town, the cast was given the use of a company van to take us wherever we needed to go. Trouble was, it didn't run well. It was old and broken down and wouldn't start for love or money but *would* crank whenever DeeDee and I washed it and talked nicely to it. "See it happening," she'd mumble once we'd spruced it up, then she'd croon sweet praises to it and turn the key. The damn thing started for us, every time.

The Magic of Believing book had a blurb on the cover by Phyllis Diller saying it helped her move from housewife to standup comic. It was fascinating. I started to realize that my belief in what was possible was shaping my world. That—and my imagination. *How much was I willing to stretch it? What did I really want out of living the life of an aspiring actor?*

When I'd first arrived in NYC, I told Bill and Peggy Simmons, the couple who rented a room to me, "I don't know if I'll ever make it as an actor, but I'm going to have a good time trying."

How willing was I to really go for it? To see myself working in the big city, to taste and smell a career and try drawing it to me, like cards in a poker game?

When I got back to town, I stumbled into a metaphysical bookstore on Sixth Avenue or possibly Broadway...somewhere in Midtown on the West Side. A title caught my eye: *Psycho-Cybernetics* by Maxwell Maltz. I bought it.

By that time, I was living in the Longacre House for Women at the corner of 50th Street and Eighth Avenue. Today it's a grand apartment building, but back then it was a dingy hotel with tiny rooms, each with only one window, and a community bathroom down the hall. When I say tiny, I mean just enough room for a single bed, one chair, and a dressing table. The head of the bed was near the door to the hall. Beyond the foot of the bed was the window. I could see the sky while I stretched out to get some rest. A lot of ex-WACs (the skirted soldiers of the Women's Army Corp) lived in Longacre, too. It was just west of the heart of Broadway. Funky and functional. I stacked my sheet music next to my dressing table and taped index cards with encouraging quotes to my walls. I did the Royal Canadian Air Force Exercise routine out in the hallway each morning.

I loved it.

Maltz's book, *Psycho-Cybernetics,* focused on programming the subconscious mind to produce life changes. It taught me how to induce an altered mental state and allow myself to "see" the reality I wanted.

In those days, when you went to casting calls, you could sometimes get scripts and bring them home to work on and prepare for your audition the next day. I used those times to practice my new magic.

I'd read a scene, then lie down on the bed, relax my mind and all my muscles, close my eyes, and imagine a bare stage. Then I'd watch myself walk in from the wings and wait to see what I'd do next. Often, I'd laugh out loud. I got some great ideas in those sessions and could actually carry them off at auditions.

But could I create an actual job by programming my subconscious mind? Wasn't that cheating? Some kind of magic?

Was it okay to try to consciously generate the reality I wanted, instead of waiting for some heavenly force to give it to me after I'd worked so hard and been a good girl?

The answers I needed came in a most unexpected way.

I was still working then at The Plaza's Palm Court, and one evening I staggered into work after getting some very bad news. My best friend from back home, Diane, was encountering a devastating loss, the kind of thing that happens in many of our lives, so brutally painful, so unexplainable that the mind reels in the face of it.

At The Plaza Hotel, in the employees' dining room, I sat with a man named Lou, a "checker" (one who watched our trays out of the Palm Court kitchen and into the dining area to "check" that there was no stealing from the bar). I was a mess. This Mississippi tragedy of my best friend did not seem like the work of God.

The All-Loving Force at the Heart of the Universe had not done this. Human beings had a part in it.

But what part? How did it work?

Mysterious ways weren't an answer for me anymore.

Lou gave me a book that he thought might help, *Learn to Live* by Ervin Seale. It was a book of Jesus's parables explained in metaphysical terms. Inside me, a light turned on.

I'd always felt a deep connection to Jesus's teachings about love. Now I saw that he was speaking the same language as my metaphysical books. That was the puzzle piece I needed: To know that this new way of viewing the world wasn't arrogant or irreverent. That I wasn't being greedy, manipulative, or reckless with forces that I was only beginning to understand. It was mine to create my reality. I could have anything I wanted and believed in.

I could stretch my imagination, expand possibilities, and ride on dreams as I'd done all my life, except now with clearer, more specific intent. I could actually start living my dream.

Did I dare?

I was going to try.

It was seeing the Broadway musical *Hair* that gave me the focus for everything I'd been learning, that started pulling the pieces together on the puzzle of Life and condensing them into a glowing sphere of understanding and power.

It was the source of a dream.

The dream that changed my life.

CHAPTER 22

ROAD TO
OH! CALCUTTA!
ACT 2

I don't remember how I got in to see *Hair* in the summer of '69. But I do recall that a cousin came to town that year and was stunned to learn that I hadn't been attending any of the theatrical productions on Broadway. *How was I going to work on stage if I didn't know what was going on in the business?*

She was right, of course. I'd been working nights at the Gaslight Club as a singing waitress, wearing high heels, fishnet stockings, and a roaring twenties version of what Hugh Hefner's bunnies were poured into just a few blocks away. Because I was so tall and couldn't fit into any of the hand-me-downs that most of the new girls wore, the boss, Victor Bennis, had the costumier make me two gorgeous outfits. Both were velvet, one emerald green with rhinestones, the other royal purple with pearls. The Gaslight was housed in an old three-story mansion in Midtown on the East Side. In its basement was a restaurant for fine dining. Upstairs on the first floor, Tommy Furtado (a pal of Frank Sinatra, who also sang the national anthem at Yankee and Shea Stadiums) played piano in a jazz trio on a bandstand in a big open room. I adored him; he could break your heart when he sang. For quieter drinkers, a tiny private library, complete with shelves of books and two or three small tables was situated in a little nook in the far front corner of that same room.

On the second floor was a piano bar, and a "secret" entrance to a stairway leading to the speakeasy upstairs where girls danced the Charleston, kicking strings of pearls into the air, which they'd spun around their ankles and toes, catching them over their heads to loud applause and huge tips. I worked the two rooms on the lower levels, singing two songs with every set that various musicians played. Being too tall for the speakeasy with its low ceilings, I missed out on the big money being thrown around up there. One girl was even given a luxury car by one of her clients. This without his even knowing her real name, as all the girls working at the Gaslight were required to use aliases. It was absolutely forbidden to tell our true identity to customers.

At the Gaslight, I was known as Stacy.

I was having a ball, busy with voice lessons and sessions with my musical arranger, Howard Hodge, a cool, black jazz man who helped me fake my way through several easy songs that I had in my repertoire for the club, among them "The Look of Love" composed by Burt Bacharach and Hal David, and "Can't Take My Eyes Off You," a gold-record hit for Frankie Valli. When I first met Howard, he'd asked me to sing with my eyes closed so he could get a feel for the kind of musician/singer I was. When I opened them, he raised an eyebrow and said, "Well, okay. Let's just go with what we got." Then he showed me how to sing each note, gently bending some of them to make it sound like I was improvising.

Of course, I was auditioning for plays whenever I could, but I wasn't seeing any, other than to occasionally "second act" a production, slipping in at intermission to stand in the back and watch the rest of the show.

My cousin may have actually given me money for my ticket to the legendary rock musical *Hair*. However it happened, I landed a seat at the Biltmore Theatre for a matinee performance—and entered a different universe. One that was at direct odds with the Gaslight Club, which wallowed in and profited from the lush, good times of men with sizable expense accounts, dining and drinking and flirting with scantily, luxuriously clad young women, dropping big sums into their palms or tip jars in the downstairs' rooms, or popping bills into their garters upstairs in the speakeasy.

Hair was billed as an "American tribal love-rock musical." It was alive with energy. It presented a culture that was anti-business, anti-structure, anti-work, anti-war. Against underwear, makeup, and manicures. Against money. Against being poor. It was a chaos of crumbling and crashing value systems without clear ideas of how to replace them. It was the first rock musical ever done, with book and lyrics by James Rado and Gerome Ragni and music by Galt MacDermot.

I can still taste the excitement in the crowd that afternoon and feel the magic of Director Tom O'Horgan's staging (who also did *Jesus Christ Superstar*). Scaffolding around and above the stage let cast members (there must've been fifty of them) literally climb the walls and hang from the ceiling. They passed joints and sang and danced and loved and cried and, once in a while, got naked.

My mind was completely blown. I was overcome with knee-weakening, soul-wrenching desire.

Musical theatre had drawn me to New York City in the first place. By the end of high school, my *star*-struck days as a young teenager had become *stage*-struck days. Plays like *My Fair Lady, Flower Drum Song,* and *The Music Man* had landed in Memphis, Tennessee, and set me on fire, and *The Fantastics* enchanted me during its long run at the Front Street Theatre.

In college, I'd played small roles in *South Pacific; Kiss Me, Kate;* and *Damn Yankees.* I knew I didn't have the splendid and distinctive voice for those big musicals, but I was training what voice I had and hoping for the best. Dreaming of somehow beating the odds.

But while I watched *Hair,* an altogether different kind of dream was born. A dream of belonging. Of celebrating a freedom new to this Earth. Of exploring the Age of Aquarius with all its mysteries. Then and there, I set sights on becoming a member of the cast of *Hair.* I wanted it as much as I'd ever wanted anything in my life—and was determined to have it.

Back in my room at the Longacre House, only a few blocks from the Biltmore where *Hair* was playing, I took an hour every morning and an hour every night to dream.

When I say dream, I mean dream from a deep place. I knew how to go into altered states, had been prepared for it when, at the age of thirteen, my teeth stopped responding to Novocain and my Memphis dentist, Dr. Bledsoe (if you can believe that) used hypnosis to do deep and potentially painful, hours-long work in my mouth.

I used his hypnosis technique now at the Longacre to dream the dream of my dreams. I dreamed every aspect of being in that play. There had been no particular part that had called to me. I didn't care what character I'd play. I just wanted to be up there with those people, singing and dancing to that music.

I dreamed of myself auditioning, getting hired, signing autographs—not necessarily in that order—as all my future images floated and changed. I'd see myself at Joe Allen's Theatre Bar for hamburgers and beer, still flushed with the glow of performance, then switch to breaking into a sweat, dancing and singing on stage in the heat of a song. I dreamed of myself losing weight and getting fitter from all the exercise, from the thrill, the lift, the flight. I'd let myself experience the senses of that world, where *Hair* was my life. I did this both mornings and evenings for one hour for about two weeks.

One night or maybe it was one morning, while I was living in my dream, I had the sensation that I could open my eyes, step off the bed, and be in that world for real. I could just step into a dimension in which I was in the musical *Hair*. I felt certain this was true.

At that moment, without any forethought, I blurted out, "Dear God, that's my idea. If you've got a better one, I'll go with yours!" I don't know where that came from, but as a child I'd always talked to God directly. And then, I felt my prayer land.

And that finished it.

I stepped off the bed and stopped all further dreaming. I didn't think about it again and just reentered my life. But the big wheel was turning. I had tripped it. It was starting to roll and was gaining momentum. A giant wheel it was. A water wheel at an old mill, as I think of it now, coated with wet mosses, ancient.

Heavy.

And finally—on the move.

Two weeks later, I left for Boulder, Colorado, to visit my brother in grad school. His wife and some friends took me out on a mountainside and casually proceeded to drop acid. When I asked what it was like, they said, "You'll never know unless you try it." So I did. I must have had a great trip. People kept looking at me and muttering something about "good karma."

I remember wanting to get naked out there on the mountainside, though I didn't dare. I also remember gold dust gleaming in a tiny stream of water, and ants marching across my arm as I lay there in *bliss* to the max.

Back in NYC two weeks later, I showed up at the Gaslight for work and was told I wasn't scheduled until the following week. My job was nonunion. I had no recourse. My boss swore he hadn't instructed me to come back to work before another week was out. Stuck in a smelly New York summer and jobless, I started roaming the streets and angrily declaring, "Something wonderful is going to come out of this! Something outstandingly wonderful is going to come out of this! I swear on all that's holy, something wonderful is going to come out of this!"

Every time I saw a payphone I'd stop and try to find someone, anyone, a friend to hang out with. Finally I reached, of all people, DeeDee Winner, the skinny blonde actress I'd toured with on *Guys and Dolls*. The one who first introduced me to metaphysics and gave me the book, *The Magic of Believing*. When she heard my voice, she shrieked with joy, "Oh my God! You'll never guess where I'm working, in the concession stand in the Eden Theatre down on Second Avenue near St. Mark's Place. The play is called *Oh! Calcutta!*

"Get on a bus and meet me there now, Sam. Everybody is naked and all the guys are straight!"

CHAPTER 23

ROAD TO
OH! CALCUTTA!
ACT 3

W e've all had it happen. A moment when everything changes. When the kaleidoscope image of our life is altered by the slightest turn of a cosmic wrist and a completely different snowflake forms before our eyes, shifting its shape in stages, then settling into the space of the one there before, revealing portals into hitherto unknown destinies.

From the moment I stepped into the concession stand with DeeDee and helped her sell Pepsi colas and candy in the Eden Theatre basement, I could feel the excitement of a hit show being born. The play *Oh! Calcutta!* was still in previews, had been for months, and everybody who was anybody was getting downtown to see it.

Standing behind the counter, I was surprised to see a girl from my days at Ole Miss. She'd been Cathy Johnson then, a tall and slim Texas blonde with deep blue eyes, a huge belting voice, a dry, dark and daring wit, and more than her fair share of nerve. She'd played several leads in the school's musicals. After watching her in a couple of productions, my dad said if the university didn't lose her, I'd never get cast in anything. Well, my father was mostly right. The fact is, if she'd made her grades, I wouldn't have gotten the part of Hattie, the backstage dresser in *Kiss Me, Kate*, singing and shamelessly strutting the opening number, "Another Op'nin', Another Show." The part still had her name beside it on the casting announcement sheet but fell to me when she had flunked too many courses.

Recognizing me behind the counter, Cathy launched into the high points of her resume since arriving in New York. She'd changed her name to Kathleen Dabney and was living with Jacques Levy, the director of *Oh! Calcutta!* She'd also just appeared in a movie with Arlo Guthrie, *Alice's Restaurant*, a 1969 comedy directed by Arthur Penn, and she'd had another movie written about her called *That*

Crazy American Girl. Here's how she explained her name change to me, "Honey, how could I ever play Lady Macbeth as Cathy Johnson?"

I was duly impressed.

There was a door to an office just to my left, and no sooner had Cathy walked away when it opened and DeeDee's roommate, Sue, emerged and joined us. I guess she had some kind of job in the production, but I never found out what. Things were starting to move, and it was all I could do to keep up.

"They are holding auditions for the San Francisco production of this show tomorrow," Sue said. "I'm too fat and DeeDee's too skinny. You're going for *us*."

"But I can't audition," I started protesting, following her into the office. "I haven't sung in weeks and my accompanist is out of town." There was a group of men playing poker in the corner. One of them was Jacques Levy, the show's director.

"Are you a trained singer?" he asked, glancing up from his hand.

"Well, yes," I said, stretching it a bit.

"So, sing anything," he offered, then put his eyes back on his cards.

They scheduled me for a 10:30 audition the following morning, and stunned, I went up to see the play, as the house was going dark.

The experience of watching that show was surreal. The writing was uneven, but the spirit of the show and the players was something to be seen, heard, felt, smelled, tasted. It was as if each actor had discovered a unique brand of freedom, of love, daring, independence, playfulness, and wit.

The play itself was sometimes brilliant and extremely funny; other times embarrassing, shocking, titillating, and occasionally even downright trashy, but always (at least barely) within the bounds of decency. The performers were unashamed, raucous, joyous. They looked like they'd been released from some kind of prison. Light beamed in and through and around the whole cast.

Basically, they were having a blast.

For a brief moment, I felt like they all looked like me up there, and everyone in the audience looked just like my parents.

At the end of the show, I somehow got myself home to the Longacre House and stumbled into my room and got to work. I didn't stop to question what was happening. I knew it was coming from the dream work I'd done, and that that final prayer, the "better idea" to which I'd surrendered, was now in play.

As you may recall, I had a rather vivid relationship with my subconscious mind at that point. I lay down on my bed and relaxed, then said, "Okay, subconscious, if you're so fucking smart, what am I going to sing tomorrow?"

On the top of my large stack of sheet music next to my dressing table near the foot of my bed was Burt Bacharach's and Hal David's "I'll Never Fall in Love Again."

Inspired by something that happened on the road while I was touring, I wrote alternate and rather risqué lyrics to that song.

The next morning I arrived early and overheard a girl singing on stage. She had a gorgeous soprano voice. I waited my turn. Eventually Jacques opened a door to a small sitting room away from the main stage. I sat down with him, and he smiled.

"So tell me about yourself…what have you done in show business so far?"

I opened my mouth to speak but couldn't get a word out. I started to tremble and shake and before I knew it, I was crying like a baby. Tears streamed down my cheeks as I fought for control.

"Did I say something to offend you?"

"Yes!" I blurted out. "Everybody asks me what I've done. And I haven't done ANYTHING! Nobody asks me what I want to say."

"What *do* you want to say?"

"I saw the play," I wailed. Then stopped and looked him in the eye. "And I'd be wonderful in it."

"Do me a favor," Jacques leaned forward, his hands on his knees. "Turn around and walk out of here and don't look back."

"Please," I begged. "Just let me sing."

"If I let you sing, and I like it, I'm going to ask you to read and to dance, and if I like that, you're going to be in this show before you know it." I noticed the ease in his eyes, worn-out jeans, heavy leather belt and soft plaid cotton shirt—looking like a transplanted Texas cowboy. "I live with a girl from the South. I know what it will do to your family. Just turn around right now and go home."

I took a deep breath, "Just let me sing."

So he got up and escorted me into the theatre, where Margo Sappington, the choreographer; Mike Thoma, the stage manager; and an actor named Bill Macy, sat in the house. At the piano was Stanley Walden, one of three composers for the controversial off-Broadway show. The other two weren't present at my audition: Peter Schickele (of P.D.Q. Bach fame, his satirical alias), and Robert Dennis, composer of "Milk" for *Sesame Street*. Together, the three of them cut an electronic-jazz album called *The Open Window*.

I slipped my sheet music to Stanley and whispered, "I'm going to sing different words." Then I went on stage and stood there in my wine-colored mini-skirt and white polyester scooped-neck tulip-sleeved blouse, with a vest laced over it to match my skirt. Stanley played the intro as I sang:

"What do you get when you fall in love?

A guy with a pin, to burst your cherry

That's what you get, unless he's a fairy

I'll never fall in love again
I'll never fall in love again
What do you get when you give your heart?
You win a new friend, who'll sit and rap
Long enough to say, 'You've got the clap!'
I'll never fall in love again
I'll never fall in love again

Don't tell me what it's all about,
Cause I've been there and I'm glad I'm out
Away from the shots, the snickers, and grins
That's the kind of shape I don't want to be in!

What do you get when you fall in love?
The least of your cares is gonorrhea.
So for just now, I'm ending my career
I'll never fall in love again
I'll never fall in love again!"

I don't know what I'd have done if they hadn't laughed. But, thank God, they did. After a silence that sucked the wind from my soul following "unless he's a fairy," they started to crack up and continued to laugh till the end of the song.

Then Jacques spoke up. "We have a problem. The show is all cast except for one part, and we need a soprano."

"Then, you're up shit creek," I smiled back at him, "because I can't sing soprano."

Stanley motioned me to the piano. He played and I sang "Happy Birthday" in a high register while fending off that crazy Bill Macy, inspired by Jacques who'd told him to loosen me up by doing outrageous things—once even grabbing me, bending me over backwards, kissing me deeply, then dropping me on the piano bench. *What a nut*, I thought.

"Happy Birthday" is a horrible song and I wasn't getting anywhere with it, so Stanley moved on, having me sing arpeggios. He worked them higher and higher. I reached and stretched. I folded my elbows and flapped my arms like wings while I tried for those notes.

And then, suddenly, I was singing them. Notes an octave higher than I'd ever sung in my life. I was a fucking soprano.

"She can do it!" Stanley yelled.

We settled down for a while, me sitting near Jacques in the house, when he turned to me. "Was there a scene in the show that particularly offended you?" he asked.

"Only the one about wife swapping."

"Guess which one I want you to read," he smiled.

"Well, at least I won't have to watch it."

I looked the scene over and went back up on stage. As I was delivering the monologue, he interrupted me. "Where is your Southern accent?" he asked.

I protested that I *was* using my Southern accent, gentle and genteel as it was, so he turned to Margo, who was playing the part in the NYC production. "Show her." Margo took up the monologue where I'd left off, sounding *very* rural Texas, like she just stepped out of a trailer park. She ended it with the words, "Do ya know what I mean?"

"I wish I did!" I sailed back to her, kind of dumbfounded but unconsciously mimicking her twang.

That cracked everyone up. "Oh!" I put in. "You don't mean *Southern*. You mean from the

Hills!" I picked up the monologue sounding like her twin sister, and from then on, had the part nailed.

So I was told to take an hour break and come back for the dance and then—the *nude* audition.

Wandering on the street near the church at St. Mark's Place, I bumped into a young man, a heroin addict staying at a nearby halfway house. We sat on a car hood and he asked what I was doing.

"I'm going to go do a nude audition." I was drained and in shock, but also liked the feeling. He sat and didn't react. "I know I can do it. I take my clothes off every night, so I'll just go take them off on stage."

"Come back later," he said gently. "Maybe we could have dinner."

I headed back to the theatre, where Margo took me through some dance moves. She was a rebel ballerina who'd opted for a style of her own, with yoga, jazz, modern dance, and ballet swirled together in her imaginative mix of movements.

Though only twenty-one, she was a born leader. I found out later that Michael Bennett, producer and co-choreographer for an uptown musical called *A Chorus Line* had originally been asked to choreograph *Oh! Calcutta!* but at the last minute had chickened out and sent Margo in his place. Sometime after, she was leading dance auditions on the stage with Jacques, the director, looking on. Next to him was my future husband, Bill Macy, who'd already been cast in the show.

Jacques turned to Bill. "Watch Margo. She's getting ready to audition for me." Sure enough, the next moment she threw off her top and danced bare-breasted while she worked out the dancers behind her. After that, it was a done deal. She was in. She quickly took on her role as a creative force in the show, and a spiritual force as well. She could coax moves out of the stiffest of actors, energizing and inspiring us with her humor, freedom, passion, and vision.

Dancing with her was easy. She made me feel I could do anything. Her moves were fluid, sensual, earthy, and fun. I found myself in a dream where I could do no wrong. After fifteen minutes or so, Margo turned to Jacques, seated in the house. "She can do it!" she said and beamed a big smile.

So now it was down to the dreaded nude audition. It was to be an improvisation.

Jacques gave me directions while a crew member cleared the stage and laid a sheet on the floor stage right.

"You have written a novel," he said, "and today you've gotten a notice in the mail saying it's been sold. To celebrate, you've taken a train to upstate New York and dropped your things off at a friend's cabin and are walking in the woods. You notice a small pond over there where we've placed the sheet. I want you to take that walk on stage, see the water, take off your clothes, lie down in the pond, and compose a letter out loud to the person you feel closest to in this moment."

Well, I don't have to tell you how prepared I was to play that little scene. Fresh off my acid trip in Colorado where I so longed to get naked out in nature, realizing that the "novel" I wrote was actually this job that I was going to get, I was primed. The letter I composed was to my first lover who'd dealt me a blow to the heart from which I hadn't fully recovered. The letter was about gold dust that glistened beneath a stream of shallow water, too fine to be extracted, and about the beauty that had to be experienced in the moment, or not at all.

I found myself lost in the wonder of what was happening. As I spoke my thoughts…the letter, as it were, and gazed into the lights, it was as if time had stopped. I could stay here forever in suspended space if I wanted to. I didn't mind being naked with these people, not at all. I loved it. And I would love being naked on stage in front of hundreds of strangers. I was where I belonged. At the end of what I had to say, I staggered up off the sheet and wandered toward the wings. People rushed to bring me my clothes, helped me put them on, and ushered me down the stairs and back into the house.

In the dimming light, as I sat in a row behind Jacques, and my fellow future cast members, he turned to me. "Well, Samantha, what are you going to tell your mother?"

"Oh," I shook my head, "I can't do the show unless my parents say it's okay."

His jaw dropped, as did everyone else's.

To say there was stunned silence is an understatement.

Finally Mike Thoma, the stage manager spoke up. "We'll give you till the crack of 10:30 tomorrow morning to let us know."

Long story short, I went back to the Longacre and dived onto my bed, quickly slipping into a meditative state. I visualized telling my folks of my adventure and imagined them hearing what I had to say. After an hour of that, I called them.

I waited for them to each pick up an extension line, then took a deep breath and launched in. "I have to warn you, I've been communicating with you on other levels for over an hour." I let that sink in. "Today I auditioned for a play that's in previews here in town. It's naked and raucous and vulgar, but it's with the most creative group of people that I've ever met, and I think it has my name on it." The silence almost swallowed me. I cleared my throat, then barreled on. "I've been offered a job in the San Francisco production of the show, with rehearsals starting in a couple of weeks. But if you can't okay it, I'll walk away and not look back and never blame you." I let out my breath. Whatever they said, I could live with it.

On separate phones, my dad, a Presbyterian elder in our church and my mom, a high school English teacher, in unison said, "Do it!"

I was blown away.

"Do you want me to change my name?"

"You do whatever you want to do." Daddy, very gently, spoke from his heart.

The next week, when the spread in *Playboy* magazine, featuring a story and naked photos of the New York cast of *Oh! Calcutta!* hit the stands, my parents called me back.

"If you want to change your name," one of them managed to say, "that would be alright with us."

Me in the film version of *Oh! Calcutta!* (1972)

Me in the film version of *Oh! Calcutta!*

Me and Mitchell McGuire on the set of *Oh! Calcutta!*

Mitchell McGuire, myself, and Mark Dempsey from the movie *Oh! Calcutta!*

Me and future hubby, Bill Macy, in the movie *Oh! Calcutta!*

Bill Macy in the movie *Oh! Calcutta!* (the leg shots belong to Margo Sappington and Nancy Tribush)

Me obviously baring a breast in the movie *Oh! Calcutta!*

CHAPTER 24

NOTORIOUS IN SAN FRANCISCO

A little should be said about our year in San Francisco rehearsing and performing *Oh! Calcutta!* at the end of a decade and the start of a new one, how that city worked on us, and how we worked that city.

A psychedelic collage of memories, images, sensations come flooding back. The smell of the sixties in the heyday of '69. Hippies on the streets, in the parks, everywhere. Girls in sheer skirts with tops hanging unbuttoned and loose off their shoulders, offering glimpses of bare breasts, dancing, singing, getting high. Young men with beards and long scruffy hair in worn-out jeans and sweatshirts ripped at the seams. Warm breezes flowing in from the Bay

Area at our company's get-acquainted party on the famous Fishermen's Wharf. Haight-Ashbury, the neighborhood that birthed the '60s counterculture movement. The kid who asked, "Do you want a flower?" to which I cheerfully called back, "I *am* a fucking flower!" then kept strolling in the autumn sunshiny afternoon, in a heaven that would never end. Chinatown with its shrimp, tender greens, eggrolls, and fortune cookies. The Mystic Eye, a store full of crystals and incense, magic potions, frankincense, myrrh, and black smoke. Blues guitarist and singer-songwriter B.B. King's Christmas album spilling out from surround speakers in the Northridge record store, just down the street from our avant-garde theatre, crazily named the On Broadway. Roaring bars opening onto streets with tables flowing across sidewalks. Strip shows in small dives and an extravagant transvestite revue on a side street second-floor site above a bar, its performers prancing joyously to packed houses.

We dubbed San Francisco "the city of the married man," because the straight guys had been scoffed down by the locals long ago. The single guys that remained were either gay or broke.

Our cast consisted of four women, four men. Our first task was to find places to live during our run in San Francisco. One of the actresses, Cassia Besson, was married and moved into a small apartment with her husband. The other three of us, Ronda Copland, niece of the famous composer, teacher, writer, and conductor Aaron Copland; Pamela Pilkenton, a young dancer who was to do the *pas de deux* (a ballet duet dance) with its death-defying leaps and landings; and I took the second floor of a duplex on Jackson Street in Pacific Heights, an area inhabited mostly by schoolteachers, like those on the floor below us, and other such respectable citizens. Our place became well-known to all in the neighborhood, as well as most cab drivers in the city.

Ronda was flamboyant, with long dark hair and a full figure. She had a trunk full of vintage clothes, hip jewelry, over-the-counter and prescription pills, plus recreational drugs for all occasions, which she unpacked and placed in an armoire in the back bedroom. Pamela was petite, perky, and a hoot. She brought her big, yellow tomcat, Morris, with her in a carrying case, took the central bedroom and hung little bells on strings with thumbtacks from the ceiling to outline her bed. She burned incense in her room and around the apartment and lived on thin slices of cheese and the occasional marshmallow cookie, shedding a few pounds in the six weeks before we opened. For the rest of the eight or so months in that apartment, Morris the cat would wait by the door every night for us to return home and watch *The Tonight Show Starring Johnny Carson* while we ate and got stoned. He'd sit on our dining table and let us blow smoke on him till he got mellow, his glowing eyes alert but half-closed. Then we'd put ornaments on his head—matchbooks, jewelry, rolling papers, and anything else that struck our fancy. He was a good boy. I slept on a mattress in our big, gorgeous living room with floor-to-ceiling windows and a wood-burning fireplace. Over the mantle hung a large painting of three naked ladies, seen from the rear. I forget how we came by that piece of art. It may have been a poster that one of us found. The female in the middle was taller than the other two and had by far the biggest rump. (I asked a guy who slept over one night which one he liked best, to which he quipped, "I'll take the two in the middle.")

Our dining room was situated between where I slept and the kitchen, and it was a magnet for all sorts of people that one or the other of us had met and invited over, and who stayed to hang out as long as we'd let them. They overflowed into the living room where I slept, in the ways of a commune.

A middle-aged black man who'd installed our telephone brought a sack lunch and ate at our table for several weeks. He'd call first from the top of telephone poles to see if it was okay to come over. A bearded postman who passed us by, sitting on our front steps waiting for a cab, overheard us complaining that we didn't know where to buy good weed and volunteered to be our dope man. He delivered for us big-time, and no wind, rain, or fog could stop him. He supplied not only our grass, but all kinds of various drug samples that he'd found in the mail. One young man came into our home and silently stood on his head in a corner of the living room every day. It took us over a week to realize that none of us knew him. We'd all assumed he was a friend of one of the others of us.

We finally had to put our foot down and start throwing people out so we could get serious about rehearsing.

Rehearsals were a story unto themselves. We worked for four weeks without ever seeing a script, doing encounter exercises developed at the Esalen Institute in Big Sur, California (a nonprofit retreat center that played a big part in the Human Potential Movement birthed in the '60s), to prepare to be nude with each other and in public.

Our director, Jacques Levy, had been a psychologist before he was a theatre man, and he was brilliant at both. Margo Sappington, who'd choreographed the show in New York joined us in San Francisco to do the same. She put us through a routine of warm-up exercises every day, moves based on yoga and modern dance, helping us develop more flexibility for our roles and our dance moves, toning and reshaping our bodies.

When we arrived at the theatre on our first day of rehearsal, we were instructed to go to our dressing rooms and put on rehearsal robes. We were to wear nothing else, no underwear, jewelry, or adornment of any kind. We were also asked not to sunbathe nude until the show's opening and to keep any tan lines left over from our previous summer. The robes were a tan cotton with threaded-through belts that tied at the waist. We were instructed never to be half-dressed, only fully clothed or fully naked, and when naked, it had to be for our work on stage.

The encounter exercises that Jacques gave us started out gently but intensified steadily throughout the ensuing weeks. In an early one, all the cast members stood in a circle in their robes. We each took turns moving to the center of the circle, removing our robe, and allowing the others, all fully dressed, to look at us unhurriedly, up and down for a long minute or two, then turned to face the other direction, so we could be seen front and back by all. Then we put our robes back on and stepped back to the outer circle, allowing another actor to take our place.

Every Sunday, I called home to Mississippi, with less and less to say each time. Culture shock was upon me. I hardly knew myself, but I wouldn't have changed any of it for the world.

By the end of the fourth week, the entire cast finally became naked together. At that point, the exercises had become more and more athletic, and we'd become more relaxed with one another. The rehearsal robes had become a real nuisance. They were a pain to keep tied and kept getting in our way whenever we needed to move quickly. In a final crescendo of a sound and movement exercise, as we grew sweaty, frenzied, and exhausted, we heard Jacques call out, "Drop your robes!" We did. All of us at once.

Then he quietly said, "Lay down in a pile in the center of the room and close your eyes."

Lying there together in the dark, sprawled in a tangle with each other, Jacques, continued: "If you give it some thought, you will see why it is important that you do not fuck each other during the run of this play. In most companies, on your first day of rehearsals, you look around to see who you want to take to bed. And then people start pairing up. And someone feels left out, gets hurt. And for the ones who get together...well, things don't always work out. Now you've got a company of unhappy, estranged actors trying to get over disappointing romances.

"That can't happen here. I want all the excitement, all the mystery, all the desire, all the fantasies to be *on the stage and in the performances*."

We saw that he had a point and from that day forward, adhered religiously to what we called the no-fuck rule. At least, that is, until after the show opened and he'd left town.

After that final encounter exercise, we were at last given our scripts. We had two weeks to rehearse the sketches and songs, and the cast became dizzy with getting the play, which was intricate, onto its feet. But we now had under our belts what we needed most. We could be nude and unembarrassed, not throwing down the gauntlet as a challenge to our audience, and also not begging to be liked. We could allow the public the freedom to respond as it would.

And then came opening night. Dress rehearsal had been a disaster, with sets falling down and actors stumbling frenzied from scene to scene. We were very uptight. Jacques called for a rehearsal that afternoon. We were incensed at the thought, feeling put-upon and martyred when we arrived.

Jacques had us sit in the house. He then dimmed the lights and showed us Marx Brothers' movies all afternoon. We laughed the kind of laughter that can break a spell. It helped us remember something of who we really were, tasting the thrill of what we were about to do. In the early evening, we rolled into our dressing rooms and started applying our makeup.

"Professor" Irwin Corey, a stand-up, improvisational comic who billed himself as "the World's Foremost Authority," warmed up the house for us and put the audience in a great mood. Jacques already had them tipsy, as he'd served champagne in the lobby before the play. As the audience was settling in, a few stragglers still making their way down the aisles with glasses in hand, our director walked out onto the stage, raised his arms and announced to the crowd, "You know, you're more ready for this than we are. We don't know what's going to happen. This evening will be as much a surprise to us as it is to you. We're glad you're here. Enjoy the show."

Music in, and off we flew, into a night like no other. Everything worked. No sets fell down. We got laughs beyond those we'd hoped for, felt a high vibrating throughout the house, and experienced wonderment as we sensed the audience allowing themselves to be altered by what they were witnessing. The crowd that was tentative at the beginning and shocked in the middle was on its feet stomping by the end. We'd had a great opening-night party that lasted till dawn, then dissolved into bed in our respective homes.

In the following months, the three of us Pacific Heights girls bought old, secondhand black velvet coats at a local thrift shop and often wore them to the theatre with nothing on underneath. We liked to catch the eyes of strangers and flash them a bare breast, then cover up deftly. We'd do this in cars or in bars, hoping that the guys we teased were wondering if they'd seen what they thought they'd seen.

We did interviews on radio and, in one instance, in the rain in a hot tub on a distant mountainside, with a reviewer from a San Francisco newspaper. We sailed across the Bay Area around the infamous Alcatraz and hiked and camped on Mount Tamalpais, a peak in Marin County.

My first lover, who's name as I have often said, I will not mention, came to visit and see the show. Pablo Ferro did, too, and took me to spend a night in the home of Victor Moscoso, a master psychedelic artist, where we watched satirist R. Crumb and a half a dozen other underground cartoonists working on a new issue for *Zap Comix*, an adults-only comic book series.

My brother, Sterling, dropped acid, came to the show, hitchhiked back to the University of Colorado where he was still in grad school, but got lost on the way and wasn't found for almost a week. He was troubled for some time.

It was a rumbling time with bittersweet drama and shakeups till the end. But it was a rich time, too. A true time. A precious time.

Just recently, I emailed Pamela, the perky, petite dancer from our show, to ask for more details on Morris the cat. She wrote me back about some things I'd forgotten, then ended her note with these words, "Those were the days, my friend."

Yes, my sweet Pam.

Those were the days.

CHAPTER 25

A SECOND NIGHT
TO REMEMBER

Traditionally in theatre, the second night of a production is a nightmare. Coming off the superhuman effort it takes to open a show, there's usually a letdown, the cast and crew taking for granted that all will go well...how could it not, when everything was so great last night? What follows is either a total fiasco with shit hitting the proverbial fan, or perhaps worse, a sluggish evening of theatre that fails to move its audience.

Neither of these was the case with our show, though our second night was as dramatic as could be imagined and weathered only by the grace of providence (and most likely the divine intervention of guardian angels).

Ironically, the multiact segments in *Oh! Calcutta!* required a lot of costumes. From the elaborate Victorian lady's and fine gentleman's attire in Sherman Yellen's satirical "Delicious Indignities," to coveralls for both actors from an excerpt of Sam Shepard's *The Rock Garden*. In-between, there was a short negligee and pajama bottoms for Jules Feiffer's "Dick and Jane"; ties and tails and sleek, black formal gowns for Stanley Walden's "Suite for Five Letters"; children's fantasy playclothes for Leonard Melfi's "Jack and Jill"; doctors' and nurses' uniforms for Jacques Levy's "Was it Good for You, Too?"; a miniskirt with a see-through calypso top, a woman's pantsuit, two sports shirts, and men's trousers for "Will Answer All Sincere Replies" by David Newman and Robert Benton; and last but never least, street attire for all the men in John Lennon's "Four in a Hand."

I'm not sure where the costumes for our production were made, probably by seamstresses working for A.C.T., the American Conservatory Theatre in San Francisco. Once they were delivered, a young actress from A.C.T. was hired to be in charge of them, keeping them clean and ready for performances, and supervising the dressers who helped us make quick changes backstage. She worked hard, there was no doubt, but as a costumer working on *Oh! Calcutta!* she likely got a lot of ribbing from her peers.

The morning after our opening, she called the three of us Jackson Street girls, Rhonda, Pamela, and me to say she'd like to bring over some pumpkin bread to have with our coffee. We were exhausted and delighted at the thought of having breakfast delivered to our kitchen. When she arrived, she unpacked the freshly made bread and mentioned that she'd baked some marijuana into the dough. "Not much and not very good stuff," she said.

She might have actually told us that earlier. Either way, I paid it no mind. I smoked a lot of pot, but I was relatively inexperienced with edible drugs. I actually thought that putting grass in brownies and breads and the like was just a story concocted to make people who didn't smoke feel like they belonged. I had no clue that ingesting grass could get you high, much less mega-stoned.

So much for ignorance!

We cut large slices of pumpkin bread, buttered, warmed them, and ate. Then had second and third servings. We'd started our late breakfast around two in the afternoon and by three o'clock, had entered an altogether new world. A new universe, as a matter of fact, where the long and short hands of a clock spun around in quickened time and walls tilted back and forth, seeming to mirror our movements as we staggered from room to room in our flat. Now the clock was suddenly saying four. Moments later it was five...then six...then six thirty.

We had to get to work. We called a cab but couldn't get down to the street to meet it. It left our place empty. We called another. Same deal, we couldn't move.

We called a third time and somehow managed to get down the stairs to the street, poured ourselves into the backseat of the waiting taxi, and ordered the driver to rush to the theatre. We arrived late, past half-hour (the rule for a theatrical show is to be "in house" when "half-hour" is announced), struggled through the stage door entrance, climbed the stairs and sat, the three of us in a circle, holding hands in the hallway, while the other cast members watched us from their dressing room doorways, aghast as they realized we were stoned and seemingly out of control. They stared, mouths agape, as we prayed out loud like high school footballers in a huddle, alternating tears, groans, and occasional shrieks, then scrambled to our feet and sped into our dressing rooms to smear on makeup and, after several gut-wrenching attempts, to paste on false eyelashes. Needless to say, the rest of our cast was furious.

In a recent email to me, Pamela said she would never forget the sound of my laughter as we headed downstairs for the opening number. I really don't recall laughing, but I love knowing that I did.

The first number was called "Taking Off the Robe," one of three scenes that involved total nudity for the entire cast, and in a way, told the story of our rehearsal process…how we came to be who we were.

In semidarkness, we actors filed in from the wings and moved to the upstage wall, removed our street clothes and placed them on hooks, and put on long, white Grecian-style robes. Next, the eight-paneled louvered wall rotated to swallow up our clothes, closing to create a smooth, curved backdrop. Its surface was white and images were projected onto it, like a movie screen.

The actors moved down stage and stood in single file, facing the audience, each in a different colored spotlight.

Music in. Quiet and sensual, sung and played by the four musicians in the pit, the *Oh! Calcutta!*

theme song, as each actor began a slow dance, all his own. After a few bars, the singular-colored light on the actor stage left turned bright white. Still shots of him rehearsing his various sketches were projected onto the surrounding backdrop. In the center of the screen, moving pictures of him naked, in the wilds, filmed on location outside the city, playing among his fellow actors. Then that actor's light reverted back to color, and the white spotlight moved to the female actress that stood beside him, again with images and movies of her on the screen behind. Each player's dance was more revealing than the preceding one, and as the dance progressed, the earlier players abandoned their own steps to mirror the movements of the one who'd just entered the spotlight. This formal, slow striptease continued until the last player was naked, twirling her robe above and around her like a bullfighter's cape, while the rest followed suit, before allowing our robes to drop to the floor, still in the grasp of one hand, as we froze, all of us back beneath our original, colored light. A single drumstick rapped against the rim of a drum, signaling a percussion piece that rose to a heart-pounding crescendo as—starting from stage left and proceeding along the line of actors to the end—we performed high-speed jazz versions of our dances, ending in a flurry of movement with all of us twirling our robes over and around, then finally, flinging them again to the ground.

Lights up.

Full lights for about ten seconds.

Then semidarkness shrouded us again as we each lifted our robe, hung it over one shoulder and exited, pausing after each step, in a slow, formal march.

And, so it was.

On that fateful second night, Rhonda, Pamela, and I found ourselves standing in our long, white robes, facing a new audience in a packed house— and utterly zonked out of our minds.

The music started and I began my dance. It was in that moment that I knew for certain that if I tried to hold it together and pretend that I wasn't smashed out of my gourd, I'd be hauled away in a straitjacket before the first act was over. I felt incredibly vulnerable even thinking of trying to pretend to be straight. Shaky. Scared. It would've been a disaster if I revealed the seriousness of our dilemma. Instinctively, I decided to go in another direction. To take it all lightly. To pretend I was at a party, as it were. So, I began sailing my robe on imaginary winds, getting lost in the dance. Giving in completely.

It was a good choice, one that Rhonda and Pamela must have discovered for themselves as well.

As I said, by the grace of angels.

Later that night, the three of us talked about what had happened once when we got home. Rhonda had hung in there very well during "Dick and Jane." Somehow, I'd remembered every word of my monologue in "Will Answer All Sincere Replies," and got a lot of laughs from the scene, my native ear for Southern speech making me feel safe and authentic.

The three of us sang our parts in "Suite for Five Letters" during both the chamber music section and the rock and roll part without a hitch. It was definitely miracle time.

We had little memory, however, of the finale of the first act, "Was it Good for You, Too?" but given that it was a Marx Brothers' free-for-all, rather in keeping with our states of mind, it wasn't hard to pull off.

We had zero memory of intermission, but somehow had gotten ourselves back on stage afterward to do the second of the three nude scenes involving the whole cast. It was a softly lit montage of various couples discovering each other, while films of us previously shot in the woods and the surrounding wilds, naked and in love with nature and ourselves, were projected on the screen. At scene's end, all exited except for Pamela and Joe Roma, who stayed to dance their *pas de deux*.

Rhonda and I stood offstage, hands on our hearts and holding our breaths to watch Pam and Joe, a tall, well-built drink of water who could catch her over his head as she ran and leapt to climb his body, reaching for the sky. He'd then let her slide through his hands behind him, dropping her slowly until he could grasp her ankles, at which point she'd curl upward around his body, and he'd kneel to meet her in an embrace. Later, she laughed that all the lifts had gone well, but in her solo stuff, when she'd to come to a dead stop on her tiptoes, contracting her middle in response to his presence behind her, she'd tended to wobble a bit. The truth is, if she'd fallen in one of those lifts, she could have been seriously injured. As it turned out, she met those challenges with guts, style, and grace and was spectacular in doing so. Our respect for each other, for our individual strengths and for the strength of our friendship, was deepened that night.

We'd gotten through the show—and through the next few days. Ingested cannabis doesn't leave the system immediately. All in all, we were stoned to some extent for a good three days.

The rest of the cast forgave us after they came to understand what had happened. And we never spoke the costumer's name out loud after that night. We referred to her, when we had to, by initials only, which I won't repeat here. Her intent may have been benign. Whether it was or wasn't, her little gift of pumpkin bread almost did us in.

As for myself, I've never again performed stoned anywhere, on stage or screen, and never will.

For me, once was definitely enough.

CHAPTER 26

OVER AND OUT

I didn't leave my heart in San Francisco, but I did leave some of my exuberance, joy, innocence, and wonder there, and though I regained much of those beautiful emotions in coming months, the colors were now different. With a bit of bruising still to heal, I returned to New York, feeling her welcome me back as I stepped onto the hot pavement baking from a day in an early summer sun. I was to find my footing soon again and with a touch of panache but couldn't have predicted this at the time. My feelings got hurt in San Francisco, and my ego took a sizable hit, leaving me confused, embarrassed, and stunned—looking once again to the heavens and to deep places within myself.

The details of my brief encounter with an actor in a musical revue of *Jacques Brel Is Alive and Well and Living in Paris*, which had been running in town at the same time as our show, aren't important. I will confess that I projected onto that actor/singer the soul of the poet/songwriter whose words he sang.

The truth is, we had little in common. I should've known this, when after we'd made love the first time, and I offered him another toke on the pipe, he said, "We're not going to stay up all night, are we?"

And, it should've also been obvious a few weeks later when we took a trip to Big Sur and had nothing to talk about. I loved his artistry but didn't know how to express that, couldn't articulate it. His work was passionate and his voice quite wonderful. I was shy. We were stuck.

Our fun to that point had centered around sex, food, hanging out with Rhonda and Pam, and playing with Morris the cat. But on the road together, we were in Nowheresville.

Perhaps more importantly, he was from the establishment and the established theatre. I was in a rogue show, the mistress of "real" theatre, so to speak. I was rebelling against the manicured culture of the time. He was cultivating it. I must've been a wild card in his hand, as he was in mine.

At the end of our time together, after a starry night and mystical sunrise camping on Mount Tamalpais and clear sailing around the Bay the next afternoon, I, along with some of the crew from my show who'd sailed with us, went to his theatre to see him perform in *Jacques Brel* (our show being "dark" that night), then met him backstage for dinner. An actress, and unbeknownst to me, a former lover of his, had just rejoined his company that weekend. She greeted our party backstage and said she'd like to join us for dinner. She ended up sitting at our large table but well on the other side of it from the two of us, though she talked over everyone to enter our conversations the entire night. As the party was breaking up, she invited the two of us to her place to show us her newborn kittens. We agreed and walked her home. As she opened the door to her apartment she said over her shoulder, "Samantha, let me call you a cab," picked up her phone and proceeded to dial. I was jolted. Something was off. Or up. Or sideways. We visited with the tiny kittens until the cab arrived, and he and I were walking outside when she followed us and called his name, "Oh my! You're not leaving, too, are you?"

He hesitated, then turned back to her. "No. I'll stay and have some coffee." He left me there alone standing by the open taxi door.

That, my darlings, was a tough moment for me.

The full impact of it resonated all night and for some time after. It stung.

Seeing it now, they were two people who'd loved each other before and wanted to love each other again.

But back then, I took it personally.

It's one thing to be thought of as a "naughty lady from shady lane" (a witty lyric about a provocative young woman), another thing to be discarded with no care whatsoever, no "I beg your pardon," no nothing, like a piece of used Kleenex. Or an old, soiled towel, which is what I felt like in that moment. All my self-doubt, shame, and self-judgment were triggered and fired through my brain. I spent that night lost and wounded. Several nights, in fact. *Who was I to think it was okay to prance around naked and to love freely any man I took a fancy to?*

Part of me, the puritanical me, believed I'd gotten what I deserved. Another part of me, however, was outraged at the unkindness, rudeness, and calculated meanness of the whole episode. Inner voices clambered in confusion. Beneath them all, I deeply felt the hurt of it. That week, I gave a month's notice to the production. I was ready to go home.

Rhonda and Pam and I moved into a smaller apartment, which they would keep after I'd gone. But before we left Jackson Street, I sat by the small altar in my room, with incense and candles from The Mystic Eye and a sign that read the same as with all my personal altars since I'd first moved to New York.

"Ask and you will receive, seek and you will find, knock and it will be opened unto you."

I lit the candles but couldn't think of what to ask. Finally, I prayed to be given the right prayer. It came immediately, though I didn't know what it meant.

"Dear God, please give me half a relationship."

Two days later, the phone rang. It was my first lover, my first love, from New York. He said, "Harriet. Come back to the city and live with me."

Arriving at his place in the East Seventies, I was stunned to see the condition of his one-bedroom street-level apartment. There was almost no furniture. Just a mattress on the living room floor. He was there to greet me and help me with my luggage, before he had to leave, for work, he said. But with him, you never knew. Intimacy wasn't his strong suit.

I suppose I could've chosen to start setting up housekeeping, but I sensed that I was in over my head. Cooking for him was out of the question. He was part owner of a trendy restaurant. Buying furniture wasn't an option. Both of us were broke. Before I'd arrived, he had borrowed the thousand dollars I'd managed to save on the road, merged it with his own money, then lost it in the stock market. He'd spend that summer paying me back a little at a time. So that first night, I locked the apartment and went to the movies.

MASH, the 1970 Korean War comedy-drama starring Donald Sutherland, Elliott Gould, Tom Skerritt, Sally Kellerman, Robert Duvall, Roger Bowen, David Arkin, and Jo Ann Pflug (among others), was playing at a nearby movie house.

I sat there in the darkened theatre and laughed till I cried. Then came home and began a summer with him in our little Uptown, East Side pad. Our friendship was solid and our affection for each other ran deep. His sense of humor and mine and our shared pleasure in the absurdity of our predicament—being still a bit in love but completely out-of-sync—made for odd times. Friends, his and mine, wove in and out of our place at strange and, sometimes, awkward moments. We laughed a lot.

He met his wife-to-be that summer, while I reconnected with Pablo, and made a film called *The Inflatable Doll* (written by Julian Barry) with him, then a few weeks later shot the movie version of *Oh! Calcutta!* and joined the off-Broadway production shortly after. Along the way, I reconnected with my future husband, Bill Macy, who I'd met at my audition in NYC (but who'd immediately left to do the London version of *Oh! Calcutta!* and was now, a year later, back in town to rejoin us off-Broadway).

Later that year, after I'd moved in with Bill and we'd moved *Oh! Calcutta!* to full-on Broadway, I was backstage and ready for my entrance in "Will Answer All Sincere Replies" when a musician from our pit approached me and said, "Oh! I ran into an actor who did *Jacques Brel* in San Francisco when you were there. He said tell you hello."

As I mentioned, I was just about to make my entrance onto the stage. Those words were a punch to my gut. I knocked on the door and the actor on the other side opened it. As I walked onto the stage, I knew I couldn't even pretend I was okay.

My opening line was, "Hi honey, I'm Cherie!" Usually an upbeat moment, but I couldn't pull it off. So I just let myself be where I was.

I uttered the line with all the defeat and despair that had been triggered by the memory of that ex-lover treating me so carelessly and tossing me aside. To my astonishment, the house almost fell down. The audience exploded with laughter. They roared and kept it up. They laughed at everything I said and did until the very end of the scene. It was a lesson for me.

Honesty reads, even if it's not fully understood by actor or audience.

That night I went home and told Bill the whole story. He listened quietly, then said, "I'm so sorry that happened to you."

We were closer for the telling of the tale.

CHAPTER 27

CATCHING UP WITH
MY BOY BILL

In the fall of '69 while I was doing *Oh! Calcutta!* in San Francisco, I spoke to my mother about once a week on the phone. In one of those conversations, I mentioned that I was thinking of writing about my experiences in the show.

"Then who will ever want to marry you?" she said. That was before the internet at a time when you could reasonably expect to keep some things secret, but I doubted that it could be kept quiet for long that I was tearing my clothes off on a San Francisco stage six nights a week and twice on matinee days.

In fact, my roommate from Ole Miss, Kaffie Mallette, "the other wild virgin," had just called me a couple of nights before, drunk—and *collect*—to put me on the spot.

"Harry," she said, "people are saying some terrible things about you, and I want to tell them all to go to Hell."

I, of course, asked her what they were saying.

"They're saying you're in that play, *Oh! Calcutta!*" she wailed.

"Yes, Kaffie, I am."

"Is that the one where everybody takes their clothes off?" she asked, taken aback.

"Yes, yes, it is. "

"Well, do you take *your* clothes off?" She was incredulous, her voice rising.

"Yep."

"Well…when you take them off, do you take them *all* off?"

"I do, Kaffie, and I have to tell you, it's the most fun thing I've ever done in my life."

She was quiet a long time. When she could speak again, she braved, "Well, if *you're* doing it, I guess it's okay."

Those words, coming from her, were the definition of true friendship. I thanked her, but she wasn't through yet.

"I'm going to tell them all to go to Hell, anyway," she spat through clenched teeth.

"Oh yes, please do," I grinned into the phone.

Neither my mother nor I realized that I'd already met my future husband, Bill Macy, at my NYC audition for the show that I was now doing on the West Coast.

Bill was a close friend of Jacques Levy, our director, and was sitting beside him when I first took the stage to sing, and later to act and dance, and ultimately to disrobe, mainly to prove that I had the nerve to do it. Jacques had thought I was talented from the start but also saw that I was nervous. He whispered to Bill, "Go up on stage and loosen her up."

For the next five hours, Bill had popped out of nowhere and everywhere to surprise and startle me. While I was studying a scene offstage, he jumped out from behind a pillar and exclaimed, "Which production are you going to do? I'm going into the London show. Come to London with me!" He scrabbled around making me laugh. I thought he was nuts.

But I got the job.

When I returned to New York after my nine months in San Francisco, I went to Central Park to watch the *Oh! Calcutta!* softball team play against another production in the Broadway Show League, pitting Broadway and off-Broadway actors and crew against each other every summer. Bill was coaching behind first base. I walked up to thank him for helping me with my audition, but he just looked at me with a raised eyebrow and rudely said, "Excuse me, Miss. I'm watching a ballgame here."

Meanwhile, I'd been cast in the movie version of our play, but in a part that I had not yet played. In San Francisco, I'd performed the Southern piece, "Will Answer All Sincere Replies," a sketch about wife swapping. In the movie, I was to play Helen, the heroine of the Victorian English sketch, "Delicious Indignities."

The role of Helen had a lot of dialogue, including two long monologues, and the producers wanted me to do the piece in front of an audience for a while before we filmed it. I wasn't currently in the NYC production, but they injected me into the show for two weeks to get my feet wet.

The first night I went on stage at the Eden Theatre, Bill watched me from the back of the house. He flew backstage after the show and ran up to me, "My God! You were WONDERFUL!"

I brushed his hand from my arm. "Excuse me, sir, but I was just on my way out!"

The first day of rehearsal for the movie, he was waiting for me when I stepped off the elevator. He grabbed and kissed me, then walked away. It was a good kiss. *That was interesting,* I said to myself. Through the week or so of shooting, he asked me out several times, and I gently turned him down each time. He was twenty-one years older than me, forty-eight years to my almost twenty-seven, a Jew from Brooklyn who'd driven a cab at night in New York for the twelve years before his first break into show business. He was rough around the edges, daring, unpredictable, loud, and crazy. As my acting teacher, Joan Darling, once said to me years later, he was odd packaging for me. But every time I said no to him, it seemed that he'd be called on stage right afterward to act and, wow, he'd be brilliant. *God, he's strong*, I thought. *He can take care of himself.*

We finished the movie and moved on with our lives. One day, about four months later, we bumped into each other on a street downtown and decided to go hang out with Margo, the choreographer of *Oh! Calcutta!* and our close, mutual friend. Sitting in her apartment, both of us smoking her excellent weed, he asked me again to go out with him.

"Look," I said, "we both know it's going to happen, right?"

He was quiet for a minute. "Right!"

"Well, it's not now," I added.

He wrote his phone number on a scrap of paper and handed it to me. "Let me know when it's happening."

Actually, he'd already turned my head while we were shooting the movie. He continued his habit of grabbing and kissing me out of the blue. And, when we went on location to film the outdoor scenes projected on the screen behind us, something happened that made me look at him more seriously.

We'd taken a bus to Upstate New York, and on the way home, I took it upon myself to entertain the troops. I stood in the aisle up by the driver and told them my stories all the way back to town. Naughty stories about my sexual exploits with, among others, a dentist who seduced me while I was in his chair, an assistant Episcopal minister who I met at a church service in New York and traveled with to Scarsdale, where we climbed a ladder to his belfry apartment and made love all night listening to the Beatles and the Stones, and, of course, Pablo on some of our assorted adventures around town and in his infamous pad.

When the bus came to stop on my corner, the driver, who was black, showed signs of the more conservative way he'd been raised when he turned to me and said, "Wow. My ole lady won't even let me make love to her with the lights on." Bill got off with me, took my hand, and said these ultimately winning words.

"If I were a girl, I would want to be you."

Who knew (certainly not me or my mom) that I'd find a man who liked me for who I was.

Months after I took his phone number up at Margo's, I thought about him again. I'd taken a trip to Bermuda with four women connected to the show, DeeDee Winner being one of them. She turns up everywhere, doesn't she? It was October 5, 1970, my twenty-seventh birthday, and sitting in a small boat, fishing off the reef that ringed the island, I announced that I was ready to have just one man in my life. The other three girls almost fell into the water laughing. I insisted, "No! It's my birthday, and if you say you want something on your birthday, you can have it!"

When I got back to town, I searched through my little black book, looking for company—and I saw Bill's name and number.

I called.

He answered.

It was the start of something *big*.

My boy, Bill, and I

PART III

Samantha and Bill

Getting Down to It

CHAPTER 28

CRAZY LOVE, BILL, AND MY FAMILY IN NYC

The first night I spent with Bill, I confided in him that I had a problem—my parents were coming from Mississippi to visit me in less than a week, and I had no idea how to show them the city or make them feel good about my life. They'd never been to NYC before, and this would be the first time I'd seen them since I'd been cast in the San Francisco company of *Oh! Calcutta!* nearly a year ago. Back in the Big Apple now, with the movie version of the show complete, and before I'd be cast in the New York production, I was again unemployed. My parents had informed me that they didn't intend to walk the streets after dark or ride the subways at all, day or night.

Bill said, "Don't worry. I'll help you take care of them."

On the day of their arrival, I picked them up at the airport for a harrowing cab ride into town, then dropped them off at their hotel and promised to come take them to dinner after they'd rested up. At the appointed hour, Bill and I were at their door. He wore his cowboy hat and a long pigskin coat, his pockets stuffed with subway tokens. They were fascinated by the man—his happy, good-natured attitude, his exuberance and the joy in his eyes, and didn't protest when he escorted us underground. We took a subway to Chinatown and sat at a round table and were served a scrumptious, bountiful meal. Bill explained that he'd been divorced twice. "My second wife asked me who was going to cook for me after I left her. Well, that Chinaman cooks great, and I don't have to sleep with HIM!"

My parents burst out laughing. Suddenly, they were native New Yorkers.

Bill made a date with my mom to take her to the Frick Museum, (more formally known as the Frick Collection) the next day. Daddy and I weren't invited. The Frick is one of the preeminent small art museums in America. On Fifth Avenue above

59th Street, it had once been the private mansion of Pittsburgh industrialist Henry Clay Frick and was the most opulent personal dwelling in a most opulent part of town, with private gardens both on the avenue's front and an interior courtyard. It houses some of the best-known paintings by the greatest of European artists, fine sculptures, eighteenth-century French furniture, porcelains, enamels, and various other treasures. Many of the rooms are still arranged according to Henry Frick's design. My mom got to see how the family that once inhabited such a magnificent house had lived, the beauty that surrounded them and fed their instincts for art and life. She was enchanted. Every day of her stay in NYC after that, she packed a little lunch and went to another museum. She was stunned at how many beautiful things there were to see for *free*. She drank the city in, slurped it through a straw.

Dad was fascinated by European history and the origins of its banking system. Bill got us all tickets to *The Rothschilds,* a Broadway musical based on a book by Sherman Yellen, with lyrics by Sheldon Harnick, and music by Jerry Bock. It was about a European family of German-Jewish origin that had established banking and finance houses in the late eighteenth century. Dad, a veteran of WWII, was aware of the great wrongs that had been done to the Jews, not only to the financially successful, educated, and powerful among them, but also to the working masses and the poor. He was deeply moved by the play and loved its message of courage and transcendence in the face of devastating circumstances.

Over dinner one night as their trip neared its end, Bill insisted that they come and see our show. I wasn't in it at the time, but he was. They said yes without hesitation. I stood in the back of the theatre and watched my parents (in the fifth row) watch Bill do what he did best—naughty and outrageous comedic shenanigans that brought down the house, again and again. Only four of the scenes involved total nudity. The first, which opened the show, was called "Taking Off the Robe." It was formal in the beginning, with soft music and shadowy lighting, and introduced each of the actors slowly disrobing in a style unique to them, then became a wildly percussive dance and ended with the entire cast standing naked in bright white lights, before retreating into the shadows for a dignified exit upstage.

I couldn't believe my parents were actually watching this. They were absolutely and totally cool about it.

As I said, I wasn't in the production at the time, but Bill talked me into making an appearance on stage that night. The first act ended with a sketch called "Was It Good For You, Too?" It was a takeoff on the pioneering Masters and Johnson sex response studies and done in the style of a Marx Brothers' movie, with Bill playing Harpo. The scene ended in a free-for-all dance and song, complete with gypsies and a small dog dancing around a nude couple all hooked up to electrodes on a table centerstage. Egged on by Bill, I went backstage during all the commotion and took off my clothes, donned a bathrobe, put my hair in rollers, and crossed the stage from one side to the other carrying a roll of toilet paper. Just as I opened the door to exit, Bill wheeled himself over on his rolling "doctor's" stool and goosed me on my way out. I was lucky that Actors' Equity never heard of my stage appearance that night.

After the show, the four of us went to a little Italian restaurant near the theatre for drinks. My mother was very quiet while she drank one martini, then another. When we were ready to leave, she suddenly cried out, "I don't want to go home and sit around talking about Joe Namath's sex life! I want to stay *here*, where people are having a good time!"

Before they left town, they invited Bill to come to Mississippi for Christmas.

He accepted.

CHAPTER 29

JUMPING OUT OF A CAKE

Shortly after my parents left town, Bill quit the cast of *Oh! Calcutta!* to do other projects. At almost the same time, I joined the company, taking on the role of Helen Axminster in the witty Victorian sketch "Delicious Indignities," which, coincidentally, was written by Sherman Yellen, author of *The Rothschilds*, the play so beloved by my dad on his visit to the city.

Being in a racy New York stage production made for unusual opportunities. In those NYC days, you could freelance, making rounds of casting, modeling, and advertising agencies, dropping off headshots and resumes, looking for work.

One such visit to a modeling agency led to a job that most would've found too outrageous to even consider, but one that I couldn't resist. It was to take part in a joke being played on a CEO of a Midtown West Side business. He was moving into a prestigious job with another firm, and a goodbye celebration and "btw, we'll miss you" party was in the works.

His underlings hired me and another model, a tall blonde from the same agency, to attend the party dressed only in slinky break-away dresses. The plan was to let the party progress, have us move close to the guest of honor, then stand on each side of him and reach for his hands, at which point, two jokesters would produce handcuffs and snap them on our wrists and his, then rip off our break-away dresses and leave him standing there chained to two naked ladies.

Why they thought that the joke would be on *him* was beyond me, but I was intrigued.

My parents had left NYC completely enchanted after Bill helped me show them the town. My relationship with him was deepening. We spent most nights in his tiny East 5th Street apartment, though I had a place, a dump on the Upper West Side that I shared with another actor who'd migrated from the San Francisco company of *Oh!*

Calcutta! The kitchen had a bathtub in the middle of the floor, which actually sagged. It wasn't one of my favorite abodes.

Meanwhile, Bill and I, as close as we were starting to feel, hadn't agreed to be exclusive in our relationship. Both of us were rascals, and we knew it. But we also sensed what was in store for us. On our first night out on a real date (I had taken him to see the movie *Performance*, starring James Fox and Mick Jagger, as that was my test for all the men I dated…either they *got* that movie or they didn't get me, as it were). Bill got the movie big-time, and when he took my hand in his that night, I felt something click. I knew. All he needed was for me to help him balance his wild passions and talent… and his career would soar. I felt a commitment from him too, in that moment, to care, to anchor me, to mentor, love, and support.

But at the time that I was offered this gig, the gag on the CEO, which to me was the equivalent of jumping naked out of a cake at a bachelor party, I wasn't quite ready to give up my freedom and settle down.

Late in the afternoon on the day of the party, my blonde partner and I showed up on an upper floor of the building, which housed the company that had hired us. We were ushered to a large common room at the end of a corridor flanked by suites of offices for the company brass. We were wearing long dresses sewn with Velcro holding the spaghetti straps on our shoulders, high boots up to our knees, and nothing more.

Almost immediately, the room began to fill with employees from other floors and eventually some of the brass themselves. There was an office party buzz as people made their way to a makeshift bar and accepted *hors d'oeuvres* from trays passed around by waiters hired for the special occasion. More of the brass arrived, among them the party boy himself, to whom we were introduced, as well as one of his close friends who stepped into the room a short time later and spotted me just as I zeroed in on him. He had light red hair and good looks, a kind of angular face, and an unexplained charisma.

Shit! I hadn't expected to be attracted to anyone at this party. We caught each other's eyes from across the room for the next hour or so as the party escalated. *What the hell is he going to think of me when they start tearing my clothes off?* I wondered. *Damn!* The perils of show business. But the ball was rolling, and there was no going back now.

We spotted the guest of honor near the center of the room and wandered close to him, then stood on either side. When we saw that our pranksters were in place, each of us casually took one of his hands, and *bam!* just as planned we were cuffed to him. The next moment we were stripped out of our dresses, and there we stood, naked except for our leather boots, laughing, him sandwiched between us.

What happened next was a total surprise. He looked at us and winked, then said "Run!" We obeyed. The three of us tore down the corridor toward his office, the redheaded guy right behind us as we flew through his open doorway and closed and bolted the door behind the four of us. Obviously, the man was no slouch. He'd been way ahead of everybody. He even had keys for the cuffs, which he unlocked, setting us free. We couldn't stop laughing.

There was a storm in the hallway as befuddled guests banged on the door and tried to open it. Our boy paid no attention to the melee. He invited my blonde companion into his inner office and closed the door behind them. I stayed in the outer office with my new redheaded friend.

"Hi," I said.

"Hi," he replied.

He put his jacket on me, and we sat down to talk, but it was clear that we were going to have sex, and that it was going to be hot. "Just so you know," I said, "I'm seeing someone and it's serious. This is a one-time thing. It can't go further." He said okay.

And then we had a few fine hours engaging in the elements of lovemaking: sailing winds of freedom, sparking fires, swimming in deep waters, playing, experimenting, plunging at last back to reality and Earth. It was a sweet ride. When it was clear that all the partygoers had given up banging on our door and gone home, I slipped out to the common room, found my clothes, and prepared to leave. He looked at me as I was heading for the door. "You're sure?" he said. "This is it?"

"Yes, I'm sure."

I slept in my apartment on the Upper West Side that night. I called Bill the next morning and told him what I had done. He'd always gotten a kick out of my wild side, but something in his voice made me know that I needed to get to him, and fast. I took the subway, changing trains on the way, and walked the several blocks to his apartment on East

5th Street, then climbed up five flights of stairs to his place. The trip to his door seemed to take forever.

It was ajar, as he had buzzed me in from downstairs. I found him sitting on his low Asian-style bed in his tiny room, a woolen cap on his head, eating chicken soup, and reading a women's lib book he had just bought in a shop down the street. He looked at me and said, "I know if it had been me in your place, I'd have done exactly what you did. I'm reading this to try and figure out why it hurts so much."

I put my arms around him and said, "Oh baby, I don't ever have to do anything like that again. And I won't. I won't. I just want to be your girl."

CHAPTER 30

BILL COMING HOME
TO MISSISSIPPI

B ill and I didn't marry until four years after the
Mississippi Christmas he spent with my family
in 1970. But that December morning, as we buckled
our seatbelts to jet down South, we somehow knew
that marriage was in the cards for us. The deal was
further sealed the first night we arrived in Batesville.

Naturally, my folks wouldn't hear of us sleeping in the same room. My mother had become a
psychologist after finishing her teaching career and
had an office behind our garage for her therapy work.
It was equipped with a full-sized bed and private
bath, and she sometimes used it for guests. Bill stayed
out there while I slept in my old bedroom in the
main house for his visit. My dad, who was totally

in love with Bill and still smitten by the production of *The Rothschilds* that he'd seen in NYC a couple months before, thought it would be humorous and entirely fitting, given Bill's heritage, to put a sign over the entrance that read: THE GHETTO. (As was depicted in *The Rothschilds*, in most cities, the Germans locked Jews inside walled-in and gated villages within their city limits. Known as Ghettos, they were in fact, prisons that Jewish people were allowed to leave during the day for work but forced to return each evening.)

The guesthouse, as Momma called it on such occasions, had an intercom connection to the big house. Every morning, my dad rose early and made coffee, then woke up Bill by announcing via the intercom:

"The Ghetto is now open!"

Bill was a good sport about the teasing, mainly because he knew it was from a man who adored him. The two of them were a pair from the start. But Bill had a more profound reason to feel secure with my family because of something that had happened the first night of our arrival. As soon as he'd plopped his luggage in "the ghetto," he was invited to join us in Dad and Mom's master bedroom in the big house where he was given a seat of honor and asked to read aloud a passage from a book that Dad had handy. I don't remember all of what it said, or even who the author was, but as Bill neared the end, I'll never forget these words as he read them: "You are accepted." These three words were repeated in the text, and Bill could hardly get them out a second time because he was so full of emotion saying them:

"You are accepted."

He put down the book and broke into tears...

After that, Bill was family, and no amount of teasing could take that away from him. And, nothing, through all the years of ups and downs with the Harpers, ever did. Though the teasing went on and on, even after we were married and kept traveling to Mississippi in subsequent years, in a style wholly unique to Southerners, where ribbing each other and the occasional well-liked Yankee has become an art form unto itself.

The high point of his visit was meeting my maternal grandmother, Alma LeMaster, the same Alma who'd later show up as one of the magical sisters in my coauthored novel, *The Two Sisters' Café*. (The other sister, Vannie, was fashioned after the maternal grandmother of my writing partner, Elena Yates Eulo.) Alma, or Mammy as the family and all my friends called her, wasn't feeling well at the time. She was, in fact, sick in bed. But like all great Southern women, she could "buck up" whenever a gentleman came to call. She lay there, piled up on pillows, as she charmed and flirted with Bill. He pulled up a chair to sit next to her, and at one point, she gazed at him and said, "Bill, what church do you go to?"

"I don't go to church, Mammy," Bill replied. "I'm Jewish."

In a millisecond, I watched a thousand thoughts flash across her face. Then she gently reached over, patted his hand, and said reassuringly, "Well, that's alright!"

I've often laughed about that moment and wondered how she knew she had the power to dispose of such trivialities with a wave of her hand. But she did, and she knew it. Just like that, two thousand years of theology flew right out the window.

That was my Mammy.

The Pope had nothing on her.

On the car ride to the Memphis airport, in front of my whole family, Bill proposed. I took a beat. Saw the anticipation on everyone's face. Then I quietly said no, I wasn't ready. It was an awkward moment, but not for long. Bill always had taken my rejections in stride. I think he would've been surprised if I said yes. He'd only asked me in front of my family as a way of stating his commitment. Everyone knew it would happen for us. Just not when.

And, sure enough, a few days after we got back to the city, I gathered my things and moved into his one-room apartment, just in time for New Year's Eve. We made love listening to the countdown at the start of 1971.

That spring, Bill was cast in his first Broadway show, *And Miss Reardon Drinks a Little*, a dark comedy by Paul Zindel, a Pulitzer Prize and Obie Award-winning playwright. Besides my Bill, it starred Julie Harris, Estelle Parsons, Nancy Marchand, and Rae Allen. The NYC show lasted only a few months but then went on tour, including a couple of weeks in LA. Before he left, Bill turned to me and declared, "I'm going on the road with this show, and I'm going to get a television series."

And that's exactly what happened—he landed a major role in the comedy sitcom, *Maude*.

For Bill, it was a great adventure to be starring opposite Bea Arthur in Norman Lear's *Maude* (a spinoff of *All in the Family*) and later, Norman would cast me in one of his other hit shows, *Mary Hartman, Mary Hartman*, a satirical takeoff on soap operas that struck it big on late-night TV. From the start, Norman nurtured and protected Bill and me, and helped us get established in Hollywood.

From then on out, we were a team, Bill and me.

But before delving too much into those wonderful times and all that followed our new LA acting careers, I want to finish the tale of how we finally managed to get married.

And, oh yes! To tell you about the one last leprechaun who showed up just before I said goodbye to New York City.

CHAPTER 31

ONE LAST LEPRECHAUN

Ahh, New York City. Always to love it, but never to live there again. Before I left, Woody Allen would become the last leprechaun I'd encounter there. Well, maybe he's not an *actual* leprechaun, but most definitely a magical being. One enchanted day, Mr. Allen lifted my spirits and left me with this story to tell.

By 1971, *Oh! Calcutta!* had moved from the off-Broadway Eden Theatre on Second Avenue and 12th Street to the Belasco Theatre at 111 W. 44th Street, an aging, legit stage with a long tradition of Broadway hits.

At the time of the move I was still in the show, but Bill, an original cast member, was not.

At our final downtown performance, Bill stood behind the last row of seats in the back of the theatre holding an empty suitcase meant for packing up my belongings at show's end.

Although he was no longer in the production, during the finale, while the whole cast was nude and rocking back-to-back and belly-to-belly in single file across the apron of the stage, his performer's instincts kicked in. I peered out from under the lights and saw him running down the aisle in his long pigskin coat and cowboy hat, carrying that suitcase. He leapt across the orchestra pit onto the stage, placed himself at the end of the line and rocked along with us, luggage still in hand, yelling "Uptown, Uptown!"

Being on Broadway had brought us new challenges as well as new opportunities. Casting agents from uptown theatre saw the show, and a number of us were called in to audition for other stage productions and movies. One of our new understudies, Jennifer Nairn-Smith, who'd danced for George Balanchine in the New York City Ballet, was cast from those auditions in *Follies* and later in *Pippin,* two Broadway megahits.

I was called to audition for the part of Honey, Lenny Bruce's stripper wife in Julian Barry's *Lenny*, directed by Tom O'Horgan (famously known for the hippie musicals *Hair* and *Jesus Christ Superstar*). I also got to meet Anthony Quinn and read with him for another project. I was charmed by his old-school courtesy and that touch of class that so many great artists seem to radiate from their souls.

By far, however, my most memorable time was with Woody Allen. Juliet Taylor, the casting agent for all his films from forever until present date, saw *Oh! Calcutta!* and asked me to meet with him at a suite on the Upper West Side. As everyone knows, Woody never lets his scripts be seen by anyone in advance of production, so I had no idea what the part was or even the title of his movie, much less what to wear for the audition.

One member of our cast, Raina Barrett, had a killer outfit that she loaned to me for the occasion. As I recall, she'd also loaned it to Jennifer for her winning Broadway auditions, too. The ensemble was a pair of kelly-green loosely-crocheted hot pants, flared to make them look like a teeny miniskirt, with a short-sleeved low V-neck matching top. The only shoes that seemed to go with it were my black-suede platform heels, worn with pantyhose, of course, for modesty.

Just as I was leaving to go meet Woody Allen, Juliet, the casting agent, called me. "Go looking short," she advised. I laughed, knowing even in my bare feet, I was taller than Woody. I slipped on the platform shoes, anyway, as they were all I had, and headed out for my uptown audition. Once I'd found his suite and knocked, I instantly lost my nerve and took off the shoes. When Woody opened the door, I was standing in my stocking feet, shoes in my hand, dangling by their straps. "Juliet said to come looking short," I said. He smiled and let me in.

I entered a room with a long, shiny wooden table and chairs all around it, a vacant one for me in the center. The rest of the chairs were filled with people who I had guessed were connected to the production. Woody took a seat at the head of the table, and I sat and gazed down at the pages laid out for me to read. I suddenly froze. Fear rolled up from my toes and swallowed me whole. Slowly, I slid down in my chair and managed to climb under the table, where I sat, looking at everyone's feet. No one spoke a word.

After a bit, Woody slid down in his chair, climbed under the table, and crawled to where I was sitting. "Are you going to come out?" he asked.

"No," I said. "Not until they leave."

He climbed back up on his chair and told everybody to go. When the door closed behind the last of them, I climbed out, too.

I remember reading for him, but the memory is a blur. Not unpleasant, but a total wash. I don't even recall what the script was about. When he thanked me and said goodbye, I rushed out of the building straight to the nearest payphone and called Juliet.

"I am so, so sorry!" I wailed. "I'll never do anything like that again! Please don't stop sending me out." I was practically in tears.

"Well actually," Juliet said, "Woody liked you very much. He thinks you could really take off with the right kind of material. Unfortunately, he doesn't think this movie is for you."

I cried and could've kissed the ground.

Whether he meant it or was just being gracious, I'll never know. But for me, Woody Allen was my last New York City leprechaun.

Someday, I would love to tell him.

CHAPTER 32

BILL AND ME, GETTING HIGH AND ENGAGED

Tales of Bill's special brand of magic—his intuitiveness, alertness, and raw talent that made him such a hit in *Oh! Calcutta!* and brought him Broadway success in *And Miss Reardon Drinks a Little*, then landed him a fantastic TV sitcom role on *Maude*—and of the serendipitous happenings that propelled us toward work in this land of oft-broken dreams are woven throughout this book. But I haven't yet told you of the very best of him.

His most outstanding quality was his generosity of spirit. From the time I moved in with him and the rest of our lives together, he'd always introduced me to every person he'd ever known in (and out of) show business with the intent of promoting my talents, sharing not only his own financial wealth, but the wealth of opportunity that had come his way. In NYC, I was his darling, and he showed me off every chance he got, making me feel at home, valued, and safe with actors, producers, agents, makeup artists, costumers, dressers, stage managers, directors, and even stage doormen.

And though that attitude in him never changed, after we moved to the West Coast, the dynamic of our relationship shifted. Suddenly, I found myself living in the Pacific Palisades (a beautiful coastal town and LA suburb), an out-of-work actress living with an up-and-coming television star. The confidence that came so naturally to me on stage was slipping away in the unfamiliar atmosphere of television acting. Movies seemed even more out of my reach and, consequently, so did my sense of value and self-worth.

In the Big Apple, I had always pulled my own weight, made my own money, and felt independent and free even before my time as an actress there. I was happy and completely optimistic in all my non-acting jobs: hosting at Patricia Murphy's 49th Street Candlelight Restaurant; waitressing (serving light dinners, desserts, fancy drinks, and coffees) at the Palm Court in The Plaza Hotel; and singing as a barmaid at the Gaslight Club. And, of course, my stage work on the road in the Barn Dinner Theatre Circuit and in productions of *Oh! Calcutta!* on both coasts, which led to modeling work and small movie roles. I'd reveled in and relished working my way up from the bottom, financially and professionally. My whole life was before me—and I was on top of the world.

That dynamic changed, however, when we moved to LA. Out of work, I felt like a kept woman, or worse, a pseudo-housewife. I struggled to find value in my days. I vacuumed, took the cats to the vet, cooked suppers for Bill, and attended all the tapings of his shows. I was blown away watching a whole new level of his talent unfold and dumbstruck by his courage in the face of tremendous pressure of that groundbreaking show.

He'd take on one fantastic, challenging script after another, learning lines for a whole new episode every week. The show was shot on three cameras at once and done with no stopping, no retakes, just like a stage production. The cast would get a new script and start working on it the morning shortly after taping the previous show, usually into the wee hours of the night. Bill unfailing performed with utter panache and often by the seat of his pants, with guts and gusto. He made playing the role of Walter Findlay, Maude's husband, look easy, even though (in truth) he was often exhausted, frazzled, and half-crazed.

His writers and producers were witty and sharp, but very demanding and rather strict about staying on schedule. Their humor won out and they blew the cast away with a great joke the morning after the first show was taped. Bill had overslept and was late to the script table reading to be shot next. When he arrived, everyone around the table looked grim and put out. Bill pled, "Wait just a minute! Please! Just let me get some coffee!" He rushed over to the coffee urn, poured a cup of black, and then raced to his seat. When he opened his script, the title jumped out and hit him like a punch to the gut. It read, "WALTER'S FATAL HEART ATTACK."

The writers had put that title on the first page of every script at the table, just in case he might see it over the shoulder of one of his fellow actors. Bill screamed and then laughed, hooted and guffawed till he cried, and the rest of the cast joined him.

Meanwhile, I was in limbo. The casting agent on *Maude* was Jane Murray, and I heard her describe me once as "shy about my talent." That pretty much summed it up. I *was* shy. A fish out of water. Lost in LA. And to put it bluntly, I was boring, both to myself, and even, I suspected, a little bit to Bill. We were stressed and didn't recognize each other anymore—and we were drifting apart. The more I tried to prove myself dutiful and worthy, the more estranged we became.

Somewhere during that time, I went to see a shrink and spilled out all my confusion and frustration. He said to me, "You are trying to make Bill love you. Just be yourself. If he is going to love you, he will. If he isn't, he won't." I went out that very week and joined a theatre group that met in the evenings. Shortly thereafter, I announced to Bill that I wouldn't be home to make his dinner most nights. It was just about time for a hiatus from *Maude,* which meant weeks of rest for the actors and time for the writers to pound out new scripts. Bill was planning a road trip through the Pacific Northwest for his vacation. We decided that he should go alone.

The first stop for Bill, after driving his beautiful, golden BMW through the desert, was Las Vegas. He called me the night he arrived. He'd had serious second thoughts, and I could hear in his voice that he was remembering who we were together, and he didn't want to lose me. He asked me to fly to Vegas to meet him and accompany him on the rest of his trip.

Funny how these things work. I had totally let go. Now life was bringing him back to me, and I knew he was back all the way. Nothing could stop us now. I said yes, I'll fly out tomorrow (and still have the pictures he took of me getting off of the plane in that hot, hot town).

After a few nights of gambling we traveled to the Grand Canyon, then through the Painted Desert in Arizona, and the otherworldly Bryce Canyon of Utah (where we played Pink Floyd's "Dark Side of the Moon" while gazing up at those steep canyon walls). Then we headed north to Spokane, Washington, for the World's Fair. In our motel room there, Bill asked me, "Is this the way it's going to be? Are you just going to do your own thing all the time and not be around to take care of me?" I told him yes, that was the way it was going to be.

"Then let's get married."

I told him he'd have to ask me on bended knee. He knelt and proposed.

Never being the types to rush, we set the date for one year later.

When we finally got married, we celebrated across five cities. Six, if you count Austin, Texas.

That, my darlin', was one fine run of parties.

CHAPTER 33

GETTING MARRIED, RIDING IT

Many couples choose to write their own wedding vows. Bill and I improvised ours in the moment, on the spot. I myself, never gave them a thought beforehand. I'm pretty sure Bill didn't either. It was a purely spontaneous moment. And though I don't remember the exact words we said, I do remember gazing into his eyes and telling him with all my heart that I wanted our marriage to add goodness to this world. I saw he agreed, soul deep, as he nodded yes.

We were married in the Pacific Palisades' backyard of Andy and Irene Robinson, two transplanted New Yorkers, like us. Andy had made a name for himself playing the sadistic serial killer

"Scorpio" opposite Clint Eastwood in Don Siegel's hit film, *Dirty Harry* (1971), and Irene had been business manager to the singing star Judy Collins for over a decade.

There were twenty wedding guests in all. Bea Arthur was one of them, and she arrived in pedal pushers and flip-flops, no makeup, sporting fashionable sunglasses and a great attitude. I wore a snow-white, full-length draped crepe Holly's Harp gown with gorgeous lace sleeves and a garland of flowers in my hair by the same designer (and in the same style) as Vanessa Redgrave's Guinevere in the "Merry Month of May" scene from the movie, *Camelot*.

My mother attended, but my father did not. I never asked him why because I didn't have to; I knew. He approved of our marriage. He just didn't need to see it in person. Besides, we had a big reception planned for a few weeks later at the Batesville Country Club in Mississippi, so he was covered, and all was well.

Before the ceremony, Andy and Irene's house was rocking. The caterers were in a stew over having to make a salt-free, low-fat wedding dinner as per my ridiculous plan to have everyone eat "healthy" that day. Bill was in the backyard telling jokes and getting more nervous by the minute. And my mother and I were drinking champagne in Andy's bathroom while I pinned the wreath of tiny white flowers to my hair—all the while fighting rising steam on the mirror as Andy took a shower behind us.

Finally Bill had had enough of waiting and barged in and hollered, "Sam! Come on! Let's get married!"

We had asked each guest to say something to contribute to the ceremony. A poem, a written passage, or just whatever they wanted to say. Even though everyone there was a dear, precious friend, the only remark I can remember was Bea's. When it came her turn, she peered from under her sunglasses and said, "Well Bill, I think it's safe to buy furniture now."

Two of my closest women friends were there. One from my NYC theatre days, Raina Barrett, the beautiful redhead in *Oh! Calcutta!* and one from my new life in theatre on the West Coast, Judy Kerr, who like me, would become a prominent acting teacher and writer in subsequent years.

After the wedding, we celebrated for a month all across the United States, taking the party to our friends rather than having them try to come to us. We honeymooned in Maui and then flew to Mississippi, where a huge crowd greeted us at the Batesville Country Club. Bill tried to learn everyone's name as he was introduced to them in the receiving line, but after the first hundred or so guests had passed through, he ducked out to the bar and downed a couple of shots of Jack Daniels, just to get his eyes uncrossed. He missed meeting the Clarksdale branch of my family, but one must do what one must do. I will say this for him, when those first hundred or so guests left, he said goodbye to each and every one of them *by name.*

The next morning, as my whole family lay in bed exhausted, Bill was up wanting breakfast. When our darling maid, Eloise, asked, "Mr. Bill, why are you up when the whole family is dead asleep?" He quipped, "This is my third marriage."

We still had two parties to go, one in Brooklyn for his family, and one in Manhattan for our theatre friends. They were marvelous affairs. Bill's family took me to their hearts and never let go. His mother beamed love that I can still feel today when I look at snapshots of that great afternoon. In Manhattan, my future writing partner, Elena, and her then-husband, Bill Knight, threw us a bash.

We had a yards-long Subway sandwich and beer and wine for the *Oh! Calcutta!* crowd and every other amazing actor that Bill and I had worked with through the years. Pablo came and was the hit of the night. He joined Elena in her hammock and told her she had great legs. He wasn't hitting on her. Just stating a fact. Pablo is not a bullshitter and has never tried to ingratiate himself. He's never had to because he's the most self-accepting man I've ever known. That night he was very fine.

All evening he was quietly moving among the guests, offering various ways of getting high.

At one point, he gestured for me to meet him in the bathroom. I walked in and said, "Pablo, this is my wedding party, for Pete's sake! I don't want any more grass or hash. No acid, no peyote, no mescaline, no nothing!"

He was stumped for a minute, then spoke up, "Don't you want some coke?" he smiled.

"Oh," I said. "Coke. Well, sure, why not."

He was a hard man to resist, especially when he was in party mode.

Somewhere along the way, between parties, or during one, Bill and I got a call from St. Edward's

University in Austin, Texas, asking us to be guest artists in one of their summer theatrical productions. It would fit in perfectly with Bill's hiatus from *Maude*. We were thrilled to say yes. It was a gift to have made it full circle, seamlessly moving from personal celebration back to work—and in the theatre—our first love.

We took our show on the road, and in a way, we never left.

Bill and I get married May 4, 1975, at the home of Andy and Irene Robinson in Pacific Palisades

CHAPTER 34

A LARK IN AUSTIN, TEXAS

As everybody who's anybody knows, Austin, Texas, is one fun town. A great place to visit, with lots of nightlife and a variety of daytime pleasures. Not only is it home to the University of Texas and St. Edward's University, it's also the shooting location of *Austin City Limits*, a long-running, renowned doc-music television show that airs the work of fine singer-songwriters performing country, blues, rock, folk, and more. It was a wonderful place to go after our flurry of wedding parties. The last stop before heading back to Hollywood, now husband and wife.

St. Ed's had a theater arts program from 1962–1982 called Stars Over St. Edwards, which featured celebrity Hollywood actors performing on stage with students. Both Bill and I were to act in a play called *The Sudden and Accidental Re-Education of Horse Johnson*, Bill as the character Horse and me as his long-suffering wife. The director that summer and for many years before and after was Ed Mangum.

I might mention that Bill had a compulsion to teach. He taught anything he knew about to anyone who would listen. And, he had it in mind that summer to teach the student actors in our play *his* method of acting, which could be summed up in these words: Don't act. Be yourself (within the imaginary circumstances, of course). Break the rules. Make fun your highest priority. Be daring. Explore. Be outrageous. Don't set your performance. Go moment to moment every night as if it were for the very first time.

What could possibly go wrong?

As we drove toward campus on the day of our arrival, we picked up a young man, a theatre student at St. Ed's, thumbing a ride. His name was Mark Jantzen, and we became fast friends. As it turned out, Mark had been cast to play Bill's best friend, and they became quite a team on stage.

Mark was at ease with us from the start. Completely himself. It was as if we'd known each other forever. Throughout rehearsals and performances, he'd sometimes hang for a while with Bill and then come visit me in my dressing room, where he'd sit on the floor, prop himself against a wall and read me passages from Carlos Castaneda novels. Extremely mystical stuff, Southwestern characters with few possessions, unique and deceptively powerful personalities who could traverse regions within themselves beyond space and time.

I got hooked on Castaneda and in the following months read everything he ever wrote.

On stage, Mark took to Bill's teachings as naturally as an eagle takes to flight. Every night the two of them would create a subtext of actions completely unrelated to the lines in the play. They'd take it to the limit. One night, while they were having a conversation at the kitchen table on set, Mark picked up a sugar bowl and turned it upside down on Bill's head. Bill shook up a cola bottle and sprayed it all over Mark in retaliation, happy with the game.

Through all of this, Ed Magnum, the director, didn't *seem* to put up any resistance. He just let Bill and the kids play. He did, however, suffer some kind of attack as rehearsals neared their end and was wheeled off on a gurney to the hospital. Bill trotted alongside down the hall toward the open doors of the ambulance chatting with him all the way. I don't know all that he said, but I do remember his last joyful shout to Ed as they were closing the ambulance doors, "Don't worry! We're going to do the play our way!"

And our way, when it came to me and Bill on stage, was to use as much of our real life as possible. To blur the boundaries between fiction and reality. My mother and father came to see the show during its run. There was a scene in which I had a fight with Bill and screamed at him that I wanted a divorce. I had saved up every instance of anger with him that had come up in our day-to-day life that week, and when the lines in the play let me, I blasted him with all I had. Once we got offstage and headed to our dressing rooms, Bill turned to me, "How dare you talk to me like that in front of your parents!"

Naturally, we both cracked up.

Offstage, we played a lot with Mark and his friend John Sanders. We were easy buddies, the four of us. During rehearsals we'd work during the day, and often we'd go out and explore the town at night. Mark once took us to a bar with soggy sawdust on the floor amid puddles of spilled beer, where the four of us danced with each other and anyone else who joined in until we were drenched in sweat from the Texas muggy heat. Mark and I got on a roll and were dancing together a lot and having some great laughs. Bill scuttled up to us and shouted to me over the music, "You're having more fun in Texas than I am!" Then he trotted off to dance with one of the girls at the bar, chortling at his own joke.

Mark and John hung out at our apartment some in the evenings, leaving just as we went to bed. In the mornings we'd often discover that they had rolled our car in toilet paper before heading home. They were fond of driving over to our place to share coffee and donuts on the way to rehearsals, leading the way in John's old pickup truck as we followed them later to work. On those occasions, John would drive, and Mark would hang his naked torso out the passenger window to soak up the sun and the Texas breeze.

They were exceptional, funny kids. We adored them.

And at the end of our run, we treated the cast to a beer bust, buying a keg and letting them pick the picnic spot. They chose the pebbled bank of a small but fast creek that rushed downhill, through boulders, sometimes shallow, sometimes deep, but always swift.

We ate hot dogs and Texas shredded barbequed pork on buns and drank drafts of beer, then climbed up the slope to jump on and ride rubber inner tubes down the stream, dodging submerged boulders to shouts of "Hold your butt up!!"

While writing this I flipped through some literature about the Stars Over St. Edward's program. Granted, I only skimmed it, but I saw no record of us ever being there. Maybe that's because we were in the summer program. Or maybe it's because St. Ed's is still recovering from our stay. At the opening night party after the show, a small, well-dressed lady walked up to Bill and me where we were gathered with the rest of the cast. "Is this a new kind of acting?" she asked in honeyed Texas tones.

But proof that we were there came in the form of Mark Jantzen, who upon his graduation, moved to LA and joined the acting class that I'd just begun teaching. He was one of my first students and stayed with me seven years. I never charged him a dime. He more than paid me with his spirit: the adventurous, joyful fun that he brought to the class and his fellow students.

There was something a bit mystical in our relationship. His birthday was one day after mine, and one year we had a joint birthday party at a fellow student's beach house. It was a large gathering, as many of my students came to celebrate. We danced in the sand near a bonfire past midnight and into the wee hours as my birthday turned into his.

He had a nice part in a good movie *Johnny Dangerously*, starring Michael Keaton, Joe Piscopo, Marilu Henner, Maureen Stapleton, and Peter Boyle before he was done with LA.

Soon after, Mark got married and moved to somewhere in the Southeast, perhaps Chapel Hill, North Carolina, to raise a child and pursue other passions, disappearing from our lives as suddenly as he'd appeared ten years before.

Searching deeper into St. Edward's archives on my last hunt for reports of our time together there, I found an old playbill from the summer of 1975. "Bill Macy in Douglas Taylor's *The Sudden*

and Accidental Re-Education of Horse Johnson...
with Samantha Harper."

We really were there.

It wasn't just a Castaneda dream.

CHAPTER 35

JON AND ME

It's my opinion that every job an actor ever gets to do is a little love affair—with the other actor(s), the director and his/her assistants, the cinematographer, and (please God) the makeup artist, hairdresser, and costumer. It can extend to the crew, the caterers, the truckers, i.e., the entire movie family that has come together for that one moment when he or she gets the chance to dance outside of time and space in an act of cocreation. It was because of my intuitive awareness of the intimacy involved in acting that even from a very young age, I had dreamed of "going to Hollywood and kissing all the movie stars."

And, indeed, my dream came true. I came to Hollywood and kissed my fair share of movie stars and danced—sometimes in wild flings soaring through the sky with sudden, plummeting crashes through the floor—other times more sweetly, in light steps and breezy twists and spins with some fine directors and producers. But the standout memory of my life in the arts, even surpassing the fun of performing, was the seven years I spent teaching acting—all the while learning from my students as much as I taught them. Jon Voight was a huge factor in the magic of those years, for in a very real sense, he taught alongside me.

As I mentioned before, in 1976, Norman Lear cast me as Roberta Wolashek in his late-night spoof of daytime soap operas, *Mary Hartman, Mary Hartman.* The show was to become a smash hit, and made stars out of several of its players, including Louise Lasser (coincidentally, a former wife of Woody Allen who played Mary Hartman herself), and Mary Kay Place who became America's new sweetheart as the winsome wanna-be country singer, Loretta Haggers.

Norman handed the show over to the direction of Joan Darling, whose creative genius and unique sense of humor favored the show with its off-the-wall, totally unpredictable style. Joan had a background in improvisational theater, being one of the many illustrious alumni of Old Town Chicago's famous Second City comedy and improv club, as well as extensive training in the acting techniques of Lee Strasberg. To make matters even more interesting, she was, and had been for several years, my acting teacher in one of three small private classes she taught once a week on Melrose Avenue. When Norman told her that he wanted me for the part of Roberta, she excitedly said yes. I didn't even have to audition.

Naturally, all Joan's acting classes were put on hold while she directed *Mary Hartman, Mary Hartman*. She resumed teaching when the show's first season was over, but with only one class instead of three. Her secretary called to say that Joan wanted me in that class, but I hesitated. Much as I loved the idea, I felt guilty saying yes.

For years, there had been a miles-long waiting list to study with Joan. Her classes were fun and productive, joyous, with lots of revelations in the minds of her students, much hope imparted, and plenty of success for a lot of actors. On the phone with her secretary, I said kind of casually, "Well, if I'm going to take up space in her class, I should at least teach some of the sense memory techniques and theatre games to people on her waiting list."

Those were magic words that brought a dizzying manifestation almost instantly. Joan jumped on the idea, and my friend and fellow student Judy Kerr followed suit, volunteering to be my class secretary, and she immediately went to work.

The following Tuesday night, I stood facing a class of some twenty-odd fledgling actors, all paid up and waiting eagerly to begin.

Abracadabra! Poof. A puff of smoke, and suddenly, my whole world had a new spin.

Judy had rented studio space, made calls to those at the top of Joan's waiting list, filled the class, collected their payments, and was efficiently keeping my books. Lo and behold, I was in business.

Well, I and my angels, that is. Every Tuesday night on the way to class I sensed two of them backing me up, whispering over my shoulder as I came in from the street. "I don't know a thing about teaching acting," I breathed. "You're going to have to do it for me." And, of course, they did.

Everything rocked along for a couple of weeks. Then, all hell broke loose.

Out of the blue, Jon Voight called Joan hoping to secure a place in her class for a friend of his,

Stacey Pickren. Joan said her class was full but recommended that he call me. He did, and I made room for Stacey among our motley crew. Jon came to watch her first night in class, and when it was over, he wandered up to me and said, "You know, I never learned any of this stuff. Can I be in your class, too?"

I somehow managed to say something in the affirmative. He smiled. "See you next week."

I don't have to tell you that I was terrified. In fact, I called Joan in hysterics and told her what had just happened. After a long pause, when I thought maybe we'd been disconnected, she finally spoke.

"I could kill you!" she breathed in ominous tones, then laughed. We both did for a while, me with tears of all sorts flowing from my eyes. Then she said some wise things. "First off, you don't have to teach Jon Voight how to act, he already knows how to do that. He probably just wants to figure out what he's doing when he gets it right. My advice is to shut up and let him teach. While he's putting things into words for other people, he'll be teaching himself. And if there is anything you want him to know, tell it to another student when you're giving notes to the group, after the sensory exercises. He'll pick it up."

I followed her advice "to a T."

And so it began. I had to expand to three classes to make room for all those on *my* now miles-long waiting list, and Jon attended all three classes every week for quite a while (my memory is about a year). He was a generous, kind, and benevolent fellow to those working alongside him, whether they were beginners or veterans, as a few seasoned actors had also joined my classes. Sensitive, playful, funny, and thoughtful, he was undeniably cool. A great teacher, I might add, when he felt he had something to contribute. When he got ready to film *Lookin' to Get Out*, he brought the casting agent, Lynn Stalmaster, to see my class in order to give every actor and actress in it a chance for a part in the movie.

Pablo had also entered the class in an unexpected way.

He had reentered my world and added to the artistry of my acting classes, and to the wonder of my life.

CHAPTER 36

PABLO — OH! HERE
YOU COME AGAIN

In 1979, Pablo Ferro moved to LA. By that time, I'd been married to Bill for four years and had acted as a semi-regular on the Emmy-winning late-night soap opera, *Mary Hartman, Mary Hartman,* in its opening season, then moved on to *The Lorenzo and Henrietta Music Show,* a short-lived syndicated TV series. (Lorenzo was better known as the voice-only character of Carlton, the doorman on the TV comedy series *Rhoda* with Valerie Harper.)

Like *Mary Hartman, Mary Hartman,* Joan Darling also directed *The Lorenzo and Henrietta Music Show.* It featured her ex-husband, Erik Darling, a folk singer and gunslinging guitar and banjo player who'd replaced Pete Seeger, founder of The Weavers, a group that reawakened interest in American folk music. Louis Arquette (father of Rosanna, Patricia, and David) and Murphy Dunne of *The Blues Brothers* sang and played as part of Lorenzo's group, performing several numbers in each show, the cast of which also included writers and improvisational actors doing sketches. But the show quickly tanked.

I was happily teaching acting again and making good money at it, as I taught three packed classes a week.

Pablo, himself, was dealing with a saga that began on January 10 or 11, 1970, just a few days before his birthday, when he'd been shot in the neck after answering the door to his apartment.

There was a lot of mystery around the event. Nobody knew exactly what had happened, or more importantly, *why*. Theories blazed, but they led nowhere. What was known was that someone had rung his doorbell claiming to be a neighbor wanting ice, and when Pablo opened the door, he was facing a gun. When he tried to slam the door, the gun fired, and a bullet ricocheted off the doorframe, hitting the left side of his neck.

Pablo's company had just grossed its first million dollars that year. He'd only recently turned down Steve McQueen's request to move to the West Coast and create all the title sequences and trailers for his films (Pablo had done the title sequence for McQueen's crime-thriller *Bullitt*), saying his commercial business needed him in New York. In short, my friend was at the height of his career. The wound almost killed him and shook him to his marrow.

When I'd left him in NYC in 1969 to do *Oh! Calcutta!* in San Francisco, his thick, dark brown hair reached almost to his waist. He was vibrant and alive: slim, strong, a savvy, unique dresser, happy, brilliant, innovative, street smart, witty, and sexy as all hell (as many a girl who loved him in those days will tell you).

He was a knockout, that five-foot-six Cuban Indian, with his Aztec nose and light brown skin, his many scarves and love beads, and all that gorgeous hair. A lady killer who never tried—and never had to. Stanley Kubrick called him a genius and Jonathan Demme called Pablo "the best designer of film titles in the country."

A girlfriend that I was getting to know in the months that followed his arrival in LA told me a story about Pablo driving her home one night. They were both working at the time for Hal Ashby on a movie. Pablo asked her to come to his place. She said she'd better not, she had a thousand things to do at home. He said, "Not tonight, Josephine" and kept driving. The "not tonight, Josephine" did her in. She did not go home that night.

I was a bit jealous when I heard that story. Pablo was never jealous of anyone and wanted his women to be that way, too. He didn't understand possessiveness. I learned a lot from him. I wasn't jealous of his other women, as long as I was one of them.

At this time in my story, of course, I was not. But I remembered the fun we'd had together and missed it. Needless to say, there was a spark and a bond between us that had always been there. My husband Bill loved Pablo. They shared a mutual respect. All was in pretty good balance, as I walked the tightrope of memory.

When we'd parted after our "summer of love" in 1970, I sat with him on his staircase for a talk. We'd just finished shooting his short film *The Inflatable Doll* with Don Calfa and had spent the summer together mostly in his apartment with

Don along with various other artists, lovers, and friends, leaving only to find food (we never knew if it was day or night before stepping out of his pad) at great little restaurants—my favorite being a Cuban-Chinese place uptown.

On the day of this conversation, we'd gone to a nearby pier where most of the group had dropped acid, though I had not. The entire day, Pablo and I were on opposite ends of the pier, watching others trip.

When we got back to his place, sitting on the staircase, I said to him, "Pablo, if all of us love each other, and one of us goes away, what does it matter?"

He turned to me, "If you're asking me if I love you, I love you. But when two people love each other, it's not always happening. You'll go away and I'll go away. But we will always come back."

I left then, after a last romp with all my friends and lovers of that memorable summer in a blast of a party that lasted all night. At dawn, I met Pablo in his downstairs bedroom for our own private sweet goodbye, then left and walked the sixty or so blocks up and across town to the small studio where we began our first rehearsals for the movie

Oh! Calcutta! There I met Bill, who courted me until he won me and who I ended up marrying.

Now, the year was 1979. It had been quite a stretch, almost a decade since the "you'll go away and I'll go away" talk, and suddenly Pablo was back in my life. Coming to be near me and in need of healing.

He had called one day out of the blue to say he'd had moved to LA, and I had invited him to audit the acting class I was teaching. When he showed up, he was almost unrecognizable. Very thin. Skinny, in fact, and had cut off all of his hair quite close to his scalp. But his appreciation for "art in the making" was still alive, and his eyes glowed softly when he approached me at the end of class.

"This is not an acting class," he said. "This is a creation. Okay if I, and maybe Frank Cavestani, come and bring our cameras?" Frank had been in NYC with us back in 1970 when he was an actor, director, and guerilla filmmaker. Now he was broadening his scope, and a short time later helped to produce the eerie TV series *Tales from the Darkside*. Later, he'd also play a key role in founding the free alternative newspaper *The LA Weekly* with publisher Jay Levin and actor Michael

Douglas. Of course, I said yes to having them film us in all stages of our work. As my acting teacher had said before me, and I'd repeated at the beginning of every evening that I taught, my classes were run like a zoo. The free-for-all atmosphere prepared us for doing work on sets where everything around constantly moved with scant regard to the actor. The more liveliness the merrier, and having cameras there was a boon to us all.

Things rocked along for a few weeks, with Pablo and Frank dropping in to shoot whenever they felt like it. Then Pablo was hired by Hal Ashby to do titles and trailers and publicity art for his comedy-drama *Being There*, starring Peter Sellers, Shirley MacLaine, Melvyn Douglas, Richard Dysart, Jack Warden, and Richard Basehart. From that day until Hal's death, Pablo worked on *all* his films.

While he was working on *Being There*, Hal housed him in Calabasas, California, up in the hills west of the Valley.

I visited Pablo one day, and he was showing me photos of himself in earlier days. "Nobody had the courage to tell me that I was too fat," he said. He kept flipping through photos. Then again.

"Nobody, *nobody* had the courage to tell me that I was too fat."

As he turned a few more pages, I quietly said, "Pablo, you're too skinny." He raised his head up from the album and looked at me. "And you need to let your hair grow out. Nobody is going to hurt you now. It's safe to come out of hiding. Let yourself be beautiful again."

He heard me that day and, thankfully, he did get gorgeous and healthy again, emerging with a whole new style. He'd reinvented himself many times in his life, as artists do, and he did it again. He remade himself into a slim, well-dressed man with short hair and that distinctive Pablo flair.

He and Bill and I had some wonderful times together back then. There was a particularly fun night in a sushi bar when Bill was so outrageously loud and off-the-wall that I climbed under a table, took off my wedding ring, and handed it to another girl. She kept it on until Bill got outrageous again, pretending to be a seagull going after the raw fish that was carried to a table on a tray by a sushi chef. She got so disgusted that she passed my wedding ring to another woman seated nearby. By the end of the evening, that ring had traveled around the entire room when I finally, though reluctantly, slipped it back on my finger.

Then there was the night of a birthday party thrown for me in the home of two of my students, a couple who'd met in my classes. When it came time for the cake, Pablo and Bill fought over who'd bring it out of the kitchen and present it. So they both ended up carrying it, each holding onto one edge of the plate, to raucous applause. Later that night, they both passed out on a bed in our hosts' back room, drunk as skunks and peaceful as babies.

The truth is, Pablo and I were getting closer to each other than we'd planned. There was an unexpected deepening of feelings between us. I was out of my comfort zone, and I think he may have been, too.

Something had to give.

Pablo in Robert Downey, Sr.'s film, *Greaser's Palace* (1972)

CHAPTER 37

A NIGHT WITH LYNN STALMASTER

Lynn Stalmaster, the man Jon Voight brought to audit my acting class that one fine summer night, was a premier Hollywood casting director from 1950 to 2000. Over his career, he cast three hundred and eighty movies and television series, many involving Pablo, but with other artists and directors, as well, on many notable films, including *The Wind, The Graduate, Deliverance, Superman, The Right Stuff, The Great Escape, The Greatest Story Ever Told, 9 ½ Weeks, Fiddler on the Roof, Silver Streak,* and *The Rose.*

He was a favorite casting agent of many directors, among them Hal Ashby, for whom he cast *Harold and Maude, The Last Detail, Sham-*

poo, *Coming Home, Being There,* and *Bound for Glory.* In 1982, Hal had Lynn begin casting a new film, *Lookin' to Get Out.* It was to star Jon Voight, Burt Young, and Ann-Margret, but there were many smaller parts to be filled, and Jon talked Lynn into coming over one evening to watch our acting class, thus, giving his buddies a shot at parts in the picture.

It was a kind, bold move on Jon's part, one that will not be forgotten, ever.

It should be noted that I ran a very loose class. There were only two rules. The first was that all class fees had to be paid in advance at the beginning of each month. The second was that during class time, the students couldn't harm anyone, including themselves. After that, they were on their own to use the class as they saw fit. They could come late, leave early, or not attend at all. If they wanted to come in and pick a partner, warm up, and go to a restaurant across town and improvise a scene there, then come back and report how it went, that was fine with me. They were adults, and I treated them as such. This attitude, like so many of my techniques and policies, was patterned after that of my own acting teacher, Joan Darling.

There were rows of seats inside the entrance to our studio that held a number of people who audited the class for free. Some were actors, but other artists came too, including a woman who sculpted and another who created pottery. As I mentioned in the last chapter, my friends, Pablo Ferro and Frank Cavestani, came by with their movie cameras and roamed around shooting anything that interested them. It was their opinion that I wasn't teaching acting, but was instead creating a live event, "a happening" as it would've been dubbed in the '60s.

Often, if someone was absent from class, I'd let one of the auditors work and pay for that night only. As I said, the class was loose. It was a zoo, by design.

As the class began, the students would lie down on the floor to relax, then I'd wake them singly and assign each a different sense memory exercise. The smell of his or her childhood bedroom on a rainy night, for example, remembered in the nose, instead of the mind. Remembering sensually can evoke unpredictable emotional responses in an actor, adding color, texture, and surprises to a performance. Sense memories, as they are called, are also diversions for that part of the mind that can become self-conscious, getting it busy with a task and out of the way, thus freeing up the actor's instincts. For me and my students, these exercises were a great adventure and a lot of fun.

Once my actors were on their feet and doing their sensory exercises, they were free to move about and improvise with others. As more and more students were awakened and assigned their work and joined the crowd, the energy built up to a roar. Later, we'd sit around, and I'd critique what I'd seen and heard, then we'd play theatre games and watch two or three scenes in various stages of development.

The night Lynn Stalmaster attended the class was packed. Word had spread that he was coming, and it seemed that every student I'd ever taught showed up. They poured in. I had to open the back door to the studio and let some of them do their relaxation exercises in the parking lot behind the building. With all the bodies lying about, it looked like the railroad station scene from *Gone with the Wind*.

Lynn, sitting alone in his chair, seemed a bit overwhelmed. A light sweat shone on his forehead, but he was stoic taking it all in, and there was a lot to see, as one by one, the corpses came to life and joined the mass improvisation.

Ken Place, brother to Mary Kay and one of my more rambunctious students, had brought his Hasty-Bake grill and set it up in the parking lot. There he donned a chef's apron, made us *hors d'oeuvres,* and brought tray after tray of them in through the back door to serve his fellow actors.

Pretty early on, I saw we had a problem. There were so many students working that there was no way I could showcase each one in a scene.

Not only that, but they were all gravitating toward the far wall and working in the shadows, facing *away* from Lynn. On instinct, Jon and I started moving through the crowd, singling out an actor and pushing him toward Lynn, saying "Tell a joke!" or "Sing a song!" Or we'd grab two actors together and have them improvise a short sketch. We'd make up the circumstances of the scene for them, then have them act it out.

Actually, it was all going fairly well till we reached the last two actresses on stage. One was a former ballerina and good friend of mine, Jennifer Nairn-Smith, who'd been an understudy for the nude *pas de deux* in the Broadway production of *Oh!*

Calcutta! The other was a tall, classically beautiful blonde model named Maggie Smith. I'd never been able to crack either one of them. They'd resisted showing any signs of vulnerability, no matter how smart or clever I tried to be in designing exercises for them. Jennifer was a well-spoken Australian aristocrat. Maggie, smooth as honey, seemed to be living a life totally devoid of angst. I needed to find a way to give Lynn a glimpse of who they really were.

Stuck, I turned to Jon. He took the two women aside and whispered imaginary circumstances for an improvised scene, talking to them separately, each out of earshot of the other. He knew and liked them both, and they'd shared secrets with him that he then used in devising a plot. He told one actress that she was a Catholic psychiatric therapist who wanted more than anything to have a child and the other that she was unmarried and pregnant, seeking advice about whether or not to keep her baby.

Suddenly, my ballerina and my model became intensely focused. Taken off-guard, they played a scene that was surprisingly powerful, poignant, in fact. It reminded me of scenes that I'd seen in movies by the Swedish genius Ingmar Bergman.

At the end of the night, Lynn bid us goodbye and left. We were all spent but felt alive and sated.

As it turned out, I was the only person in class who was cast to act in the movie with Jon. Hal already had me in mind to pay Burt Young's ex-wife, Lillian. Lynn agreed and brought me in to audition, and I got the role. It was a great lesson for me. Being so focused on others that night in class, I was more visible than I might've been otherwise.

Playing the scene with Burt Young and Jon Voight in that film under Hal Ashby's direction was a fine adventure. A great thrill. I'll tell you all about it; well, everything that can be told anyway, as at last, I saw my dream coming true. I was in Hollywood. And, wouldn't you know it? Playing with movie stars. Perhaps to even kiss a few.

PART IV

La La Land

New Birth, New Life

Stars of the hit comedy *Maude:* Bea Arthur, Bill Macy, and Conrad Bain, *TV Guide* (1974)

Bill Macy and Bea Arthur of *Maude*

Me with Bea Arthur and Bill Macy, along with cast extras from *Maude,* "The Office Party" first Christmas episode (1973)

Bill and I had a blast on *Tattletales* (1974–1977), the celebrity-couples' game show hosted by Bert Convy

Bill and I scoring some pins on *Celebrity Bowling*, hosted by Jed Allan (1976)

CHAPTER 38

AS HOT AS THEY COME

My passion and deepest-held heart's desire had always been to act in movies, and as I've mentioned before, to play love scenes with movie stars. When I finally got a chance to do both, and under the eye of one of the all-time greatest movie directors ever, I thought I'd died and gone to heaven.

I'm referring, of course, to the film I mentioned before, *Lookin' to Get Out*, a comedy starring Jon Voight, Ann-Margret, and Burt Young that was just beginning to shoot under the direction of Hal Ashby.

Jon had won an Oscar in 1978 for Best Actor in another of Hal's films, *Coming Home*, a mega hit in a string of mega hits by the same director over the previous decade. It received eight nominations at the 51st Academy Awards, including Best

Picture and Best Director, and took home another two wins in addition to Jon's: Best Actress for Jane Fonda and Best Original Screenplay for Waldo Salt and Robert C. Jones.

Now four years later, in 1982, in preparation for *Lookin' to Get Out*, Jon had brought Hal's casting director, Lynn Stalmaster, to the acting class I was teaching (as you now know), providing a kind of informal audition for all the students, and a surprise part for me in the movie itself. Hal, as I have said, had already been thinking of me to play Burt Young's ex-wife, Lillian, and shortly after Lynn's night of watching my class, he called me in for a meeting with the director.

When I arrived at Hal's trailer on the studio lot in Culver City, he informed me that the scene wasn't yet written. All that was known was that I was coming to see Burt to hit him up for money. His character, Jerry, along with Jon's, were gamblers and down on their luck, so I was the last person they needed to see. My scene was to be with Burt, but Jon would come in and shoo me out at the end of it. Hal and I chatted a bit. I told him my ideas about why Lillian wanted money. Not for the kids, as she was claiming, but to buy cocaine and a pair of hot shoes. He said I had the job, let me choose my own wardrobe, and told me when to show up to shoot. I'd never been given that much artistic freedom, ever.

I was up all night before the shoot, thinking of what would make the scene interesting and fun. I hadn't met Burt, but I loved him as Talia Shire's brother and Sylvester Stallone's fight manager in *Rocky*. He appealed to me. I planned to wear the same clothes that I'd worn to the audition: a blue-green fitted silk shirt with the top button open, a push-up bra, and tight-fitting jeans. I had wanted to wear expensive, hot and trashy heels with that outfit, but didn't own a pair, and that's what gave me the idea for the "audition story" I told to Hal. I ended up wearing the closest thing I had in my wardrobe—metallic strappy high-heel sandals. I vowed that if I got the job, I'd use the money to buy those super-hot shoes. I carried the energy of my secret promise to the meeting with Hal—and it worked.

I planned lots of curls in my long hair, pulled back from my face and big rings on my fingers. Instinctively, I wanted the scene to be a seduction, but didn't know how Burt would feel about that.

Early the next morning, as I sat nervously in my trailer, all dressed but having no idea of the scene I'd be shooting, there was a knock at my door. I opened it, and there stood Burt, looking sheepish. I invited him in, and he said rather tentatively, "How would you feel if this scene got a little sexy?"

"Oh good grief! That's just what I was thinking!"

He blinked, then said, "Let's go find Hal."

We burst into Hal's trailer, talking over each other with our ideas. I remember telling Hal, "There is a reason I'm coming here that is more than just hitting Jerry (Burt's character name) up for money. I like it that I have power over him. I like messing with him. It gives me something. It feeds me."

Hal looked me in the eye and said it better. "You've got his number." (For those too young to remember, see Cy Coleman's music and Carolyn Leigh's lyrics of "I've Got Your Number," a racy song made famous by Tony Bennett, Ella Fitzgerald, and others that implied if you've got a guy's number, you have the keys to his psyche.)

The three of us were like footballers coming out of a huddle with a loud YES!

I don't know how we came up with the dialogue, if we wrote it together or had the help of writers, but we ended up with lines that revealed I'd been married to Burt for a few years a long time ago, had left him for another man, had two kids and now was divorced again and broke. I was hitting him up for money supposedly for the kids, who weren't even his.

We shot the scene over and over for a week. I was sure that we had it in the can that first day and thought I'd be sent home with a thank you. Hal wanted to play with it some more. We shot it from numerous angles and were not held to doing the same thing in every take, but instead were allowed to let the scene evolve over time.

Burt would start to giggle when I flirted and teased, getting a little physical, and then he'd get out his checkbook and pen and offer more money than I was asking. This would crack us both up and I'd put my arms around him and tell him the lesser amount would be fine. Tears would roll down his cheeks. I kept my hands on him while he wrote out my check. Then Jon came in and abruptly put a stop to things, made fun of how I spoke, and put out the fire. I managed to get out of their apartment with the check in my purse before Jon caught on that I'd gotten it.

At the end of a week, the scene was done. It was late, after ten at night, when I went back to my trailer to pack up for home. But as I was leaving, there was a knock on my door, and an assistant director hollered out, "Hal wants you back on set."

I walked through all the lights and equipment, watching the next scene being set up, but when Hal saw me, he halted all activity, took me aside and said, "Sam, it's a rare thing to see two people who really like each other working together on-screen. What you and Burt did; it doesn't get any better than that. That was the real thing."

Anyone seeing the film today would see me riding up in an elevator with an eccentric, offbeat guy, then a scene with Burt reluctantly letting me into his room, us gradually finding our footing with each other. Then a glimpse of Jon coming in through the downstairs lobby before a final scene with Burt when Jon interrupted us. They might wonder what possessed Hal to hire me as a Brooklyn girl, dyed-in-the-wool Southerner that I surely was, though I did have the benefit of the many voices in my head of my in-laws, Bill's Brooklyn family, to help me make a decent stab at the accent.

But I learned some things about film and art that week. It's not the size of a part that matters most. Not perfection and not neatness that makes magic. What does, when we're blessed enough to find it, is spirit, passion, enjoyment of the moment, heart, and daring. Taking chances.

I'll always love Hal for making me value those qualities in myself. And I'll thank him forever for the joy of working with him.

He was a shy man. I was also shy and very green. He never approached me with notes. But when I was by myself, rehearsing the scene in my mind, I'd look up and see him peering in at me from the other side of a doorway. He'd nod in a silent message of approval, then move on.

Jon had his own way of adding to my confidence.

Once, early on in the week, when we were getting ready to shoot my entrance from outside "Jerry's" door, just when we were starting to roll, Jon, waiting behind me for his own entrance later, loudly whispered, "Sam! Wait!" I looked up, annoyed at having my concentration broken. He said, "Do you have any ideas for me in this scene?"

I shushed him and smiled. It was a smart move, reminding me of my strength, at a moment when I might have felt insecure.

And Burt. Oh, my. In our free time he shared part of his life story with me, the amazing circumstances that led him to study with Lee Strasberg and become a member of the Actors Studio, a huge accomplishment for a man coming into the field well into his adult years. I loved his naïveté, the innocence of his approach to his craft. I also loved how still and present he could be, willing to just be there, honoring the moment, fully enjoying himself and me.

As I said in my last chapter, every job an actor ever gets to do is a little love affair.

A few years ago, we had a screening for Hal's cut of *Lookin' to Get Out*, which we thought had been lost (the studio took over the original and cut it badly). Burt stopped and introduced me to his daughter, a gorgeous young woman who he'd talked a lot about in the days when we were shooting. "This is Samantha," he said, "she really went for me."

Yes, Burt, I did.

And strange as it seems, that was the end of my desire and need to "kiss all the movie stars." I never kissed Burt in the scene, but I encountered the sweetness of his soul and the kindness of Hal's and Jon's as well, as we made art together for that one week. I never again longed to do love scenes in movies. I had experienced something much more real.

Postscript: Hal's cut of the film was brilliant. The con scene in the casino was wonderfully funny. Hal had edited the film while listening to music from The Police (Sting's group) to give the movie its rhythm and pace. He wanted the studio to secure that music for him to use as his soundtrack. They did not. They didn't realize what he'd brought to his previous two decades of hits and his sensibility of how music can inspire a film.

Me, Burt Young, and Jon Voight in 1982's *Lookin' to Get Out*

CHAPTER 39

HOT L BALTIMORE

In the spring of 1973 while Bill and I were visiting NYC, we went to see a play, one that would lead to a break for me in my career as a television actress, though I didn't know it at the time. Bill had just finished shooting his first season of *Maude*, and the show was on hiatus, giving the actors some rest and the writers time to write more episodes.

Lanford Wilson's *The Hot L Baltimore* was playing at the Off-Broadway Circle in the Square Downtown. We wanted to see it mainly because it featured Trish Hawkins, who'd been in the *Oh! Calcutta!* cast with us. She'd replaced Boni Enten in the "Jack and Jill" sketch after Boni moved on to other shows, including the 1974 LA stage production of *The Rocky Horror Show*, starring Tim Curry, no less, where she truly rocked.

Trish had a delicious innocence about her: soft brown eyes and shoulder-length, sandy blonde hair with long bangs that hung over her forehead. She also spoke with a gentle lisp, making her all the more appealing. We loved her work. And besides, we'd seen her naked.

Winner of the New York Drama Circle Award, the play also featured Conchata Ferrell, Judd Hirsch, Jonathan Hogan, and Mari Gorman, and won the Obie Award for Best New American Play that season as well as the Outer Critics Circle Award.

Set in the lobby of the Hotel Baltimore, a decaying structure soon to be condemned and drawing its title from the hotel's neon marquee with a burned-out letter "E" that was never replaced, the play focused on the residents, many of them prostitutes, facing eviction—a loss of shelter and home, such as it was. There's enormous humanity and credibility in the characters, and the actors playing them that night hit all the right notes, giving distinguished and inspired performances. As I sat in the dark theatre, I felt my heart pulled, both with empathy and envy.

From early childhood I've never been content to just sit and watch a play, or even a game, being performed for me. If something moves me, it moves me to *action*. My mother was always disappointed whenever she took me to The Barnum & Bailey Circus to see "The Greatest Show on Earth," expecting me to enjoy the beautiful girls in their colorful tights and tutus doing tricks on trapezes or walking tightropes or juggling in the various rings. "Why do you want to do everything you see?" she would say through clinched teeth. "NO, YOU MAY NOT RIDE THE ELEPHANTS! PLEASE, JUST CALM DOWN!"

Watching *The Hot L Baltimore*, I was definitely *not* calm. I ached to be in that play.

Flash forward to the following fall.

Bill and I were back in LA for the second season of *Maude*. All Norman Lear shows at that time were shot at the CBS studios on Beverly Boulevard at Fairfax Avenue. I went with Bill to tapings every Tuesday night, and on those afternoons, we rode up the slow elevators with producers and directors and actors from Norman's other shows.

This particular afternoon, as we stepped through the elevator doors headed for the third floor, Rod Parker and Charlie Hauck jumped in with us. Other writers were with them. They were talking freely about the new show they were mounting, and I suddenly realized the show was none other than a television version of *The Hot L Baltimore*.

My heart was racing. They got off on the second floor and we continued up to the third where *Maude* taped. I bolted from the doors and charged into Bill's dressing room, grabbed the phone and called Rod and Charlie.

"I know you guys only see me as Bill's girlfriend," I blurted trying to calm my breath. "But I'm an actress, and I saw *Hot L* in New York and I have to tell you, I want...I *need* to be in your show." I plunged in further, "I play naughty girls, hookers, strippers. And because I look innocent, it's funny. I've never asked for anything from you before. Please, please let me read for you."

There was silence for a long few seconds. Then one of them said, "Sam, the show is already completely cast." I stayed quiet, but hung on, waiting. "Tell you what," Rod said. "Come down here and pick up a script, take it home, and come back tomorrow and read for every part in it."

And so I did. I came the next day with a box of jewelry, various belts and scarves, lipsticks, blushes, and eye shadows. I quickly altered my appearance for every character and read for every part. When I finished and was walking out the door, Rod stopped me. "Sam," he said, "this will not be for nothing."

The following week they handed me a script. It had a guest-starring role for me. I was to play Evie, a disarming young woman dating the Richard Masur character. His problem in the show was that while he was working among so many ladies of the evening, he had a secret that he could tell none of them: he was a virgin.

The segment we shot was rewritten from a script that originally had my character come to the Hotel and accuse him of being the father of her child, which of course, he couldn't have been. I ended up playing a girl who just had a crush on him and was willing to be patient while he found his courage.

I came to his office, dressed in an off-white embroidered blouse under a blazer of the same color and a light-pink flared skirt, proper attire for a date. My hair was cut very short, and I wore small pearl earrings that I still have today. The two of us went out to MacDonald's and while there, had a misunderstanding that hurt my feelings, but later we made up in his office. The scene then went to black, at that point, where my character supposedly made a man of him right on his desk—and later we copped to it in front of the girls, thus saving his reputation with them.

Bear it in mind that Bill had been trying to get Norman Lear to hire me on one of his shows for over a year. Norman ignored him and always said, "Bill, please! Just leave the casting to us." So other than an appearance in the *Maude* first Christmas episode as Audrey, the friendliest girl working at Walter's appliance store, a guest in Maude and Walter's house for a Christmas party who was later discovered on their bed with a man under a big pile of coats, I hadn't yet worked for Norman.

As it happened, he was in Europe when I was cast in *Hot L Baltimore* but got home in time to see the show being taped. He walked backstage afterward to where I was standing with Bill and said, "Bill! Why didn't you tell me she was an actress?"

That guest shot was a stepping-stone toward a semi-regular part on *Mary Hartman, Mary Hartman*, leading to a decade of guest appearances on other hit TV shows of the day, among them *The Bob Newhart Show*, *Mork and Mindy*, *Hill Street Blues*, and *Hardcastle and McCormick*. Plus, my bit as Audrey, the friendliest of Walter's employees at Findlay's Friendly Appliances became a running gag on several of the *Maude* Christmas shows.

When all is said and done, we owe a lot to Norman Lear. Ah, the stories I could tell. But then, maybe not.

As Norman once said to Bill, if you're playing second banana, you'd best hang with the bunch.

CHAPTER 40

HAL NEEDHAM, TERRY BRADSHAW, AND MEL TILLIS

S trange as it may seem, I did play a love scene in my very next acting job after finishing work with Burt, Jon, and Hal. It was on a television pilot with a bunch of cowboys and marvelously fun. And the part came to me in an unexpected way.

I'd spent the better part of two decades working my way into Hal Ashby's family of artists, starting with the little movie I did with Pablo Ferro that first brought me to Hal's attention.

I'd also invested a lot of myself in cultivating my relationship with Norman Lear, acting in small parts in his shows until my first guest-starring role on *Hot L Baltimore*. My teacher, Joan Darling, had directed me in Norman's hit late-night soap opera spoof, *Mary Hartman, Mary Hartman*, and because of my relationship with her, I was cast as a regular in *The Lorenzo and Henrietta Music Show*.

But that cowboy pilot was won on my own from a man I'd never met, on the fly and by the seat of my pants, using audition skills I'd been trying to master for years. It was a joy to find out they could work in a world of first encounters and cold readings, in my new world as a grownup in Hollywood.

It was unusual for me to have two auditions in one day, but my agents had called and told me that I was to see two prominent directors the next day, each with excellent projects, and that I'd have no time to change clothes and restyle my hair and makeup between interviews.

The first meeting was with Frank Perry who was directing the movie *Mommie Dearest*, with Faye Dunaway playing Joan Crawford, based on an autobiography by her adoptive daughter, Christina Crawford. The movie garnered good reviews and became a commercial success, and later—due to the bizarre script and highly charged acting, especially on the part of Miss Dunaway—attracted a cult following as an unintentional comedy.

I was to talk to Frank, the director, about playing the part of a fan of Joan's who became her lackey, accompanying her daily and doing all sorts of jobs in her service, a very plain woman who wanted nothing more than to be close to the star she adored.

After my interview with Frank, I was to get myself across town and meet with Hal Needham, one of Hollywood's top stuntmen and stunt coordinators who'd recently become a director best known for his collaborations with Burt Reynolds on films involving fast cars, such as *Smokey and the Bandit, Hooper, The Cannonball Run,* and *Stoker Ace*. It was a BIG step for me having the opportunity to meet him, with huge successes to his credit. His movies were big at the box office because they were wild rides, raucous, and a lot of fun.

Needham was casting a TV pilot called *The Stockers* for Mel Tillis, a country singing star famous as much for the stutter in his speaking voice (which he completely overcame whenever he sang) as for his music, and Terry Bradshaw, former quarterback for the Pittsburg Steelers, a mega football star who'd won four career Super Bowl titles in six years, completing 49 of 84 attempted passes for 932 yards and nine touchdowns—both records at the time of his retirement. He had one of the most powerful arms in NFL history and called his own plays throughout his career. At the time of our shoot, he was beginning to act in movies and on TV and was becoming a sports analyst. And he was a hoot.

Mel and Terry were playing stock car drivers racing on small tracks across Texas on their way to Daytona. I was to read for the daughter of the owner of a small-town auto parts store whose local boyfriend was taking her for granted, that is, until Terry and Mel made him jealous enough to propose to her.

As the meeting for *Mommie Dearest* was first, and as it was a feature film and a much bigger project, I dressed for that part, wearing dowdy clothes with my hair in a tight bun and little makeup. I'd been taught by my acting teacher, Joan Darling, to always have an "audition story" to tell in an interview. A story that seemed off the cuff but revealed who I was and why I was right for the part.

I'd also been influenced by Pablo Ferro to go into all interviews with the understanding that if I had a meeting with a director, I was already working on his project. "Give him something he can use," Pablo confided. "After that, if he wants more, he'll have to pay you."

I brought along a Christmas card with the picture of a large family, friends of Bill and mine. In the shot were a glamorous mother and father and several attractive, young adult children and their offspring. In the background was "Aunt Shirley," a slim woman in her late thirties with short hair and no makeup, part of the family, yet removed…a bit of an outsider. I showed the picture to Frank Perry, and he looked at it, stumped.

"What is this?"

"That's the relationship this fan has to Joan Crawford's life and to her world," I explained.

This set us off on a lively talk and a decent meeting of our minds about the character. I left and sped over to meet Hal Needham, where I read okay for him, but hated that I was dressed so awfully for the part.

When I got home, I called my agent, Steve Stevens. "I want you to phone Hal Needham right now and beg him, BEG him to let me come back with my hair down and wearing something pretty."

"Okay," he said. "I'll call you back."

A few moments later he was on the phone again. "Needham said, 'Oh Hell. Why don't I just give her the part?'"

I let out a yelp. We both did. And even whooped some as we celebrated our first big win together. He told me to go back to Hal Needham's office the next afternoon for instructions for the shoot.

When I arrived, Needham said, "Here's the map to our first location. Be on set at 7:00 a.m. We stop shooting every day at 4:00, and we have steak for lunch."

So my cowboy adventure began. It was my first show shot outdoors on various locations all over the San Fernando Valley. We shot in mud puddles between rain showers, halting the cameras when small planes flew over and threatened to ruin our sound. We did indeed have steak for lunch, and I shot pool with the other actors and crew members on breaks. And true to Hal Needham's word, come hell or high water, we rolled it all up and stopped filming at four o'clock every afternoon.

As I said, Terry Bradshaw was a hoot. And sweet as pie. The acting teacher in me showed up the first time I met him, and I actually tried to teach him a relaxation exercise on the floor of the makeup trailer we all shared. He was too antsy to settle down, but he tried for a while before his feet started twittering and he gave up the effort in a fit of giggles.

Mel Tillis showed up in the parking lot of our first location in his band's touring bus with his wife on board. She wore a giant diamond on her wedding ring finger and kept a close watch on Mel, as I recall. I don't know whether they lived on the bus for the whole shoot or if they went to a hotel for part of the time. He was funny and winsome in the part and hilarious off camera. On a day when Terry had to drive a real racecar around a track—no small task for someone who'd never handled such a sophisticated machine, even at the slow speeds being used for the shoot—Mel walked over to me after the rather harrowing ride and said, "The owner of that r-r-racecar is mad at T-Terry." When I asked him why, he said, "Because he's shi-shi-shit in it!"

The love scene I played when my boyfriend proposed and kissed me was with Burton Gilliam. It was a rare chance for him to do a straight and fairly romantic role, as most of his work was in outrageous comedy. He'd played the wild cowboy, most memorable for dancing and singing "The

Camptown ladies sing this song, doo-da, doo-da!" to a bunch of incredulous black cowboys watching him from the opposite side of a riverbank, and for eating beans around the fart-fest campfire scene in Mel Brooks' *Blazing Saddles*. He'd also played the bizarre geek of a desk clerk in *Paper Moon*, the 1973 comedy-drama directed by Peter Bogdanovich and starring real-life father and daughter Ryan and Tatum O'Neal, for which Tatum received an Oscar for Best Supporting Actress, making her the youngest winner in the history of the Academy Awards at the time. Burton's career was taking off, and we both were signed with the same agent who'd encouraged us to go to lunch together before the shoot began. A wise move on his part. We knew a lot about each other by the time we went on camera, and it showed. He was tall and ruggedly handsome, with a way of looking at women that struck home. My feeling was that he'd had his share of fun before he got married and settled down. He was definitely fun to play with on camera and off.

At the end of the shoot, the cast of *The Stockers* joined Hal Needham for a dinner at the glamorous Polo Lounge in the Beverly Hills Hotel. It was a great night with lots of laughs. Our little family of artists split up much too soon, as is the case with all jobs in an actor's life. You come together as a company and are close for a while, and then one day it's over and life must begin again from scratch. But I did love my time with the cowboys.

A few weeks later, I received a surprise in the mail. A letter from Frank Perry regarding my audition for *Mommie Dearest*. Getting a personal note from a director is very rare for anyone who isn't a star. In it he said that he very much enjoyed our time together and loved my audition but had decided to go "in another direction."

I had made a dent...and was on my way.

CHAPTER 41

MARY HARTMAN, MARY HARTMAN

There's nothing more fun in the whole wide world than to be in a production that's a hit. Whether the show is on the big screen seen by people spanning the globe or on stage with the audience right there, breathing the same air as you in a big theatre in a huge city, or for folks in a small town—either way, the sensation is electric.

I was fortunate enough to experience it three times in my life. Once on stage in the Barn Dinner Theatre production of *Ladies' Night in a Turkish Bath*, which played in small theatres across North Carolina, Georgia, Virginia, and Tennessee; and again on stage and in movie screen productions of *Oh! Calcutta!*; and a third time in Norman Lear's late-night takeoff on daytime soap operas, *Mary Hartman, Mary Hartman*.

I'm aware that the *Mary Hartman* show was likely long before many of your times. But it was a maverick and innovative. You might have fun going back to catch a bit of its off-the-wall flavor. It was fresh. Sweet spirited. And with things the way they are today, it was important.

Every evening at eleven when the show aired, waiters disappeared from the floor in fine dining places from LA to Las Vegas to theatre bars in NYC, and I'd suppose, also in eateries across the Midwest and Deep South. Diners would have to wait while their servers skipped out to watch in the kitchens of hotels as well, at least the diners who'd ventured away at that hour from their own TV sets. *Mary Hartman, Mary Hartman* was a hit—and not a show that many wanted to miss.

In 1973, Norman Lear was honored at a beautiful dinner party at the Beverly Wilshire Hotel. Bill and I went, and late in the evening, the party turned raucous. Bill was on stage with Norman, and a joke got out of hand, went too far and tanked, Don Rickles style. Norman looked down from the stage and saw how it affected me, the shock and upset on my face. He told me later that tears jumped from his eyes and landed two feet in front of him. In that moment he made up his mind to use me in one of his shows. *Mary Hartman* gave him a place to put a character like me, with my craziness, guts, and sweetness, for sure—but more importantly I think—my vulnerability.

Joan Darling was directing the show, and Norman called her to say he wanted me to play the character of Roberta Wolashek, the social worker assigned to Mary's grandfather, Grandpa Larkin, when he's caught wearing a raincoat and nothing else, and convicted of being the shadowy and long-sought fugitive known as the "Fernwood Flasher." Joan knew my work from her acting class and agreed that I was right for the part.

My professional relationship with Norman wasn't perfect, but it did have glorious moments. The first season of *Mary Hartman, Mary Hartman* was one of those moments, filled with quirky joys and mad adventures. It was a time when Norman acted as a hero for me, hiring me to play Roberta and also saving me when I veered off in the wrong direction during the shooting of one of my first scenes in the show. When he saw it, he insisted on a reshoot, an unusual thing, as *Mary Hartman* had a pencil-thin budget.

Grandpa Larkin was played by Victor Kilian, an eighty-eight-year-old veteran of the movies who'd appeared with great frequency in supporting roles from 1935 to 1950 before he was blacklisted for his political views and forced from the business. For the next twenty-six years the only acting he was allowed to do was on stage. Then in 1976, Norman cast him as Raymond Larkin on *Mary Hartman*, returning Victor to the screen—and to the role for which he was most remembered.

My character was to fall in love with Raymond, as I called him, while giving him a Rorschach test. I was thirty-two at the time, and the wide difference in our ages made for sweet comedy. Victor was easy to love. He was hard of hearing, and I had to stare into his eyes and make a strong connection with him when we played our scenes together. It was good for me as an actress, grounding me in a world that I shared with him, and it worked like gangbusters on screen.

In an early scene with Dody Goodman, who played Mary Hartman's mother and Raymond's daughter, I made a choice to be troubled over my attraction to Raymond. I tied up my character in angst, and Norman put a stop to that as soon as he saw the tape of that episode. "I hired you to fall in love with Raymond because Raymond is wonderful, not because you are neurotic."

We reshot the scene and came up with a character that the audience accepted. Roberta threaded her way through twenty-nine episodes and many perils, as soap opera characters do, getting fired as a social worker for dating her client, Grandpa Larkin; selling Lady Fashionetta (Avon-like) cosmetics door-to-door; becoming a member of S.T.E.T. (Survival Training and Existence Therapy), a takeoff on Werner Erhard's *est* "self-improvement" movement, big in the '70s; breaking up with Grandpa and then landing in a love quadrangle between Mary, played by Louise Lasser, Sergeant Dennis Folly, played by Bruce Soloman, and Cathy, Mary's younger sister, played by Debralee Scott, and of course, *me*.

Joan Darling had once commented that I was like an octopus with one arm missing. She said I had a wide emotional range and could relate to the inner workings of most people. "What you are missing," she said, "is aggression. You don't want to hurt anyone's feelings. You don't like to fight.

And sometimes you need to play rough as an actor. Think about that."

She was right. My aggression arm had been severed in Mississippi while I was in training to become a Southern Belle one day. Not all Southern ladies lose their aggression, far from it, but my training was strict and the values of my parents rigid about what was expected of me. My mother with all her books on child raising thought it was part of her job to "break my spirit" at an early age. Before I was two, we battled over shoes that I didn't want on my feet until, with enough spankings and tears, I finally gave in. And there were other painful bouts until I finally got it that aggression, even assertiveness, if it crossed her, was not to be tolerated.

Roberta Wolashek had her aggression arm missing, and that, with my other qualities made for one quirky character. It was in a fight scene with Debralee Scott's Cathy character over Bruce Soloman's Sergeant Foley that I felt the impact of my missing arm. I didn't enjoy trying to one-up her, and just kind of melted into the furniture. I have since learned the fun of battling, of standing my ground, and although the quality of nonaggression was endearing in Roberta, if I had it to do over, I'd bring just a bit more fire.

I did win a fight or two with Louise Lasser who played Mary Hartman. Well not so much of a fight as a test of wills in one case, and the ability to see through her games and show her what I knew of her secrets, in another.

The first was on the set, in rehearsal, when I'd stayed up all night struggling to memorize a page-long spew of dialogue, which I was to deliver to Mary in her kitchen, pitching my Lady Fashionetta beauty line. I brought it in for camera blocking only to have her constantly interrupt the rehearsal to ask the guys in the booth what she should be doing while I talked; she kept at it incessantly, kept it up until I was ready to scream. We were on a tight schedule, only one day ahead with our scripts and I felt tremendous pressure to get the scene shot and do a good job of it. I literally couldn't finish one sentence without her saying something like, "Maybe I should stand over here and lean on the counter and wave at Foley when she says that. Or maybe I should grab his hand and pull him over to me!"

Finally I surrendered. Just gave up, shaking with exhaustion and rage. When she saw the look on my face, she fled to her dressing room embarrassed, dashing through the set yelling, "Oh Sam! Sam!" then slamming her dressing room door behind her.

That was Louise, she loved her drama. We were used to the unexpected from her, though this was a bit extreme.

When she was safely out of earshot, the producers came down from the booth and onto the floor and asked me what I wanted to do. "We'll do whatever you say," they told me. Although I was trembling, I said, "I want to shoot it now, and if I'm not happy with it, I want to shoot it again tomorrow morning." I knew I was asking a lot. But they seemed to feel I deserved all the help I could get. They gave me a glass of orange juice for energy and to calm my nerves, and called Louise back onto the set, and we rolled tape. Miraculously, we got the scene on camera that night.

My other most interesting encounter with her was in her home. She was giving a birthday party for her personal assistant or costumer, I forget her position, but her name was Sandy. Louise had invited over one hundred guests, all of whom had arrived to find that she wasn't at home to greet them. She'd gotten herself arrested for cocaine possession that afternoon at a local toy store by insisting that a doll's house be delivered to her door, even though she had no money or credit cards with her. She told the clerk that she was famous and that everyone should know who she was, then sat down on the floor and refused to budge. The police were called, and when they arrived, they searched her purse and found the drugs.

Her one phone call was to her home, and soon all the guests were abuzz. After making bail, she arrived at the party hours late, went to her bedroom and lay in bed all evening holding court, with various guests coming in and saying something like, "I'm a lawyer. I can tell you just how to handle this."

I watched from a comfortable spot on the carpeted floor, leaning against a bedroom wall. At the end of the evening when everybody else was out of the room I said, "Louise, I'm totally onto you. You are loving this. You couldn't stand to let this night be about Sandy, it had to be all about you."

She looked at me and smiled, enjoying the moment. Enjoying me. Then we both died laughing. Guffawed till we were done.

I ran into her years later in a workout class, where she was lying on a mat on the floor behind me. She'd gained weight and, at first, I didn't recognize her. She sat up and put out her hand to me, "Hi. I'm Louise. I USED to be one of your best friends."

Life is strange. So is fame. It's enticing and fleeting. I haven't seen her since that day. But I loved that her quirky nature and wild sense of humor made *Mary Hartman, Mary Hartman* such a hit, if only for a couple of years.

I loved the taste of that high.

Victor Kilian and me in *Mary Hartman, Mary Hartman*

Me and Bruce Solomon in *Mary Hartman, Mary Hartman*

CHAPTER 42

STORM CLOUDS
IN MISSISSIPPI

Following my time with *Mary Hartman, Mary Hartman,* for a few years, there were some fine times teaching and guesting on television series, movies of the week, and playing small supporting roles in feature films before life took some unexpected turns. Hal Ashby, my favorite director and my only real link to the film business died, taking with him my expectation, hope, and dream of further developing my talents and evolving into a more serious movie actress—and by the late 1980s, skies began to darken back home in Mississippi.

My mother, Emma, who'd been my lifelong champion…befriending my boyfriends while setting boundaries for us…sweating it out while watching me practice for majorette tryouts, twirling a baton and throwing it up into the semidarkness of twilight, breaking a lamp or two whenever I continued wheeling the baton in our house...my mom, who'd taken giant leaps in her own choices, gone back to school and taken all the necessary steps to become a psychologist, had come to California for my wedding to Bill, standing next to Bea Arthur during the ceremony, the both of them looking equally gorgeous and powerful. My outrageous mother who traveled with me and Bill's family in two cars to Disneyland one Christmas holiday, then watched as all the other grownups—Daddy, Bill, his sister, Roz and her husband, Marty—got disgusted with the long lines, hiked back to the parking lot and headed for home. Mom watched them drive away, then turned to me and Bill's young nephew and nieces, and smiled, raising her arms to the sky, and shouted, "YES! TO EVERYTHING!" and played with us all till the stroke of midnight. My precious momma, Emma May, was now sinking into a depression that had manifested as an undiagnosed and ever-worsening bout with chronic physical pain.

She described it as feeling "like steel bands pulling," grabbing and clutching the internal organs beneath her ribcage and moving up to grip the muscles and tendons of her shoulders. On a visit back home, she begged me to take her back with me to California so she could see the chiropractor that I'd been raving about. And, go to a good dentist and have some therapeutic massages.

And so I did. I also got her engaged in a slew of other therapies, including a four-day metaphysical seminar to perhaps help her understand what was happening to her body and how her mind might be contributing to her condition. She seemed to love the seminar, was enchanted by the meditations that took us into rare and beautiful dimensions of consciousness but would not (or could not) see how she could use those experiences to heal herself.

As a teacher of mine once told me, metaphysics is dangerous if you only want to do the pretty stuff. There needs to be a balance, which involves facing negativity and pain head-on, feeling sorrow for our part in it, and ultimately forgiving everyone involved, releasing it and moving on. My mom had a glimpse of this, toyed with the idea that we have the power to heal maladies in our bodies by working with our minds and spirits, but she did not sustain it, and ultimately, rejected it almost violently.

In the months that followed, the search for a physical solution, a cure for her tangled nervous system continued. She went to my dentist to have her silver fillings removed, having read that the mercury in them was toxic and could be causing her pain. But her blood pressure skyrocketed in the dentist's chair and she had to abandon that plan. There was a series of massage therapists, homeopaths, acupuncturists, psychics, and spiritual healers. After almost a year of exhausting every alternative medical resource I had, she started to break down for real and sought help in the mental ward at UCLA.

On the drive there, my friend Melissa Converse rode with us in the back seat of my silver BMW and in the quiet, began to sing "The Lord's Prayer." It calmed and comforted us. Upon arriving at UCLA, we were informed that doctors no longer used talk therapy for patients in that hospital. The only treatments they could offer us were drugs. After a week or two, we transferred her to St. John's Hospital and Health Center in Santa Monica, but things turned out to be much the same.

Mother, however, was kind of a star there. She had a strong personality and a lot of humor was in her madness. Once when I was visiting her in a common room filled with other patients, she looked at her surroundings and muttered *sotto voce* (but loud enough for all to hear), "That wallpaper has GOT to go." She would wander over to the nurses' station and rearrange the flowers standing in their vases on the countertops. She was even caught in a man's room (he wasn't present at the time) with all her clothes off, sorting through his drawers of socks and underwear.

She was obliquely seductive with the doctors—and competitive. In the end, they persuaded her to undergo a series of electroshock treatments. Being desperate and at her wit's end, she submitted and gained some relief from her pain along with a rise in her energy and spirits. We bought her some beautiful clothes, and I and another of my closest friends, Grif Griffis, saw her off, toasting her with champagne as she boarded the plane to rejoin my father in Mississippi.

Unfortunately, her relief was short-lived. A few weeks after arriving back home, Momma took to her bed and never left it again. Her pain and the underlying sadness over the death of her firstborn son to AIDS, coupled with the steady mental deterioration of her second son, Peter, who would clearly never be able to live on his own and who frightened and provoked her—proved more than she could handle.

Peter had moved back to Batesville in 1977, just six years before Sterling came back there to die. Their stories are intertwined. Peter had been living in LA for two years, chasing his career as singer/songwriter and guitar/harmonica player. He'd had some success, living almost a full year with Bill and me in our rented duplex apartment just off Olympic near La Cienega Boulevard. When I heard Peter perform one of his songs, "Country," I grabbed him fast and drove him to audition in Santa Monica at the Great American Food & Beverage Company, a restaurant looking to staff singing songwriters as waiters and performers in their small chain of roaring cafés—known for loud ambiance, gigantic food servings, and rocking, bluesy, original entertainment by young musicians. We got lost on the way to Santa Monica in my trusty BMW, however, and the auditions were finished by the time we came barreling into their parking lot. The producers were packing up to leave, but I begged, saying they *had* to hear Peter, and wouldn't take no for an answer. They relented, reluctantly at first, then lit up when they heard him play and sing his wild "Country" song lyrics ending with, "Well, I barely got a dime, 'cause I paid up all them dues, and I swear that I can feel 'em, but I just can't play the blues." He rocked on his guitar, played his heart out on harmonica, and took them by storm, landing a job in their restaurant chain just a couple of miles from our apartment. Peter loved his time writing music and performing for their packed houses.

He was also part of a band that entertained at Rue McClanahan's fourth wedding (she was Bill's famous costar on *Maude,* who played Vivian Harmon, Maude's naïve best friend and wife of Walter's right-winged, *mucho* conservative friend always at odds with the outspoken, liberal Maude). Peter was gorgeous that day, strumming and singing at Rue's garden party in his white, shiny suit that we'd bought from Reel Clothes on Ventura Boulevard in Studio City, a store that specialized in great styles previously worn in Hollywood movies (I had an identical suit to his, which I also wore to Rue's wedding).

He also had a great time in my acting class (which I taught him for free, of course), as an actor/singer-songwriter for his peers, who found him hysterically funny. Definitely offbeat. Once during a scene, I noticed that a "prop" suitcase carried by an actor looked empty. It had no weight and seemed phony swinging by the actor's side. I stopped the action and said, "Somebody put some old clothes in that suitcase, anything!" Ken Place, a humorous friend sitting beside me stood up and blurted out, "Nobody has clothes older than Peter's!" He was right, Peter's everyday clothes were decades old, threadbare, and torn. Just right for his "Country" song.

Bill and I enjoyed Peter's company, but before moving to our new home in Beverly Hills, we gave him time to find his own place. We'd given him a great start, but now wanted to live on our own as a couple. He'd met the star musician Jackson Browne's brother, Severin, while working at their jobs in the music restaurant, and they moved in together. Peter wasn't happy about leaving our home and before the year was out, got tired of running after fame. I'd bought him a car with the money I'd made from *Mary Hartman, Mary Hartman.* He asked me to sell it and send the money to him in Mississippi. He was ready to head home. He moved into a trailer on a stretch of property near our grandparents' home in McKiver, kicked back, got stoned, and wandered the hills feeding the birds and the pack of wild dogs that seemed to always find him. But he was surviving—until Sterling came home and, without warning, died.

Sterling. There's so much to say of this precious, wild, delicious soul. He was a handful, always. A vibrant, alive, rebellious, raging, deeply wounded celebratory man who swore he never wanted to see the age of forty, and who died when he was thirty-nine. A self-taught painter and time-to-time writer, too, when he'd peck out a script on the typewriter kept in my father's optometry office. It was two doors down from Marion Shackeroff, part owner with her husband, Edwin, of the finest clothing store in town and who gave Sterling rudimentary training in oil painting. In spite of her warnings, he managed to catch his bedroom on fire with cloths soaked in oils and stashed in the closet. Fortunately, the flames were squelched before they brought down the house.

Sterling. Who searched the world looking for himself. Looking for home. Who was furious that Peter had time with us in LA, thought it was his birthright as the oldest brother, but didn't come until it was too late. I was in bed recovering from surgery. Bill had asked him to come stay with us, but Sterling was traveling with a man he'd just met, and Bill didn't include his new friend in the invitation. Sterling took offense and left for Mississippi before I could greet him. I never saw him alive again.

He was wounded as a small child, contracting an infection that was treated with sulfur, the doctors not knowing of his allergy to that medicine, which almost choked him as he screamed while they crammed it down his throat. His rage started, I think then, although it might have begun earlier. Either way, it was lifelong. There was a darkness in him, but, oh, what a dazzling light as he fought it. He loved battles; this is true. Conflicts, victimhood, martyrhood, chaos. Yet, he had an artistry that threatened to transcend his madness. He was gay probably. Practically. But not surely.

Peter always said that Sterling wasn't a homosexual; he was just hooked on getting attention and had learned that the best way to be in the spotlight was to shock people. That was, I think, perhaps true. Sterling discovered shock-sex in the sixth grade when he heard an announcement that all who wanted to go on a day trip to the local roller-skating rink must be dressed properly, either with long pants or a knee-length skirt. Sterling adored several girls in his class. One was Sally Holloman, and he persuaded her to lend him one of her skirts for the day. When he showed up wearing it at the skating rink, all hell broke loose. He was hauled into the principal's office, where a war broke out between his teachers and our parents' friends, most of them prominent physicians in town. He was on fire with excitement, loved the stir. And the odd gossip about him.

Unfortunately, once he was in the soup, he couldn't extricate himself. He was always stewing, brewing, always the hero/goat. At his year-end piano recital, his gorgeous brunette teacher, Theresa Dunlap, an aristocratic Spanish woman who'd married a World War II soldier from Mississippi and moved to our town, didn't let Sterling play the piano, but instead had him sing "I'm getting nothin' for Christmas, 'cause I ain't been nothin' but bad."

Flash-forward: He attended my father's alma mater, the Mississippi State University in Starkville, and was there in 1968 when the Christian leader for peace and equality among the races, Martin Luther King Jr., was assassinated in Memphis. Sterling lowered the flag to half-mast on college campus and stood alone all day, from what he told me, in its shadow. He said he wasn't afraid to stand up for Reverend King, even with carloads of kids passing by and heckling him. When he graduated, he married Mae (whose maiden name I don't remember), daughter of a plantation owner, a tall, beautiful blonde who looked like the girl in the popular folk group Peter, Paul and Mary. The two of them left together for grad school at the University of Colorado. Their marriage didn't last, and he left to live the life of a painter, imitating the works of van Gogh, Monet, and Picasso, then finding his own original style.

On his own, he moved to NYC and stayed for a couple of years, then to Key West, where he sought the haunts of Ernest Hemingway—the all-time great American journalist, novelist, short-story writer, and sportsman who'd had tremendous impact during his days and for generations to come. Sterling painted Hemingway's favorite cafés, the streets where he walked under flowering trees, and lush hotels that flavored that magical place. My brother then traveled to New Orleans and worked in an art gallery in the exotic French Quarter. Throughout his years he was abused as a homosexual, raped in NYC, and verbally treated badly in New Orleans when I visited him there. But he was so beautiful— such a brave and enchanting man, this brother of mine. A tall, handsome drink of water, any way you looked at him.

When he arrived in Batesville at age thirty-nine and with pneumonia, my parents rushed him to a hospital in Clarksdale, Mississippi. I flew down to visit him, only to find that he had died while I was in flight. I'd wondered why a friend of my father's met me at the airport in Memphis and offered polite conversation on the sixty miles to Batesville. I noticed cars parked in front of my house, then entered the living room and saw it was filled with well-dressed, quietly talking visitors. Something was wrong, but I was clueless. My dad rose to meet me, "Your brother didn't make it," he said, taking me into his arms.

I spent the night at the funeral home beside Sterling's coffin, having a long conversation with him. In this surreal place, I felt him with me. I can't remember what we said, but it was filled with hurt. Two souls speaking across a void, breaking hearts, angry and deeply sad. The next morning a huge truck arrived at our house. It was filled with nearly a hundred of Sterling's paintings. Big canvases and smaller ones, from his work in NYC, Key West, and New Orleans. My mother took the money from his life insurance, then repainted her house and hung every piece of his artwork on her walls, some even outside in her screened-in porch, and a few up the stairs to her attic. They were bold and striking paintings, each one. Many styles, many of them inspired by great masters, yet graced by his originality, humor, deep sensibility, and an eye for beauty. Six months after his death, we were informed that he was a victim of AIDS, an illness that was just waking up, baring its teeth, and threatening our world. The hospital had done research to discover this virus in Sterling. It was stunning news to us all.

As I said, after Sterling's death, my mother had tried to save herself in California with my help but was unsuccessful. When she returned to my father, she saw Peter steadily becoming more mentally unstable and was forced to face the loss of Sterling, his soul, spirit, and personality reflected from his paintings on her walls, and she fell apart… this time, for keeps.

Daddy was left pretty much on his own, working, grocery shopping, and coming home at night to cook and keep her company.

Bill and I were clearly needed back home in Mississippi.

CHAPTER 43

GOING HOME

Bill had fallen in love with my parents when they visited NYC, had adored his daylong date with my mother at the Frick Museum and bonded with my father as well. They were both World War II veterans and instant buddies, the deal sealed when Bill took us to see *The Rothchilds*, the Broadway play I mentioned earlier about the rise and fall of a prominent Jewish banking family in Nazi Germany. On his trip to Mississippi the following Christmas, he'd felt accepted and loved by my parents to such a depth that the bonding with my family was solidified. As we hit hard times, he did not blink.

Through the years, we'd traveled to Mississippi for several emergencies involving my brother, Peter, back in the days when Mother was still on her feet. Once he'd refused to eat, almost to the point of starvation, believing that if he tasted any nurturing bite of food, one of his family members would die. We'd stood praying with my mom and dad in a circle around him for many hours until he was able to take sips of soup from a teaspoon in my father's hand. And again, Bill and I hurried down there when Peter was taken to jail for threatening a man, who he saw in his delusional state as evil and supernatural. Peter had written this man a letter, calling him the anti-Christ. At that time, he owned a rifle and was living in a tiny apartment on the other side of town from my parents.

My folks called and told us policemen were on their way to Peter's place and asked us to phone and tell him not to resist when they came for him. Without hesitation, Bill dialed him, "Peter, the police will be at your door any minute. Don't lift a finger against them. Let them take you peacefully. Samantha and I will get on a plane right now and come get you a lawyer."

And that we did. Well, actually, we didn't end up needing a lawyer. Daddy was so disturbed about Peter having a weapon and threatening to use it, that he wanted to have him institutionalized. But it was in an institution that Peter had gotten really ill. He'd been scared by some recent psychic experiences, like seeing a train wreck in his mind and then hearing on the radio that the crash had just happened. The doctor said he needed treatment, so Peter checked himself into a place he knew very little about and found that he couldn't get out. I'm sure in his state of mind, he didn't read the fine print of whatever he had signed. There, they gave him psychotropic drugs that were way too much for him; he became suicidal and from that day forward, had recurring episodes of trying to take his own life.

So when we got to Mississippi, Bill hung out in the house with my parents and calmed them down, helping them to entertain ideas for other therapies that would offer my brother more freedom. Meanwhile, I walked the two hundred yards from my house down the railroad track toward the town square, crossed the track to the courthouse and county jail that sat on the near corner, where I visited Peter. I stood across from him and gazed through the bars of his cell, grateful for his humor as he smiled at me and said, "Look at me in here, for Pete's sake! Can you believe I'm in JAIL?"

We both laughed, and I could see he was as relieved to have me there, as I was to see him standing (and not dead). I convinced him to sit tight while Bill and I searched for a solution. Then, somehow, it was all arranged that he'd go to a clinic in Oxford, where he wouldn't be a prisoner, but a patient. After another night in lockdown, they opened his cell door and I walked him back up the tracks to our house.

I thought he was joking when he told me he'd found the meaning for his life by reading the Bible in his cell the night before. But he wasn't, even though he skipped and laughed as he told me the story. He'd asked for guidance, then read a passage that said it was man's purpose in life to say the name of God. He grabbed that as a literal lifeline.

From that day forward, he constantly spoke, wrote, recorded, and played all the names of God he could find throughout history. He did this for years, actually until his dying day, several decades later. He scribbled names of the divine everywhere, covered the walls with them, scribbled all through a slew of notebooks, on every page, back and front, and on every clean surface he could find, including secret spots in some of Sterling's paintings, the names of Jesus, Jehovah, Christ, Yahweh, and many more ancient names for God. And, over time, he became nonviolent, and for the most part, gentle, kind, and benevolent. Still, he had wild opinions and occasional expressions of rage toward those he considered evil, but no longer threatened harm to anyone.

He remained unable to work or function in society, but in spite of that, was entertaining and actually fun to hang out with whenever he took time off from chanting "Jesus" and "Jehovah" to play his guitar and write some music and behave in unexpected, often hysterically funny ways.

Bill and I enjoyed our time getting stoned with him. Peter had read in the book of Genesis that God had given us "all the herbs in the field..." and took that to mean that marijuana is sacred. I don't think he was far off about that. He had a little problem with responsibility, that's most definitely true, but it's my opinion that the grass he smoked helped him stay alive, and for the most part, stable. And, his offbeat and unconsciously comical doings were something to behold, almost worth what he had put us through.

Before Mother got real sick, when he'd just gotten back to Mississippi after his stint in Hollywood, Peter had taken all his dirty clothes, tossed them in the back of his pickup truck, then driven the truck through a car wash. It was one of those places where you hosed down your own vehicle by hand, so he washed his truck and his wardrobe, too, then took it home to hang on various chairs in the backyard to dry.

Now a full decade later, he was living in the living room and helping out at home, concentrating on recording chants of God's many names and broadcasting them stereophonically throughout the house while smoking so much dope that marijuana fumes wafted through the ventilation system of our gorgeous, old antebellum-style home. Bill and I could get stoned from inside our own bedroom without ever taking a single toke. Bless his heart, Bill had to put on earphones to drown out the Christ and Jehovah sounds blasting through the walls into our room.

One last little tale about Peter, and then I'll have done. After his days of threatening violence were over, he went out of his way to never kill anything, no matter how pesky, and therefore, refused to let us poison any bugs. Mind you, the cockroaches in Mississippi are enormous two-inch-long monsters, and they'd crawl through the kitchen at will.

One night I walked in and saw *la cucaracha* ambling across the middle of the floor, so sure of his safety that he might've been at a pedestrian crosswalk on a busy street. It was the last straw. I got so mad that I opened the side door from the kitchen and kicked him a good fifteen yards out of the house. I turned to face Peter, who was sitting at the kitchen table rolling a joint. He looked up and said, "Well, now you're gonna have a roach with an attitude."

Meanwhile, my mother was a difficult patient. She could seduce me with her sweetness one minute and turn as mean as a snake (as my Aunt Sadie would say) the next. I started going to Mississippi more often on my own, without Bill, and for quite a few years, spent two weeks every month with my family there, as good help was hard to find, especially nighttime help, after my father started to break down himself.

When I saw him weakening, I rented a big van, packed it with goodies, and took him to a Memphis hospital for some tests. The doctors announced to us that he had prostate cancer. I looked at him and their words didn't jolt or even faze him. He was the same gentle, unruffled man I'd known all my life. On the ride back to Batesville, I opened a little cooler and gave him a sandwich and a Coke. He flashed a bright smile and said, "This is just plain fun!" Granted, senility was beginning to settle in, but it looked good on him. He was happy and at peace, even though the doctors had predicted that he'd have a great deal of pain in his last days. As it turned out, he had no pain at all when he died. As I spent more and more time with my folks, my career in television and movies was put on hold, and my acting teaching days came to an end.

It was a time of mixed feelings, of joy to be with Dad and Mom when they needed me, but also a time of self-doubt. Had I hurt my mom by veering away from orthodox religion and introducing her to metaphysics and a broader spirituality, as my brother Peter contended? Momma seemed to agree, although she'd been eager at the time to venture into a more expanded view of our world. Now, in her pain, she couldn't feel that she was loved by an all-loving, all-inclusive divine being and force at the center of our Universe, or by a traditional God (or by me or anyone else). Nor could she sense the possibility of any healing.

Would Sterling be alive today if I hadn't stuck up for him when he came out of the closet, writing to tell my parents he was gay? I wrote them, too, asking that they might try to accept it, upsetting them mightily as they thought it was their job to set him *straight*. Would Peter have not gone nuts if I hadn't danced naked on stage coast-to-coast and on the big screen? Now my mother regretted granting me permission to do *Oh! Calcutta!* She said I never should've asked her in the first place. *Was she right? Had I brought down of the house of Harper?*

I weighed the "me" she'd wanted me to be against the "me" I'd become. I knew I'd been guided all my life by an unseen force. How could I deny it with so many signposts along the way? I couldn't believe that I wasn't meant to be part of the sexual revolution, part of altering the dynamics of relationships between the sexes, adding an element of play and fun and unconditional love to the mix—that I wasn't destined to meet Bill (as free a spirit as they come) and live the life I was living. Still, the doubts were painful. Excruciating. It was a dark time.

But also, a time of light. And of miracles, too, the biggest being two souls who arrived to help us with both of my now catastrophically ill parents. They came when I'd exhausted every resource in the county, it seemed, looking for nighttime caregivers who were willing to stay with my family more than one night.

They were May and Dan Rowland.

CHAPTER 44

MAY ROWLAND

Most of the help for tending the sick in Mississippi, at that time, came from the black community. I'd hire a caretaker for late afternoon, she'd spend one night in our house tending to the needs of my mother and father while breathing marijuana smoke that poured from every vent and being blasted with constant chants of Jehovah and Jesus from my brother in the living room, then leave the next morning never to be seen or heard from again.

My two saviors were from the rural white community just outside of town. They were angels in the form of a country nurse named May Rowland and her husband, Dan, who she called "Daddy," a minister of a small country church. She came riding up my driveway in a red-panel truck, gray hair in a loose bun, and false teeth shining a smile as sweet as they come. She heard my story and patted my hand, "Don't you worry, honey. I'm going to help you take care of your momma and daddy."

Dan helped her out some, coming to take Dad for long, fun rides on back country roads, stopping at roadside shacks for Moon Pies and RC Colas, or Cokes, nuts and chips.

As I mentioned, I'd put my screen acting career on hold and ended my teaching career as well, while staying in Mississippi to help my folks. Now that I had some breathing room, I could finally head back to LA for longer stretches of time. I'd call home and May would answer the phone in Daddy's room and rush to say, "Guess what we're doing?! We're watching midget wrestling!" Dad adored her. Mother tolerated her presence in the house, and Peter got along with her pretty well. May would sometimes join him in the living room to sing hymns, with her banging away at the piano or beating the tambourine. I began to feel free enough to start working in LA theatre productions again, finding my way into plays that were eerily related to the situation with my family back home.

Ah! But May's first night at the house. That first night she came to work for us, it won't soon be forgotten. It was full of the stuff from a Marx Brothers' movie, with surprising twists, turns, and a few pratfalls, not at all what I would've expected.

I met May at the door and walked her through the house to Dad's room, which was across the hall from my old bedroom where my mother now resided in a hospital bed. Her door was always open, so she was aware of everything that went on in the house, though she rarely spoke to anyone (unless it was to protest a caretaker there to attend to her needs, largely against her will). Momma really wanted to be left alone, but I think she loved knowing what was going on around her, nonetheless.

I'd visit with her from time to time, sitting in the far corner near the window behind her and not speaking a word. She'd keep her eyes closed and not make a sound or any movement. The truth was, she'd refused to move for so long, had resisted all attempts to get her to stand up, to take a few steps, even to sit on the edge of her bed, that now, she couldn't do any of those things. She couldn't walk, stand, or even sit. Her feet had hardened, her toes pointing down like a ballerina *en pointe*, and her legs were stiff wooden stilts. She could move her arms, but not her fingers, which were clenched, her thumbs tucked under her forefingers and nails that, as they grew, threatened to cut into her palms.

Still, at times, she was beautiful whenever her sweetness came forth. She could engender a feeling of love with just a look or a word or a memory. But then, the manipulation she'd been secretly planning would follow. The favor she wanted me to do. Like calling the Batesville and Memphis newspapers and asking them to publish editorials supporting her wish to be granted a "mercy killing." Or, like trading rooms and beds with her, me taking the hospital bed and her lying on my soft double bed where she couldn't be reached by helpers trying to bathe or change her or treat her bedsores. Or more insidiously, that I'd look her in the eye and tell her I believed she had no part in her illness. That she hadn't created it, or allowed it, or in any way contributed to it. That she was a victim and had been stricken. But I couldn't say what she wanted me to say, and that hurt. Yet, I could see in her eyes that she didn't really believe it herself.

It was a game, a painful one-on-one. We'd taken that game to a whole new level when she developed huge skin-cancer sores on her face, and I drove her to the Batesville Hospital to have them removed. She screamed all the way saying that she didn't want to go. She believed she'd finally developed a disease that could kill her and begged me to let it run its course. I told her that I could not allow her face and brain to be eaten away in full view of us, helplessly watching her in that kind of pain. And have my father witness the ugliness of all of that for one minute, much less days, weeks, months.

When we got to the hospital, she was brutal to the nurses caring for her, calling them whores and saying they were the ugliest women she'd ever seen. When the doctor came in, she accused him, in front of me and the nursing staff, of doing the surgery because he wanted to take me to bed. She screamed throughout the procedure and was taken back to a recovery room, then wheeled down the hall, me at her side, to be driven back to the house.

Suddenly, she was all sweetness and light again, and asked me again to swap beds with her once we got home. I, of course, had to say no, and when I did, she uttered a few sarcastic words under her breath and shot me a look of pure hatred.

My mother, in her madness, had been saying for some time that she was possessed by a demon.

Pushed to my limit in that corridor, trudging alongside her gurney with her hurling punishments every step of my way, I turned the tables on her.

"SHUT UP, YOU DEMON!" I screamed in her face, looking deep into her eyes. "I know you are not my mother! My mother loves me, DEMON! I don't believe anything you say, DEMON! NOW SHUT THE F—K UP! I don't want another word out of you!"

All this in the hall of the Batesville Hospital. I'm sure people were talking about it all over town for days. But it stopped her in her tracks. Then she did what she did whenever I said no to her. She closed her eyes and went stiff. Adamantly stiff. Aggressively stiff. And retreated into the utter silence that was pretty much her standard M.O.

After one of those bouts, I'd sometimes wait till she cooled off a bit and go sit in her room behind her, out of view, and actually enjoy the quiet. And sometimes amazing things would happen. Sometimes we'd fly together into a peaceful place. I wrote my first contribution to the adult faerie-tale novel that Elena Yates Eulo and I coauthored, *The Two Sisters' Café*, while sitting in Momma's room one night. It had tumbled onto the page in her presence, set in her childhood haunts just six miles outside of town in McKiver where love poured out of the hearts of two female country magicians, one of them very like her own mother, Alma.

Now, on this first night, May who'd ventured in to meet Mom was backing out of the room, gingerly stepping into the hallway. Picking up on Mom's energy and her strong will before I could even introduce them. Mother went silent and blind and May read the message correctly. "You may be here but steer clear of me."

I knew that she would.

We then turned and entered Dad's room. "Daddy, I want you to meet May Rowland. She's going to be here at night to help and keep you company."

What happened next was so out of character for him that I was paralyzed by it. He bolted from the bed and said in a loud voice, "Why are you bringing this old woman into my room? She's too old for me! Get her out, NOW!"

He pushed us out into the hall, slammed his door, and locked it. May and I just stood there, shocked. Peter came and joined us, and the three of us stood together staring blankly at Dad's door.

We stayed in that spot until after a while we grew tired and made a quick sweep through the house to find straight-back chairs, lined them up facing Dad's door, and sat to wait. Silently.

I felt my mother behind us, laughing softly in her bed.

After a bit May spoke up. "He doesn't have a gun in there, does he?" The question was like ice down my spine. I told her I didn't think so. I'd never known Daddy to keep a weapon in the house. But then, I didn't know until that night that he had a lock on his door. It was spooky. And comical, as us three stooges sat in the hall staring at a locked door. It never occurred to me that he saw May as my replacement, a way I could leave him. A way back to California and Bill. I'd spent hours with him, cutting his toenails, giving him reflexology treatments and massaging his feet, clearing his hearing passages by using hollow candles that when lit created a vacuum and sucked debris from his ears. I'd cleaned out his medicine cabinets and scrubbed the kitchen floor, done everything I could think of to make his life sweeter. He must've sensed that May spelled the end of so much attention from me. But I couldn't fathom that at the time. All I knew was that this gracious man, my father, was behaving badly.

After an hour or two, May and Peter and I gave up and went to bed. I was staying in the guest room next door to Dad. After closing my door, I pushed all my yoga equipment, bolsters, mats, etc., that I'd dragged with me from California, in front of it. I dragged the chest of drawers up against my door, too. I needed a cushion from his energy, could sense his wrath. Finally, feeling a bit more secure, I lay down to try and sleep. No sooner had I drifted off when I heard a light rapping at my door. I called out "who's there?" and a familiar voice answered.

"It's me." It was my dad.

It took a while to dismantle the stuff blocking my door, and when I opened it a crack, I saw him standing there holding onto his walker. "I think I may have offended you," he said. "And I came to apologize."

He invited me into the kitchen to share a Coke with him. So we sat at our big round wooden table and had a heart-to-heart talk. I confessed to hiding his car keys and taking his checkbooks away from him and removing all the liquor from the house. I'd been blaming all those things on the doctor. Now I came clean. It was me who'd taken charge of his life. I let him sense that I was frightened by the reversal in our roles, torn by the loss of him as my advisor, my anchor. He heard me. His heart was open.

He did protest the liquor being gone, as he'd been drinking pretty heavily and plying my mother with her share every night. I told him that wasn't working anymore, that we couldn't go on living that way. He felt the truth in my words and agreed to give it up. I know now that in that conversation between us he decided to let his love for me be stronger than his pull toward dementia. He'd made an empowered choice. A strong-willed choice from his soul, backed by the force of his beautiful spirit. Something clicked. We went to bed peacefully, feeling loved and loving.

In the morning light, May went into his room and leaned over the bed. He opened his eyes. "You're an angel, aren't you?" he smiled.

"Yes," she said. "I am."

CHAPTER 45

GOODNIGHT SUN, GOODNIGHT MOON

May and Dad were great friends from that moment on. She loved to laugh, and he laughed with her. She loved to eat, could coax him into eating by saying, "Do you want a sandwich? I'll have one if you'll have one!" He ate to please her and keep her company. He'd made a choice to enjoy every moment of his life from then on and busied himself doing it.

She got him interested in midget wrestling, this optometrist who'd never watched a TV sporting event in his life. She'd sit with him while he was reading, chuckling at his jokes and marveling at his intelligence whenever he shared snippets of writings on philosophers from *Reader's Digest*. Some of them were quite good. My favorite was one of the last ones he ever read aloud in my presence, a quote from an unknown author. To paraphrase my memory of it, "Harboring resentment is like taking poison and waiting for someone else to die."

May had trained in a Memphis hospital that specialized in elder patients with Alzheimer's and other forms of dementia. She knew how to be respectful *and* how to be a friend. She kept up with his medication, had her husband take him on joy rides, and hung out with him for three-some-odd years before he died. She didn't witness his passing. Toward the end, he was hospitalized for pneumonia and a team of caretakers, May among them, sat with him in shifts.

Coincidentally, my mother was also hospitalized at the same time. It was uncanny. The hospital had two wings that branched off from a central section. My father was in the last room at the end of the hall on the right wing. My mother was in the last room at the end of the hall on the left.

Dad seemed to be the one at death's door, so Bill and I flew home to be with him. But when we entered his room, he had rallied and looked to be better.

I left him and walked the long distance through his wing of the building, across the central nurses' station, and down the far corridor to my mother's room in the left wing. When I walked through her door, she didn't greet me, just said, "Is Billy going to die?"

"No, I don't think so," I told her. "We thought he was going to go, but he seems okay now."

I headed back to the house and fell asleep. In the morning the phone rang. It was the hospital. They said Mother was dying and wanted to know if they should use extreme measures to keep her alive. I had Bill race to the hospital with the papers she'd signed saying not to resuscitate her. And suddenly, she was gone. She hadn't wanted my dad to be first, couldn't bear to be left alone. His own threatening death was what she needed to let herself go. It was a huge accomplishment for her. She had, at last, made it out of her body.

I buried her in a closed casket, not wanting people to see the horrible job they did of making her up for burial, her face and hair so...wrong. She was no longer recognizable as the woman she'd been, yet the pain she'd lived with for decades was still visible. She looked dead. More dead than any corpse I'd ever seen. I instructed the funeral home to close the lid. I regretted later that her sister Miriam didn't get to look at her face and say goodbye, but I knew what was important to my mother and gave her what I knew she would've wanted—privacy.

At the gravesite, Dan Rowland preached over her coffin. I know she wouldn't have liked that much, as she'd always reached for a class of people, friends, and preachers, of a different sort. But I let him preach anyway. Partially out of love for May and Dan, and partially, I think, just to stick it to my mom (though I didn't know it then).

A few days after her funeral, I went into Dad's room to talk. He was back at home and relaxing in his reclining chair. I sat at his feet and told him I needed to go back with Bill to California. Bill had stayed with me, enduring the chaos of our house, with all its noise and him with nothing to do, for over two weeks. He was wearing thin. Dad looked me in the eye and said simply, "If you go, I'll die."

I thought about that. "Do you know how long we're going to be together, Daddy?"

His eyes lit up in recognition of something we both had always sensed. "Forever?" It wasn't a question as much as an answer.

I nodded yes. He smiled and also nodded, then looked away. I had his permission to go.

Five weeks later they called me to say he'd slipped away. He'd been in the hospital again with pneumonia. The nurse who sat with him said he had no pain. She hadn't, however, seen him in the moment he passed. When she'd looked over at him, she realized he'd already taken his last breath, so fitting an end for this gentle man.

I left the lid on his coffin open. Whereas Mom had looked dead, he looked alive, radiant, peaceful. Like an angel in his favorite shirt, a blue plaid cotton with short sleeves from Walmart, which he wore all the time. I'd bought one too, and still keep it in a drawer in remembrance.

During the visitation, I walked over at least a dozen times to look at him. I couldn't resist touching him, putting my hand on his heart, lightly stroking his arm, holding his hand. If the visitors thought it was a strange thing to do, they didn't show it. Love filled the room and gave me a sense of privacy. All the girls from his office were present. He'd engendered love in so many. Now it was being poured back to him.

It was a transcendent time.

After Daddy was buried, Bill and I left Peter alone in our Mississippi home. His trailer on our grandparents' land had been overrun by mice and was decaying. He didn't want to move into a smaller space than our grand, antebellum-styled home, and was adamant and hostile to us when we tried to sway him otherwise. We left him feeling alienated and hardened in his grief. It was a hard way to say goodbye to a brother, but it was time, at last, to look out for myself.

During the last decade or so of our parents' lives, when I was traveling back and forth to California, I had busied myself with more LA theatre productions mounted by Southern artists. They shared a common theme of crises of those we'd left behind in our search for bigger lives. They were full of hope and healing. And they helped me stay alive.

I'd like to tell you more about them now. They were incredibly on point. Thoughtful, witty, wise, and often, downright hilarious.

Life on stage in small theatres, like in the old days on tours out of NYC. *Déjà vu,* as they say. Now here again, but this time in LA—a gentle way to begin waking a new life for me.

CHAPTER 46

DADDY'S DYING

With brand-new stars in the sky, there's a brand-new life for us all, if we hang onto and ride the ever-changing emerging force of hope. Life keeps on giving new life for as long as we want it, need it, and have the passion to serve it. In the late spring of 1988, Bill took me to see an LA theatre production called *Daddy's Dyin': Who's Got the Will?* by Del Shores, his first smash hit, with many more to follow. We'd been told the play was terrific but had no idea the extent of the pleasure we would take from it.

This was in the days before my mother's illness was known to me and a few months before Hal Ashby was diagnosed with the cancer that took him from us. Life was sweet, smooth, and high as I settled down in the third or fourth row, feeling the crowd's excitement.

The title implied a lighthearted Southern romp, which, of course, it was. But it also had surprising depth and a moving truthfulness. Del had been witty and fearless as he put words into the mouths of outrageous, touching characters. The play was directed by Sherry Landrum, a girl from the rural South herself, and acted with unabashed authenticity by a cast of Texan and Southern actors: Judith Durand, Glenda Tremaine, Molly McClure, Rosemary Alexander, Michael Hoit, William Edward Phipps, Mickey Jones, and Patrika Darbo.

I sat gaping at the first scene, which introduced Molly McClure as Mama Wheelis and Judith Durand as one of her daughters, Sarah Lee. Molly was a hoot as the outspoken, knee-high hose-wearing matriarch of her family, which consisted of a beer-drinking, ham-and-grits-eating, sanitation engineer (aka garbage collector) son and three very different daughters: a sweet and gentle hairdresser still living at home, a righteous, and straight-laced preacher's wife from a neighboring town, and a trash-talking, sexy black-sheep-of-a-wild-thing who'd picked up a hippy on her trip back home to find out where she stood in the family inheritance.

Bill saw the look on my face, read the disappointment I was feeling of not being up on that stage and whispered, "Don't worry. In forty years you can play Mama Wheelis. And you can bet, the play will still be running then."

Over the years there've been a few times when stage productions have inspired momentous desire in me—a level of passion that unleashed my fiery will, and with it, a sense of daring, allowing me to claim some part of the event for myself. At each of those times, I received a life-changing miracle in its wake. As you know, the musical *Hair* was one such event, leading me to *Oh! Calcutta!* Another was the off-Broadway production of *The Hot L Baltimore*, which I'd seen in NYC, and years later, led to my first guest-starring role in the TV series of the same name. And now I was feeling the same yearning as I watched *Daddy's Dyin'*. I prayed that Bill was right.

As it turned out, I didn't have to wait forty years.

Just a few weeks later, the first cast of the play was invited to participate in Scotland's Edinburgh Festival Fringe. The second company (made up of all the understudies for various roles) was to perform in LA, while the first company was out of the country. I went to Del and asked if I could cover (understudy) one of the sisters in the second company while the first company was away in Scotland. Del said, "Why don't you cover all three of them?"

I recently spoke to Del, and neither one of us can remember when we first met and how he knew I could do all three roles. We both had studied with the same acting teacher, Joan Darling (though at different times and locations, he as a director and me as an actress), and he'd visited the classes of my other acting teacher, Anita Jesse, where he may have seen me work. But neither of us think that's really it. I like to believe it was his intuition of the moment. He was flying high, ready to take his play to Scotland. The second cast was in place in LA. I was Southern, and physically right for all three women. My enthusiasm for his show and desire to be part of it had me dancing on one foot, then the other. I had Broadway stage experience and, around town and among mutual friends, a reputation for good work. It felt at the time that he just went with his gut.

Memory's a funny thing. When Del and I spoke, he was in Arkansas, teaching a writing class. We agreed to have lunch when he came home to LA and mull it over some more. But it will probably remain a mystery.

Regardless of how it came to be, there I landed, in hog heaven, learning three of the best-written roles for women that I'd seen in a long time: Lurlene, the preacher's wife; Sarah Lee, the sweet, funny daughter still living at home and making her living cutting, curling, dying, and perming hair; and Evalita, showing up to see her dying father (and discover her standing in his will), dressed in the trashiest cutoff jeans you ever saw, a strapless cotton top, and high heels, dragging with her a hippy, Harmony Rhodes, whom she'd picked up along the way.

The sisters, as I played them, were a brunette, a blonde, and a redhead. I bought three wigs, had them styled, pulled together my costumes, and started learning lines. When I was ready, Del, fresh back from Scotland after watching his play open there, saw to it that I got to perform in all three parts a goodly number of times. I never tired of saying the words, crying the tears, singing the songs, and getting all the laughs I could while playing those roles. To this day, I still keep the three wigs perched on their stands on the top shelf of my closet.

What impressed me most about Del was his sense of fun about his writing and his seeming unconcern about how I'd do whenever I went on stage in one or another of those parts. All three roles were demanding and significant to the play's success. He'd come backstage while the cast was putting on makeup and tell off-the-wall, funny stories about the latest episodes in the lives of his family members back in Texas, after which he'd patterned many of the characters in *Daddy's Dyin'*. He was lit from within, his humor contagious. Whenever he came around, my work got better. Everybody's did.

There was a reason (other than the play was good theatre with characters that seemed to share my DNA) that I needed to be a part of that show at that time. My father, the first love of my life, was beginning a slow decline. He was just turning seventy and dealing with more stress than most men ever have to face. He'd lost one son to AIDS, was watching another son surrender to mental illness, and his wife, his partner in life, was showing signs that she might collapse in pain and grief, perhaps never to recover.

He was brave, kind, and valiant, but he was getting hit hard and starting to let go of his power. By the time he reached eighty, he was gently telling the same stories over and over, just as his own father had done at that age. Retiring graciously from responsibility, the Southern gentleman, giving in to senility, waving a white flag. Much like the patriarch in *Daddy's Dyin'*, who was going round the bend, but in Texas style.

It was a time of transition for me—of many deaths of many kinds. The resilience and humanity in Del's play prepared me for the couple of decades to follow in which all responsibilities for keeping my family afloat, fell to me.

As I noted earlier, Hal Ashby died that year in 1988, and with him my dream of working in more of his films. Sudden change can be frightening. The challenge of rebirthing dreams and, of dreaming, can be difficult.

As Bette Davis once said, "Getting old is not for sissies."

You said it Bette.

I see now how much help I received during those days, a pattern in the events of that time. Blessed with a new family of artists and a string of plays that would keep me on my feet and offer insight during the challenges ahead, I stayed in creative mode much of the time, safe from the harm of an over-troubled mind.

Those challenges, they keep on coming, don't they? They don't stop. Times of overwhelm. Times of seeming defeat. They come to me and to all those I know in varying degrees, but they do come to us all.

Yet it seems, miracles keep coming too…and hard-fought achievements and peaceful surrenders to grace.

Me as the character Evalita in *Daddy's Dyin'*, a hit dramedy and award-winning play by Del Shores

CHAPTER 47

HYSTERICAL BLINDNESS

Theatre has magic. The early Greeks wrote of a phenomena called a "catharsis," an emotional purging that audiences can experience while watching a story acted out in front of them. A catharsis can occur in any theatrical event; even a summer blockbuster movie has the potential to lift people or crash them through the floor—to stimulate the expression and release of intense emotion, and thus, allow a return to life, refreshed and perhaps, even inspired.

Some theatrical pieces can do more. They can reveal truths in our natures and allow us to examine them and to grow and change. They can lead us to transform situations in our lives, and in some cases, actually transcend problems that had before seemed utterly hopeless. I stumbled upon such a transcendent piece of theatre in the most unlikely of places.

In March of 1993, Newell and Rosemary Alexander produced a very funny show called *Hysterical Blindness and Other Southern Tragedies That Have Plagued My Life Thus Far*. It was written and performed by Leslie Jordan at the Hudson Theatre's Backstage space as a 10 p.m. show with a limited run. Jordan, an Emmy winner for his recurring role on *Will and Grace*, also recurred on the TV series *Ugly Betty*, *Boston Legal*, and *Reba*, and was featured as well in several blockbuster movies, including *The Help*.

Wildly successful, *Hysterical Blindness and Other Southern Tragedies That Have Plagued My Life Thus Far,* was soon moved to the much larger Hudson's Front Theatre, and later taken to NYC where it enjoyed a seven-month run off-Broadway. At that point, Rosemary Alexander (who'd I'd replaced in *Daddy's Dyin'*) asked me to step into her part, as she was leaving to do Del Shore's next play, *Daughters of the Lone Star State,* about a church group of wealthy, white women refusing to accept the world changing around them.

Leslie Jordan's new show, *Hysterical Blindness*, was essentially Leslie telling his own personal tale, a tragicomedy of a gay boy growing up in the Deep South, moving to Hollywood and starting to make good, all the while struggling in his relationship with his mother back home, who was fast losing her marbles and watching them roll under her bed.

On stage behind Leslie was a Southern version of a Greek chorus: a gospel choir singing takeoffs on hymns to move his story along, various choir members stepping into scenes with him, taking on the parts of his sisters, his mom, his psychiatrist, his preacher, and others along the way.

I loved taking over Rosemary's roles, especially that of his shrink, and loved singing in that choir even more. It was swinging! We danced snazzy steps in unison while singing witty lyrics in four-part harmony. But the greatest pull for me was getting to hear Leslie tell his tale every night.

By now, you all know about my mother's hard ending, the way it went down. But at the time, early in her illness, I'd hoped that my mother could have the kind of breakthroughs that Leslie's mom had achieved. They were a tale of transcendence, a tale worth reporting. And, a tale as hysterical as any you'd ever want to tell.

At one point, Leslie paraphrased Tennessee Williams, citing him as the utmost authority on eccentric women like his mother, who wrote in his memoirs that, "A high station in life is earned by the gallantry with which appalling situations are survived with grace."

Leslie's mom, like my own, had taken to her bed with no plans to ever get up and get back into life. It was a kind of Southern tradition that some women who were over their heads in grief and rage took to their beds and planned to stay there forever as an attempt to deal with the pain. It never worked, but many a lady tried it anyway.

Leslie's mom drove all of her children crazy with outrageous projections about them and was plagued with bouts of hysterical blindness, where her eyes were frozen shut for hours or days at a time. She took to her bed as a way of dealing with what she considered the tragedies of her life: her husband who she'd divorced and walked away from penniless, her children who'd deeply disappointed her, and her lover who, in the long run, had turned out to be impotent. Leslie referred to her as a "gregarious recluse."

At one point, Leslie confronted his mom. "When you start in on all of us, it's usually a sign that something's bothering you. Dr. Lee says that your eyes snap shut because you hold everything inside. I want you to talk to me, Mama. I want you to tell me what's wrong. What is wrong, Mama?"

"What's wrong?" his mother exclaimed. "You dare ask me what's wrong? I've got a daughter that's an anorexic. I've got another daughter that's a manic depressive. My firstborn son is a homosexual. I'm blind. I'm crazy. And my lover is impotent. WHAT THE HELL DO YOU THINK IS WRONG WITH ME?!!"

And then, Leslie turned and spoke to the audience. "Following Mama's little outburst came a peal of laughter that I swear could have ridden down from Heaven on the wings of a snow-white dove. I hadn't heard that laugh in years. She whooped! 'Leslie Allen, you know, you laugh or you cry. And Lord knows we've tried crying. Maybe laughing will help!'"

He went on. "From her lips to God's ears. If I'm lying, I'm dying. From the time that peal of laughter burst forth, my mother's eyes have never shut. Going on eight years. She says, 'It's answered prayers. Son, it's a miracle straight from God.' I'm proud to say that my mother has earned her high station in life. She survived. Drove us damn near crazy, but she SURVIVED what was an appalling situation. And she survived with amazing grace.'"

It was that miracle told by that funny, winsome little man that drew me into the show, made me know that I needed to be part of it.

My own mother's tragedies were overwhelming her. In the first decade of splitting my time between California and Mississippi and watching her decline, I held out the possibility of a miracle like the one that came from heaven for Leslie's mom. As it turned out, my mother didn't have such a moment of amazing, healing grace. But she did have the grace to gift me a great lesson in her illness, unknowingly perhaps, yet treasured, nonetheless.

In my years of recovery from an infection in my bloodstream that resulted in (stay with me): a mild heart attack, two small strokes, open-heart surgery, an impaired digestive system from massive doses of antibiotics required to save my life, and, the straw that broke the camel's back, a grand mal seizure, I've had to battle PTSD, anxiety, and depression.

There have been many mornings when I haven't wanted to leave my bed. Many noontimes and mid-afternoons when I've longed to run home and hide under the covers pulled over my head.

I've resisted those impulses. I see, and I know, where retreat ends. In spite of the curses that Mother hurled at me in the worst of her times, wishing that all that had fallen to her would fall to me, I have not fallen. I've resisted the seduction of giving up, the seeming way out that I know is the worst of horrors.

Thank you, Momma. Thank you for going there so that I didn't have to.

I would've preferred a miracle straight from God, laughter flowing from heaven "like on the wings of a snow-white dove." A healing for you like that of Leslie's mom.

But your dealings with life were more serious. Not to be messed with. You were on a tear, a rip in your psyche and a shredding of your world. It was yours, Momma, and I won't try to disturb it.

But I will accept life's gifts as they come.

CHAPTER 48

AND MISS REARDON
DRINKS A LITTLE

In 1991, while my relationship with my family was still young, my brother, Sterling, having died only six years before, my mother still on her feet and struggling to recover, Peter having a promising romp in Hollywood writing music, playing and singing it for a living, my career still having footing that could lead to something bigger, I found myself in massive credit card debt. It had crept up on me and was completely out of control. The amount was so embarrassingly high that I won't mention it here but suffice to say that it was substantial.

At the time, Bill was working, and I was on a salary from our company, Harper and Macy Productions, Inc., for running our household and paying my personal expenses. I was exceeding that salary each month to pay for holistic and preventive medicines, including acupuncture, homeopathy, nutritional guidance, and chiropractor services, and for travel to seminars where I was learning the laws and ways of metaphysics, and well, to put it honestly, of magic.

All my life, I'd been seeking a live connection to the Universe and an understanding of esoteric knowledge, and finally had been privileged to encounter one who could introduce me. I was on a path of spiritual growth based on love, light, laughter, and ease, a path of responsible action and growing consciousness, as opposed to the myriad of fear-based cults, conspiracy theories, and fringe sciences that were being passed off as metaphysics at the time. Top-of-the-line knowledge, powerful information, and expensive, what with travel and lodging and sometimes weeklong seminars. I was also buying quality clothes, getting facials and expensive haircuts to stay competitive for acting roles, of which there were a few that actually paid me decent money.

As for financing all of this, I was, as they say in gambling parlance, betting on "the come." Waiting for that one big job—or several jobs—that would pull me out of the hole I'd dug for myself. I've learned since that programming for success is a much less effective tool when you have your back against the wall. Desperation is an energy that fails to attract magical solutions. And the secrecy of my debt, the hiding of the growing fear inside me, stoked the growing negativity in me as well. Not much expectation of good outcomes from that spot. I was coming to my rope's end, it seemed.

And yet, it was metaphysics that saved me. In the midst of a deep meditation in which I visualized myself sitting at my desk paying off all those credit cards, I was suddenly hit with a solution. I sat up in bed, picked up the phone and called our lawyers and accountants and told them the mess I'd made of my finances and then, told them my plan. They were all older Jewish men and a bit shocked by both my situation and vulnerability, but they also wanted to help. We made a deal for them to pay off all my credit card debts; I, in turn, took a huge cut in salary for the next three (or was it four?) years coming. I'd be on a bare-bones budget, but I could and would, make it on what we agreed to as my monthly paycheck. They put money in my checking account for me that same afternoon. It was fun sitting at my desk and paying off all those credit cards, just as I'd seen happen in my dream.

And then, I told Bill.

All of it. I remember his jaw dropping when I said the amount. He was utterly speechless. We walked around our swimming pool in silence holding hands for a long time. He told me later that he was surprised by what I'd done. Not by my overspending, but my paying it back. "I thought you were going to say, 'I spent it and I'm glad!'"

A couple of weeks later, he came to me and said he wanted to give me a gift. He offered to produce a play for me in LA, not just any play, but the play that had launched his career on Broadway and led to his success in TV, and ultimately, movies, too. Paul Zindel's tragicomedy, *And Miss Reardon Drinks a Little*.

I was to play the part originated by Julie Harris in the NYC production, and asked Rosemary Alexander to play the outspoken, alcoholic role of Catherine (originated by Estelle Parsons). Rosemary's husband, Newell, agreed to handle the artwork for programs, flyers, and all advertising.

But Bill, as producer, wasn't through yet. He showed himself to be more than just a money guy.

His next move was a stroke of genius, and one for the ages. He asked the actress who'd played his wife in the original production and who'd won the Tony for Best Featured Actress in that same role, Rae Allen, to direct. And direct she did, with such creativity, brilliance, and panache that when all was said and done, we had the hit of the 1991 LA theatre season.

Rae cast Paul Lieber, who'd played a small part as the delivery boy in the opening scene of the NYC production and who—like the rest of us—was now twenty years older, to play the part that Bill had originated in New York. For the married sister, Ceil, played by Nancy Marchand in New York, she hired Mary-Margaret Lewis, a stunningly intelligent, tasteful, and sensitive actress to play what could've been—but in her hands was definitely not—a thankless role.

Rae's *pièce de résistance* was the casting of Gloria LeRoy in the role that had won Rae her Tony. Gloria was an old vaudevillian, highly original, blonde, dippy, and completely her own woman. Inimitable and adorable.

Paul Zindel came to see our show and was extremely happy with the revival of his witty tragicomedy. The play was full of dysfunctional, pathetic souls, but it wasn't dark (despite what the critics in NYC said). It was moving, insightful. But more than that, it was unabashedly, outright funny.

The play didn't propel me into a lucrative television and film career, as it did for Bill. But it did more for me than that. Having the opportunity to play that lovely, seemingly fragile, relentless, erudite, thundering, funny woman-child that I'd watched Julie Harris first conceive on Broadway was deeply fulfilling. Julie, who I loved both personally and professionally whenever I hung out at rehearsals and performances in NYC, had revealed a rainbow of colors in that crazed character. Stimulating and inspiring me, helping me know how to approach the part, all those years later. She had a sense of glee about riding the edges of sanity in that role. I stole everything I could from her. Lee Strasberg taught his acting students that you could always imitate a great performance because it would never be a duplicate of what you'd seen, coming through your own instrument, as it were. Be that as it may, I felt Julie's ghost and relished it, but also like to think that I brought storm clouds and sunshine and a few rainbows of my own.

Funny, but somehow, Paul Zindel's play made major life dreams come true for Bill in 1971 and for me twenty years later. Bill's dream was (and had always been) to make a living for us through his acting. My dream was to have fun in show business, and though I didn't know what that meant at the time when I affirmed it as a goal in NYC back in 1966, I know now. What it really meant was that I wanted both personal and artistic freedom, and a shot at doing work that was authentic, intensely entertaining, and fine. I wanted to make people laugh and cry and raise high the ceilings in celebration.

All the pieces of that dream came together in *Miss Reardon*. Looking back through news clippings to find the exact date of our production, I was struck by the quality of the reviews. All raves, every writer loving every actor and every aspect of our production, down to our programs with childhood pictures of the actresses playing the three dysfunctional Reardon sisters on the cover. I remember we won several LA theatre awards during our run.

When dreams come true, something lives, and something dies, to make way for new dreams.

Little did I know what all was in store next.

Me, Mary-Margaret Lewis, Gloria LeRoy, Paul Lieber, and Rosemary Alexander in the high-energy revival of *And Miss Reardon Drinks a Little*, written by Paul Zindel and directed by Rae Allen

CHAPTER 49

GINGHAM DOG

In 1980, Sheila Scott-Wilkinson asked me to co-produce and to act with her in the revival of Lanford Wilson's *The Gingham Dog*. Born in Aurora, Illinois, to local philanthropists and civil rights workers, Charles and Marie Wilkinson, Sheila had studied acting in Frankfurt and London, where she lived for many years and was a member of the Royal National Theatre. There, after a performance one night, she'd met Pablo Ferro, who was in town working on a movie with director Stanley Kubrick.

A mutual friend had mentioned that Pablo would be dropping by but hadn't described him in any way to Sheila. When she opened her dressing room door to find herself facing a small and dark, handsome man with long, flowing hair, a headband and love beads, looking like a Native American in full regalia, she was floored. And totally charmed. He took her out, and the rest, as they say, is history.

By 1980, Sheila had moved to LA and reconnected with Pablo, who introduced her to me. She was a sharp, outspoken, strong and funny lady, with long legs and gorgeous black skin and interested in doing work pertaining to race relations in America.

The Gingham Dog was just such a piece. A three-character play about the breakup of a marriage between an intellectual black woman and her white liberal Southern husband. The story takes place on their final day together, in their NYC apartment, and in the presence of his sister, an unwitting, clueless, and rather casual racist, who's there to help him pack.

When I read the play, I called Sheila right away and said, "Absolutely not! I have spent my whole adult life proving to the world that I am not a racist. I won't be seen like this. I can't! Good God. Whatever were you thinking?" Or some such words to that effect.

The next week, while I was walking on the beach in Santa Monica, the script kept running through my mind. The two women in the play begin conversing cordially, then start to bicker, and end up in an act of out-and-out verbal warfare, one in which the white Southern sister-in-law is completely outmatched, though she isn't smart enough to realize it. Just as she's leaving the apartment, carrying one of her brother's suitcases, she spins around on the landing and bellows, "Well, ha ha ha! I'm white and you're black, and I'm just as happy as hell about it!"

Remembering that line, I started to laugh, and then to trot, and then burst into a full-out run to the nearest payphone, where I called Sheila, yelling into the mouthpiece, "Yes, yes, yes! I'll do it! Absolutely! Of course! I'm in!"

"Okay," she said. "Let's go raise some money."

I don't remember exactly how we managed to finance the show. I do recall that we had some meetings with people that Sheila knew and they came up with at least part of the money. Joe Spano of the TV series *Hill Street Blues* was cast as her husband. I chose Judy Kerr to understudy my part. Judy had organized and run my acting class and was now teaching on her own. My husband, Bill, directed her privately, rearranging our living room furniture to match that of the set on stage and leaving it that way for the run of the show, while helping her prepare for the one performance that I had guaranteed she would have, come rain or shine.

We opened the show and it was well received with full houses, and the production and whole cast garnering great reviews. My agents ran an ad in *Variety* to congratulate me on mine. Today it's framed and hanging on a wall in my dining room, with these accolades (thanks for indulging me!):

> "There is more sympathetic and credible humanity to be found in the character (and the performance) of **Samantha Harper** as the bigoted Southern sister..."
> –John Mahoney, *LA Times*

> "And the production features the terrific **Samantha Harper**...who is wonderfully unnerving as the husband's Southern-belle sister...(and) who's worth the price of admission..." –S. Robert Goodman, *KABC Radio*

> "**Samantha Harper** draws a perfect bead on the buttery voiced Mississippian..."
> –Jay Reiner, *Herald Examiner*

"Harper could be a scene stealer as the Southern dumb-belle, but she is a master of restraint and understatement, adding brilliant support with her What-The-Family-Thinks morality, vapidity and unthinking racism." –Donna Matson, *Drama-Logue*

"Ms. Harper is a comic actress of enormous skills, whose timing and delivery match perfectly with the material…moments of genuine glory." –Jack Viertel, *LA Reader*

"Samantha Harper is terrific as the white sister-in-law who finally gets her chance to say what she thinks about her brother's marriage." –SRG, *LA Weekly*

And where I had feared that black audiences would hate me, I was in for a surprise. They adored me, packing the lobby after our shows to thank me with deep warmth and affection for being so authentic in that part. They loved that I was willing to show the kind of unwitting racism that lurked in the shadows of much of white society at the time, and to do it unabashedly.

The night that Judy went on in my part, I went backstage to be with her before her entrance. She was debuting in the LA theatre scene and introducing her work to absolutely everyone she knew in show business, as well as to her family who'd never seen her act before. There I found her, sitting in front of her mirror, frozen in terror. Fortunately, I knew what to do.

She and Pablo and I had been taking a hands-on healing class in Santa Monica, taught by our trusted friend, Corey Van Loon. I did what Corey would've done: placed my hands on her shoulders, and as Corey taught me, didn't do a damned thing more. Only quieted my mind and stood there, touching her. Suddenly she looked up at me. "What did you do?" Then rose out of her chair, stood tall, dropped her shoulders back, and walked toward the entrance to the stage.

I turned and raced to the back of the theatre to witness. I was in for a powerful ride. She showed up in all her glory, on fire up there. Utterly brilliant. I watched, noted her nuances and stole all I could from her performance. Judy's people are from Texas. Nobody understands the intricacies and attitudes of the Deep South like we Southern and Texan belles do. And like me, she received praise from the black friends in her audience.

I guess when all is said and done, people like to hear the truth told. Especially when it's told with both humor and pathos. *The Gingham Doll* delivered laughter and heartbreak, sometimes within the same moments.

Ah, I said to myself. *This is what dreams are all about.* Except, I didn't yet have a clue.

Who does know how, if, or when dreams will be altered, even taken away it seems for good? Or what possible things can touch us—as our future reaches back to take us by our hands—and pull us through?

CHAPTER 50

PABLITO

It was not until Hal Ashby died that I reconnected with Pablo, though only cursorily, while we sat long hours with Hal and, eventually, said our good-byes. It was a sacred time for us both, a respectful time, as we were mourning the death of our dreams as well as the death of this dear, brilliant man. But Pablo didn't open his heart to me, even then.

We hadn't been in each other's life for some time. Back while I was teaching, I had ill-advisedly taken part in giving him a surprise birthday party that he hated. His mentor, Hal, was invited while they were working together on *Being There,* and he felt humiliated to have his work interrupted without his permission. Something was broken between Pablo and me that I didn't think could be repaired.

Those four months with Hal were poignant, full of small miracles, laughter, music, and healing of the heart. It was a precious time that seemed would last forever. But it did not. In the end, Hal slipped away, and, like all show business families, we, his devoted friends went our separate ways.

A decade later, after my stint in Mississippi, and my return to California, I was unprepared for my last encounter with Pablo, a man I had loved but never thought I'd see again.

One day, out of the blue, he called. We met for lunch near the place he was living. He was overcoming a complication to the gunshot wound he'd suffered so many years ago. The doctors had told him it would worsen as he grew older. As Pablo was wont to do, he used drugs to ease his pain, had overdone it, and finally had collapsed in his kitchen. His family found a place for him: a home in LA where old people go to wait for death, but it was livable, at least for the time being.

That lunch was an awkward time for me. Pablo was so easy across the table. So much himself. Finally, I asked him what he wanted with me. He pulled out of his briefcase a biography of his life. It was huge, bigger than a Bible as I held it in my hands. Every drawing, every comic book, and all his levels of accomplishments and achievements. His special commercial businesses. His film school days of doing titles and end credits for dozens of films. All he'd ever done throughout his life—from boyhood to that moment, today.

I looked up, confused.

He told me that the American Institute of Graphic Arts (AIGA) wanted him to come to NYC and accept their lifetime achievement award. He looked at me, simply saying, "I don't have the money to go."

It's funny how when you look back on your life, you know who your friends really are. I knew that for whatever reason he had pulled away from me before, he knew me now. He was showing me who I was to him. The one he'd always known, when it came down to it, was a player and a partner. We believed in loving, of celebrating, of enjoying each other. But most importantly, we were willing to allow the other to be free. This was the breath-taking leap off a cliff, and we both had been living it for years.

I reached into my purse. I had four hundred dollars. I handed it to him. Then I took him back to his old folks' home.

The following week, I told this story to Daphne Russom, a close friend. She'd never laid eyes on Pablo, but said, "I want to help, too." So I set up a date for us both to meet him for lunch. That morning, she had a plumbing problem and traveled for miles to buy the right equipment and came home and fixed the toilet herself, saving four hundred dollars to give to him at lunch.

As I knew he would, Pablo loved her. He thanked me for giving him a new friend. It was cool. Daphne Russom, who also loved him on sight, both for himself and his talent, and I had unknowingly created a dream team. It was perfect. Two married women and our odd male companion. We batted around some ideas and came up with a plan.

Every week, we'd bust him out of that retched place for the dying elderly and take him to a sushi bar on Laurel Canyon. The place was usually packed with movie and television people who had a great sense of Pablo's history and reputation.

Pablo had always been a "two-girl guy" and loved coming out to play with us. At the sushi bar, he did, indeed, meet many people in the business who remembered his pioneering film work. One of them, Mark Kirkland, director of the animated TV series *The Simpsons*, invited us to his home to have Pablo sign a document of authenticity for a vintage movie camera that Pablo had once owned and which Mark had purchased from the legendary cinematographer Haskell Wexler.

Within a short time, Pablo regained his footing, moved into an apartment adjacent to his son, Allen, and started working again. Brilliant as always, he was getting offers to do film titles, and it was a joy to see him tackling new projects.

With some financial help from others, he made it back to NYC for his award. All was heaven. And then, by a stroke of genius, my coauthor on *The Two Sisters' Café*, had the idea of asking Pablo to illustrate our book. We were self-publishing and had eight blank pages to fill. And, we realized those pages could go anywhere in the text, near the action that called for imagery. He eagerly took on the job, and oh my. He and I had a great time working to conceive those sketches with me giving him input along the way. Blown away by his speed and creativity, we both loved watching them unfold. He even did a profile drawing of me and used it for my

"Alma" character in the café. As my daddy would say, it was just plain fun.

Then his life turned again. His son moved back to the East Coast to pursue work. After a period of time on his own, Pablo started to weaken. Daphne and I went by his house and helped him get around and run his errands, but he was having a hard time. One day, he fell and hurt his leg and called to ask if I could get him a wheelchair.

I knew this was getting out of hand and too much for me to take on and said that into the phone. He got it instantly, graciously. No recriminations. I called his daughter, and she came out and took him to live with her in Sedona, Arizona. His ex-wife, Susan, being his children's mother and his close friend, came often to visit. Julian Barry also came to play with him, and after a bit, his son moved to Arizona to be closer.

Pablo and I talked on the phone every week. Sometimes Daphne came over and we called him together, and sometimes she called on her own. Often, he'd call me whenever he was feeling up to it, sometimes when I was in the car with Bill. But much of our time was private at odd moments when I was home, sitting in my bed. Always upbeat and witty. He never got tired of telling me that he loved me. And, I never got tired of hearing it.

The week before Pablo died, his children put him on FaceTime so Daphne and I could see him. He was having trouble breathing, and we talked to him until he was suddenly back in this world and demanding a good cup of coffee. It wasn't to last long. He died the next week.

His daughter, Joy, went through some heavy grieving, then came to California and stayed the night at our house. She brought me two mementos. The first was the AIGA award that he'd received for his lifetime achievements. The second was his signature red scarf that he wore on all occasions, even at home, as the injury to his neck made him feel chilled most of the time. I have lots of pictures of a gang of us all over town, accepting his accolades late in his life. Him in that famous scarf. The rest of us in the glow.

Thank goodness we outgrew that "you'll go away and I'll go away," Pablito-san. It was, and is, so out of fashion.

We're part of each other, and that's that. We'll always be close, my darlin' man. And, I have your daughter Joy's gift of your lovely bright-red scarf to prove it. It hangs on a chair opposite my computer in my office.

Life is eternal.

Otherwise, it's just too damn short.

Me and Pablo, Grif Griffis, Daphne Russom, and Inas Anis, celebrating one of his many awards

CHAPTER 51

BILL'S LONG GOODBYE

O n his way home to a party at our house with our neighbors, my husband, Bill, was in an accident on his ninety-seventh birthday, May 18, 2019. He'd run over a curb in his car. At the time, he seemed unhurt, but now I know he was more shaken than we knew. He'd waited a couple of hours for AAA to take him home, seemed fine, but was walking slower after that. No more dashing his usual one hundred yards to the golf course coffee shop. Instead, he started having me drop him off near the shop's front door before I parked. Then he'd wait for me after we'd eaten and paid our check as I'd hurried back to retrieve our wheels. He was injured again some months later, on Monday, August 26, in an accident that eventually took his life. But not without a battle fought gallantly. Bill slipped away seven and a half weeks later, on October 17, after a long—though not long enough—time to say, once and for all, goodbye.

On the morning of his second accident, I was scheduled to work with a fellow writer, Todd Waring, to complete this book. I'd planned to meet Todd at 1 p.m. at my house for a conference, kissing Bill and wishing blessings for his day around seven o'clock. I did that every morning. I couldn't let him leave without putting my arms around him, touching the top of his head, resting my hand over his heart. I knew he was at risk: his ninety-seven-year-old eyes were wearing out because of macular degeneration. He had clearance with DMV to take another test and assurance from his eye doctor that he was safe to drive. But I was worried. Every morning he sat on my bed beside me and we called on love, light, and magic, and each morning, he'd promise to come home to me that night. That was a bond we held onto, each of us seeing him drive up safely just before dark. We both knew, however, the risk that someday it might not be so. Bill was a man who needed to keep moving—I knew that and had to live with it.

About ten o'clock, Todd called to say he needed to cancel our appointment. Bugs had infested his home and he had a battle ahead of him. I hung up and called Bill's cell.

"Oh, I didn't want to disturb your meeting," he said. "I would have called you." Something in his voice was wrong. "I hit a parked car," he said simply. "No one was in it. An airbag hit me and I was penned in for a couple of hours till someone reported it and an ambulance came to help me."

"Where are you?" I asked, incredulous on all counts of his story. Flabbergasted that he was taking it so lightly.

"At Cedars Sinai, in the emergency room."

I flew across town to find him lying in a bed with a neck brace on and cell phone in hand. I stayed with him all day into the night and finally up to a hospital room. They wouldn't let him eat or drink anything. They x-rayed his whole body. In the morning, the doctors came in with good news. No broken bones, no whiplash. They said he could go home that day, but just wanted us to keep him quiet for a while.

Bill kept celebrating that he hadn't hurt anyone. There he was in his hospital bed thanking God that although he hadn't seen the car, nobody had been injured. He looked at me and said, "I can't see your face, Sam. My eyes are shot. I thought I could see, but I can't. I didn't see the car at all. I was trying to make the light and gunned the motor. I hit it at forty-six miles an hour."

We thought we'd dodged a bullet. We hadn't. I was stumped, had no food in the house, no way to drive him all the places he'd wanted to go. But as I mulled it over, the doctors still conferring in his room changed their minds and said they wanted to keep him for a day or two.

When I came to see him the third day, shit hit the fan. Suddenly, he was screaming in pain. Eight doctors raced to his room, checking blood pressure and heart rate, and placing him on oxygen, doing all kinds of things to him, and finally drugging him till he fell asleep. They kept him on morphine and lesser drugs for three more days, but he was still awake, still functioning. I could talk to him and keep him company for hours every afternoon. Then one day, I walked in to find him asleep and unresponsive. They'd given him a drug called Ativan. His doctor came in and said it was a mistake to give him that drug. He told me I had to find him a rehab center and fast. "He's got pneumonia and he must be moved around, gotten to his feet on a regular basis."

My friend, Daphne, and I sailed around town looking at rehab centers on Labor Day and found one that could take Bill. An ambulance transported him and met us there. It wasn't the best of places as it turned out. Overcrowded and understaffed, no one could, or would, try to get him out of bed. He thought the food was poisoned and wouldn't eat it. After three days there, they called 911 for an ambulance to take him to the Santa Monica UCLA Hospital, where a miracle was worked on his behalf.

A brilliant woman doctor named Dr. Wen, worked with him. Bill's niece Dahna Brecker and her brother Stephen came out from New York to confer with her and support us. Things were looking good. Amazing, in fact. When Daphne and I got there, Bill had a tube in his throat and a machine was breathing for him. But he could hear us and respond on a notepad. Dr. Wen explained that if they removed the tube, it couldn't go back in—unless Bill wanted to have surgery on his throat and be bedridden forever. Of course, he did not.

We had one option. If they removed the tube and he could breath, he had a chance at life. If they took it out, and he was unable to function, they would keep him comfortable, put him to sleep, as it were, until he left us.

She talked to him and to me until we both understood. Then several mornings later when he was most alert, after making him hold his eyes wide open for a half hour, fighting to prove he was awake enough to handle the procedure, she made me walk away from his gaze and come stand at the foot of his bed. Needless to say, I was in a state. I didn't think I could make it if I had to watch the team "pull the plug." I went into shock and rocked on my feet.

Dr. Wen turned to me. "Get Sam a chair. It looks like she's about to faint." Then she turned to Bill and his speech therapist and very gently said, "Okay Bill, here we go. We're going to remove this tape. And this one. When we take out the tube, cough and breathe."

And that's what he did. He coughed and breathed like an angel. Long deep breaths. He reached for a pen (his throat was very sore) and wrote in dark letters, "I WANT TO LIVE!!!" We were out of the woods, or so it seemed.

The days that followed were a challenge. Daphne left town to take care of her mother in the Midwest, but I had another angel by my side for the time being.

Pablo Ferro's daughter, Joy, flew out from Sedona as soon as she heard Bill and I were in trouble. When she arrived at my home, she grabbed and held me tight. "I know you and Bill don't think you have children, but I am your child. I've always known you as my second mom. Let's take care of Billy."

Then she kicked into high gear. We traveled miles and miles looking for another rehab center. We brought him food and visited him, then hit the road again, going to outlying places and finally, finding a much better center that would take him. Me, all the while dreading, that I'd have to tell him we needed to take him to yet another place to recover before he could come home.

As usual, Bill surprised me. The day we'd settled on a rehab center, he looked at me and reached for my hand, "Sam, I can't walk. I need to be on my feet again before going home."

"We have a place that will take you now!" I breathed, happy that we were on the same page.

"Let's GO!" he said. And that very night, under the stars that he hadn't seen in a very long time, we took him by ambulance to the Brentwood Center.

Dahna, his niece, had insisted that this time he should have a person with him round the clock and she helped me pay for his helpers (caretakers). His favorite one, Clyde Narobi, took him on wheelchair rides after dark to the center's garden and let Bill sing his wonderful songs. It seemed he was getting stronger. Then suddenly, he was not.

He hadn't been eating enough. And the first x-rays were incorrect. He had bruised ribs and a fractured sternum bone from the airbag blast, which weren't on his original x-rays because fractures won't show up until weeks after they occur. He was fighting constant pain. The docs at the Brentwood Center said it was time to bring him home...with hospice care.

Daphne was back, helping me ready the room that was filled with crystals and paintings and a new sheer, soft-pink curtain that her seamstress friend had hung just a half hour before Bill arrived, to offer him some privacy, should he need it. He was brought in on a gurney with both fists clenched in the air, exclaiming, "I made it! I made it home!"

He was awake until midnight and I was able to spend time with him. He made Daphne dance in front of the curtain. Got it just the way he wanted it to hang, having her move panels around till he could see through the windows to the swimming pool outside. To his left was a large, colorful, abstract painting entitled "Three Women," two of which were human with a third figure in the shadows by Claudia Carr, wife of Jacques Levy, our director of *Oh! Calcutta!* Below it, a bowl of crystal spheres surrounded by talismans, laminated drawings with concentric circles surrounding arcane and mystical symbols.

At midnight, I gave him our last goodbye, though I didn't know it then. I tucked him in, kissed him and gave him his favorite homeopathy, aconitum to quiet his nerves (and a little bit of chocolate marijuana).

The next morning he was sleeping soundly when I left the house to run errands. Later in the afternoon, he still wasn't waking. Daphne went home to shower and change clothes. I was there when his helper called me to say his pulse was gone from his hands, only still alive in his throat. I massaged his hands and the pulse returned. But only for a short time. He stopped breathing at 7:13 p.m.

I had so wanted him to look me in the eye and say goodbye one last time, but he couldn't. But at least he'd given me a seven-week-long goodbye. I could make it now. I don't know if I would've done so well if he'd died suddenly that day he was trapped in the car with the airbag.

When I turned around there was a reverent and yet celebratory party gathering around him. It was in keeping with his spirit. He was a man to relish, even as we mourned. Daphne had returned, along with her son Zachary. Nina from next door popped in, not expecting to find him gone; she stayed to celebrate her love for him and us. Clyde, his most favorite helper who'd started his shift at six o'clock was there by his side all evening. Bill's body stayed miraculously warm, filled with love that was coming to him from all sides. We were able to stay with him until midnight, when the funeral home came to take him away. A man and a woman carried him out. They said it was their job to pick up angels.

I have never felt him gone. I still feel him here, seeing his favorite baseball hat that had Elena's and my book, *The Two Sisters' Café,* written across its front. I still feel his love whenever I see it on a stool in our living room or wherever it has traveled as it has moved from time to time in our house.

There's much to be thankful for.

Here's the poem I'd written for him to hold this spot in my book. It still fits him very well:

"My Old Man"

Sometimes he's VERY old

Sometimes he's not

Sometimes he's a pistol

Brash Rash Hostile and Hot

Sometimes a saint, gallant and smart

Wise from depths of his gentlemanly heart.

Of his chivalrous soul

Of his untamable spirit

This Ancient Lemurian, this man from the stars,

from Sirius with the Legend of Camelot in his heart

In his blood, his DNA, his old brain, and his lost memory

This baggy-pants comedian who will drop his drawers

for my Friends (if he likes them and is in the mood)

while they are over

For a quiet night of metaphysics, magic,

meditation, and grass

Who mooned all of Melrose one night celebrating

one of those

Very Women of Manhattan opening a play.

He is flying, bounding, splashing through clouds

Younger than innocence, older than hills

Pure spirit spiraling upward in blistering wind

Flying to rise, to glide open-winged, bolting, vaulting,

Catapulting, jolting, slowing to land on a feather,

Light on his toes.

A dancer, a mime, a whispering muse

Harpo. A stripper. A day tripper. A jiver. A rapper.

A child. Not quite an infant.

But a baby, and a miracle as all babies are

Crying at the wonder of being here

Curious with questions of

Why and how and how come

And who did this,

Who made us

Who made them and

Who made it all?

Trying. Trying to figure it out.

Frustrated FRUSTRATED

Honking his horn

Seeking peace in chaos

Diving through lightning, fire raging, waves crashing, to

The eye of the storm.

In quiet turning gentle. In silence being still.

In hush evolving, transforming, transcending

Becoming who he always was, who he's always been,

WHO HE IS.

A brand-new man. A new kind of guy.

A philosopher poet, a soft, sacred son.

In my sky

Under my skin

Under my feet

In my heart

In ME.

CHAPTER 52

THE TWO SISTERS' CAFÉ

There are two ends to this story, just now being finished by me a year and a half after Bill's death. One is about the birth of my first book, conceived by my writing partner, Elena Eulo, and me, and the second about a new and surprising relationship in my life, a great love, a man of music, family and beauty, a gift from *the love* that surrounds us all, as we learn to allow it.

So, beginning with *abracadabra*, the magic that manifested *The Two Sisters' Café*.

The first clue for Elena Eulo and me that something was up was Samantha, the dog. There's power in coincidence, in synchronicity. Incidences that stir wonder, curiosity, and often a sense of awe. They are, after all, so mysterious. They not only intrigue us; they can send us searching for answers and wrestling for meaning.

How are these strange events happening, we ask ourselves, these bizarre timings, where are they coming from, and what are they pointing to?

Possibly to destiny. We have many possible destinies, each of them an offering. And an invitation. Like talent, which may be developed, destiny is a choice. Something we can "take on, or not take on." This is, in fact, a Universe of free will.

Whenever I'm looking for clues from "powers beyond" for direction, I take note of coincidences and synchronicities as they appear.

That brings me back to Samantha, the dog.

In 1976, Elena Eulo and I had known each other for a number of years. She'd been married to William "Bill" Knight, one of the actors in *Oh! Calcutta!* In fact, they'd thrown a wedding party for Bill and me in their NYC apartment back in 1975. Shortly after that wild night, they'd split up and she headed back to Kentucky to stay with her family before returning to tackle the Big Apple on her own.

One dark night, after she'd returned to the city, she found herself lost somewhere on the Upper West Side of town. Nervous, she saw a man walking a small black and white mutt and felt safe enough to speak to him. "That's a pretty dog," she said.

"Her name is Samantha," he answered.

"One of my best friends is named Samantha."

"Well, *this* dog is named for Samantha Harper, the actress," he said.

His name was Ken Eulo, and he'd directed me in my first professional theatrical production, *Ladies' Night in a Turkish Bath,* for the Barn Dinner Theatre Circuit in 1966. Three months after he and Elena first met, they called me in LA from Las Vegas. They'd gotten married.

Ken was a theatre man, but he was taking on a second career as a writer, and soon published a number of bestselling books. Elena had studied writing in her early days in NYC and found herself working on novels of her own. She'd had a string of successes, among them a novel called *A Southern Woman,* for which she garnered magnificent reviews. Published by St. Martin's Press, it was translated into French and enjoyed by readers in Europe as well as America.

You'd think that was enough of a coincidence, wouldn't you—my introducing them to each other and her to her writing career—them in NYC and me in LA? And us both being Southern women, other clues showed up in the years that followed, finally making us hungry to write something together.

Meanwhile, in California, I needed to bring in more money, wanting to have a feeling of more freedom but feeling stuck. In a telephone consultation with a teacher and ally, a channeled entity who's befriended me for forty years (what can I tell you, I'm from California), I got another clue.

He said, "Samantha, this is an issue of value. How you value yourself is how you will reflect value in your finances. If you start writing you will get a better sense of who you really are. Even if you just write poetry, this will happen. And though we are not saying that you will be rolling in dough, finances will loosen for you." During the course of our talk, he repeated the words "even if you just write poetry" three times.

The next week I wrote my first poem. It was about heartbreak and healing. I read it to Elena soon after I wrote it. She'd moved to California, and I continued to read her more of my poems as they kept rolling onto the pages. That generated our idea of partnering with each other, her love for my poetry, and my (already intact) love for her novels. We started looking for a project.

We discovered that we both had magical maternal grandmothers. Each a rural woman with little formal education but with her own special talent for healing.

Elena grabbed an idea that was starting to surface in both of us and asked me to write *The Two Sisters' Café* with her, patterning our heroines after our favorite people on Earth: Topsy, as she called her grandmother, and Alma or "Mammy" as I called mine.

We married Elena's upbringing in the small café in her Kentucky hometown to my grandparents' farm and its people in Mississippi. Our plan was that Elena would teach me more about writing and I'd contribute my knowledge of magic, something I'd been pursuing for many years.

Two Sisters was a miracle event between two strong-willed writers. We created it first as a series of short stories and almost sold it to Time Warner publishing. Then spent a few more years sculpting it into a full-fledged living, breathing novel in its own right. We almost killed each other in the editing process toward the end. But we both got the book that we wanted. Filled with fun and "practical magic" and love, the most magical force of all.

Our dream had been to capture the feeling of Camelot, that magic we'd experienced in the presence of our grandmothers. Also to catch and retell what it was like to live in rural America in the 1950s, a time that's disappearing from memory but which holds much value—a time when people who had little Earthly wealth made fulfilling lives for themselves—rich with humor, wit, hard-earned wisdom, and the added blessing of knowing that they mattered, although their existence wasn't recorded, acknowledged, or represented—even as a tiny dot on a map.

Now it is ours, Elena's and mine. A dream come true.

Now we will wait to see what dreams will be born from it. May they all come true for us and for those of you who enjoy the magic of love, beauty, forgiveness, imagination, mystery, light, and the ONE beyond all names.

And of synchronicity, too.

We do, after all, have Samantha the dog's reputation to uphold.

Me and Elena Yates Eulo, coauthors of our faerie-tale novel, *The Two Sisters' Café*

CHAPTER 53

WHO'D A THUNK IT?

Agent came calling, even before we knew what he was intending.

Julian Barry. A man I have written about in this book, who lived with his wife and two children as my neighbor on the East Side of NYC in the sixties. Who introduced me to Pablo and wrote the short movie, *The Inflatable Doll,* with roles for Don Calfa and me. That film, directed by Pablo, was later shown to Hal Ashby, and started my film career.

In short, Julian and I had a history that began over fifty years ago. We've kept up with each other over the years, but I thought of him as a powerful and beautiful friend, never to know that we would someday become lovers and move in together, to live so well, so happily.

I should have known it was possible for so many reasons. In my family, the men were always good to the women, caring, responsive, protective. Julian shared those qualities. He was close to his family (as was I). In business, he showed himself to be a powerful man, functioning with passion, perseverance, persistence. and assertiveness. And sometimes, when warranted, a ferocious, delicious, and somewhat dangerous, aggressiveness.

He seduced me with his passions—for music, for cars, for theatre, for nature, for love—and for his appreciation of good work. In short, Julian is and was an achiever, and as my husband, Bill, would have said, a *mensch* (that's Jewish for all-around good guy).

How did it begin? After years of sporadically keeping up with each other by phone, email, or texting, our friends started dying. He'd already lost three of his ex-wives: Sheila, who he'd married young and stayed a good friend to until her death in her midyears; Pat, the mother of his first three children, Sally Ann and Michael, who I babysat as youngsters, and Jennifer, who was born after they left for Connecticut; and Laura Ziskin, the trailblazing female film producer and studio head at Fox 2000 Pictures, and mother of his fourth child, Julia.

Their deaths were hard, and way too soon.

Then, we lost Don Calfa. Julian sent me an email after hearing of his passing. It contained one word…"Fuck."

And when Pablo was on his way out of this world and into the next, Julian twice went to see him in Sedona, Arizona, and called to keep me up on his progress.

And, alas, when Bill died, I wrote Julian to tell him the sad news. He wrote to say anything that he might say would seem trite. Instead, he'd come to LA the next week and see me. He came. He took me to the Writer's Guild Theatre to see *The Irishman,* saying people will see us and say, "That hussy, Samantha, Bill is gone and she's already out with a younger man." A quip referring to Bill's age of ninety-seven and his own of eighty-nine. I jokingly said to friends that I had my first date for Saturday night, two weeks after Bill left on October 17, 2019.

I had no idea.

The week of Valentine's Day 2020, Julian was back in town and came over for dinner. He brought me a beautiful bouquet of red roses. Daphne was here to cook for all three of us. We had fun, so he came back again on Saturday night, then went back to New Hampshire, and our communication became more frequent. He expressed his desire to move to LA. He was planning to rent a space in Santa Monica. I said stay here, with me, till you find your new digs, though I was afraid he might be bored stuck in my house during the coronavirus crisis. He confessed then that his top priority was to be close to me.

After a great deal of planning his packing and travels, he sent me this letter, saying in the subject line, "HERE'S THE LETTER I WAS TOO COW-ARDLY TO SEND TO YOU BACK IN APRIL."

Dear Sam,

My mother once told me, "If you suddenly find yourself having feelings for someone...don't make speeches about it." I have never been able to abide by that.

That being the case, I will tell you now how much it means to me to be so in touch with you now. It has eased my sense of aloneness in this Covid pandemic a great deal.

I know we have known each other since 1966 and stayed in touch sporadically, (not to forget The Inflatable Doll), but in many ways I hardly know you. Yet of late, I feel my knowing you has increased greatly as has my appreciation for how centered you have become and how gracefully you are handling the loss of the great love of your life. I've heard you say from time to time that you are trying to "get your bravery back." I would say it's back.

Suddenly you have exposed to me how lonely I have been for so many years. The last time I let my heart out from the cave in which it was sheltering was the most unlikely relationship I had with Veronica (Ronny) when I lived in England, but that was quite a while back and has happily transmogrified into a long-lasting friendship. And since then, I have satisfied myself with non-romantic friendships with a few noteworthy ladies I have met along the way.

I don't know how many years I have left. I come from a family that lives well into their nineties. But with whatever time I have left nothing would make me feel more complete than to be loving you and perhaps if life allows we can stumble on a few "remember whens" together.

All my love,

Julian

P.S. If I actually sent you this letter it would be because I've gotten a bit of bravery back myself, and no this is not actually my handwriting, but I wish it were.

I wrote him back this note:

Julian,

You touch me so deeply. I will read this again and again. I do and will love being loved by you.

Memories hold much magic, and we are sharing that magic. And if the creek don't rise, we can make new ones together.

I confess I still wrestle with fear and anxiety and hope I can live up to the bravery you see in me.

Love that you hold me dear. I love you beyond words. Such surprising awakening in my heart, spirit, mind, and body.

All my love back,

Sam

And so, my dear friends and readers, life goes on, and love goes on.

On Julian's drive to California from New Hampshire he had several adventures.

He left Lee, New Hampshire on June 1, 2020, just at the early months of the Covid pandemic and threaded his way through places reported as the least infected with the virus at that time. He was in Harrisburg, Pennsylvania, that first night, then moved through Knoxville, Tennessee on June 2. From there he passed through Little Rock, Arkansas on June 3, and Amarillo, Texas on June 4.

While on a freeway out West he was stopped by a Highway Patrolman who had clocked him speeding in excess of ninety miles an hour.

"You are the first person that I've stopped from New Hampshire." The policeman was businesslike, but curious.

"I'm glad to be your first," Julian smiled.

"Where are you going?"

"To California."

"What are you going to be doing?"

"Moving there."

"For what reason?" The cop was intrigued.

"A woman," Julian said with laughter in his look.

"Well," said the cop, "I think she'd want you to get there safely. Drive a little slower." He walked away without giving him a ticket.

On June 5, Julian made it to Kingman, Arizona, and on June 6, late in the day, he knocked sweetly on my Beverly Hills front door.

His first words to me were, "Do you think we made a mistake?" with a grin.

"No," I said, kissing and holding him tight.

His phone was out of order on his trip, but every night he'd called me from his hotel. On his days of travels, he'd listen to the radio and memorize his favorite country songs, which he'd sing to me each night while I curled up on my bed and counted the hours till he would arrive.

His favorite lyrics of all the songs being, "Honey I'm almost sober. Can I come back home?" and his other favorite, paraphrased by him from a tired memory after a long drive, "There's a Bible on my dresser and a woman in my bed who shouldn't be there."

Viva Julian. *Je t'aime.*

Julian Barry, the Olivier Theatre (named for the great Laurence Olivier), National Theatre, London (1983)
Photo credit: Nobby Clark

My Night with Orson, Julian Barry's autobiography, published July 2011

Julian Barry "now"

Epilogue

To the Girls Back Home, Elvis, and the Good Times

Every day when I sit down to eat at my dining table, I look into the eyes of eight women smiling back at me from a photograph that was taken at a recent class reunion. The women are holding a banner that reads:

> Harriet (Sam) WE LOVE YOU AND
> MISS YOU!!! GET WELL SOON!
> LOVE!!! (with a heart drawn below
> and an arrow shot through it.)
> Signed:
> TEEN CHARM GIRLS

I'd had a serious bout with illness that caused me to miss our reunion that year—several medical events in sequence, all of which were grave enough to be thought of as life-threatening by some, if not all, of my friends and family sweating them out with me. I'd been scared by nothing at the time; I felt like Superwoman—brave, happy, optimistic, and playful.

But in the weeks that followed being released from the hospital, I found myself feeling fragile, vulnerable, and not able to digest food without pain. I plowed on with physical therapy for six months, until the spirit which had sailed me through the wildness of that storm in the hospital took a major hit.

I'd been blowing the minds of all my therapists progressing well ahead of schedule. Passing memory tests easily, counting backwards from a hundred by sevens. The tester said I was the only patient that she knew of who had made it to zero without an error. I also surprised myself and everyone else by reciting the alphabet backwards without a glitch. When my friend Judy, who took me for those tests, saw me acing them, she turned to the nurse and said, "Shoot, she's fine! If I'm supposed to be able to do that, I'm in trouble!"

So I ventured further. I took an MRI to establish that the bleed in my brain was stable, then with my doctor's help, weaned myself off seizure medication, feeling that was the source of my digestive problems. Three weeks after becoming drug free, the shit hit the fan. In short, I had a seizure.

My only physical injuries were a little crack in a vertebra in my lower back and a small cut in my scalp that happened when I was hurled into our sliding glass door, blacking out as I spun backwards and fell. But the blowout in my brain was more traumatic. It short-circuited a lot of my old rambunctious and confident neuronal patterns. In short, it shook me the fuck up. My driver's license was immediately suspended. I had to take a test three months later to get it back. Bill hired a close friend of ours, Daphne Russom, to drive me and keep me company during those months. I was grateful for her and leaned on her love and generous spirit but felt a bit lost.

In the midst of those confusing times, the package from Mississippi arrived, containing, among other things, the photograph I just mentioned.

There were fourteen girls who were close friends in Batesville, Mississippi, throughout our growing up years. But only nine or so of us were signed up during the summer of '56—or was it '57? to be hauled off once a week to Charm School in Memphis, where we were taught rules of etiquette and the secrets of how to be proper Southern ladies. Our mothers took turns driving us, four or five to a car, and saw to it that we got to class in one piece. We always managed, however, to maneuver them into letting us make a few stops along the way, to and from classes on how to cross our ankles (not our legs), to walk with a book balanced on our heads, to handle our knives and forks correctly, and to hold a teacup with a bit of *savoir faire*.

At that time, Elvis Presley had just purchased a home on Highway 51 called Graceland. That was long before the highway was renamed Elvis Presley Boulevard and before lavish modifications were made to his home, which would someday include a fieldstone wall around the property and a wrought-iron, music-themed gate.

Also, before commercial buildings were added at the foot of the hill across the highway, complete with a gift shop, a café, and ticket offices.

But during our charm school days, Elvis's home was simple; the influence of Las Vegas wasn't adding its sweat and glitter, and security wasn't all that tight. In fact, it was nonexistent. The property had no fence at all, only a muddy ditch to crawl through in our high heels and sheer hose, although every time we made it up to his house, there seemed to be nobody home (though one in our group, Joanne, distinctly remembers us talking to his Uncle Vester). That, however, didn't stop us from collecting souvenirs. We found a newspaper on his doorstep once and tore tiny pieces off its edges and tucked them away in our purses. We even took blades of grass and small scraps of paint from where it was peeling near his windowsills. Some of us collected little vials of water from his swimming pool. And according to Joanne's memory, we collected small pieces of the carpet that was being installed one day when Uncle Vester let us in.

Later we'd arrive in class a little muddy and out of breath, sporting smirks, elbowing each other and whispering fantasies with dreamy eyes.

One of my dearest friends from those days and, of course, until still now, Diane, reminded me recently when she visited California with her husband, Jimmy Eubanks, of how I reacted when Elvis was drafted. She said she met me in the hall of the high school between classes to find me crying hard, sobbing, completely out of control. She said, "Harriet, what on Earth is wrong?" According to her, I wailed, "Haven't you heard? They are sending Elvis off to war! They're only doing it because they know we like him!" She tried to comfort me by saying that he'd be back someday, but I was inconsolable. I choked back tears but blurted out, "NO! They'll keep him over there FOREVER!"

Others prodded me to remember our very serious letter-writing campaign to the president (or maybe it was the chairman of the Armed Forces) begging them not to cut off Elvis's hair. We were heartbroken to think they might shave away the soft, shiny, black tresses that hung over his forehead when he sang.

The truth is, we were all a little boy-crazy— I more than most—and when I published part of this story on my blog, the Charm Girls read it and asked me to not forget certain tales I'd left out along the way.

The best of those tales was of Coach Toy Tedford.

Darling Mary Francis, who we lost to cancer a few years ago, this one's for you.

Coach Tedford was my homeroom teacher during my freshman year in high school. He also taught algebra I. He was a tall drink of water, with black hair, killer dimple-like creases in his cheeks, blue languid eyes, and a wry sense of humor. All the girls were more or less in love with him, but I was a complete goner. My song that year was "Born Too Late," and I cried bitter tears singing it and daydreaming about the man I could never have because I was too young for him and he was way too old for me.

This was the year before my mother retired from teaching at Batesville High, which she did in order to not cramp my style, opting instead to work out the rest of her career in the nearby rural community of Crowder, Mississippi. But while I was still in the ninth grade and not officially a high schooler, she roamed the halls and kept her eye on me. She was forever passing by Coach Tedford's open door and catching me draped across his desk flirting with him.

Toward the end of the year, a rumor went around the school that "Coach" would be a counselor at the 4H Club Camp at the Sardis Dam the following summer. There was a stampede of girls signing up to be 4H Club members, and I was leading the herd. We went to 4H meetings and when the time neared, packed our gear and drove out to Sardis Lake and the camp. Mary Frances reminded me that we were lost and running out of gas and that someone had told us we could make the gas last longer if we turned on the windshield wipers. We did. I doubt that it helped our mileage much, but it was good for a laugh to see a car full of girls driving with our windshield wipers on in sunny, dry daylight.

As for camp, it was a pretty uneventful week. Coach Tedford behaved himself properly, and so did all of us girls. We honored the Four H's—head, heart, hands, and health—like the truly good citizens that we were.

But on our last night, I went out and sat on a grassy bank under the stars. After a while, Coach Tedford came out and sat about twenty yards away from me. We never said a word to each other. But it was enough to have him there with me under the tiny sliver of moonlight. My dream was fulfilled.

I would always remember stargazing on a beautiful night with that dreamboat of a guy, the love of my fantasy life.

Sweet and honorable man and a true gentleman.

And I'll always remember my girlfriends of that time, how close we were as we played and competed in talent shows and beauty pageants. And fought to become majorettes and cheerleaders.

And homecoming queens and their courts, and actors in our school plays.

But most of all, how we loved each other from the cradle to the grave that two of us have already found.

And how we still love and treasure our shared memories.

"Teen Charm Girls," left to right: Johnny Lou Marshall, Sue Evans Lobrano Womble, Peggy O'Neal Young, Ann Saxton Trusty, Betty Jane Seales, Mary Francis Harmon Woods, Claudia Phillipy, Diane Breedlove Eubanks

Acknowledgments

I'd like to gratefully acknowledge the artists, teachers, writers, metaphysicians, magicians, and friends who have helped me write and publish this book. To the members of our Artists for Artist group, including Melissa Converse, who first invited me to join; Steve Harris, who originated the group; Todd Waring, an amazing writer, actor, friend and editor; Jeff Austin, who made me commit to developing my blog into what has become this book; Hillel a.k.a. Mr. Balloon Man, who cheered me on; and Jaclyn Rose Bernstein, a genius writer and listener to my readings and contributor to excerpts of these writings.

To the members of our metaphysicians' Caldron group, Grif Griffis, Veronica Thompson, Sue Kiel Seeff, Marilyn Winfield, Merle Morgan, Carrie West Knight, Lori Leyden, and again, Melissa Converse, brilliant poet and healer in her own right.

To my closest and most intimate friends, Grif Griffis, Mary Dorn, Judy Kerr, Daphne Russom, and Veronica Thompson who listened and heard the heart in my work, giving me courage and joy in my process.

Also to Barry Strugatz for his amazing Foreword for this book and to Julian Barry, Elena Yates Eulo, Joan Darling, Judy Kerr, and Del Shores for the powerful blurbs on my cover. I also owe Julian for his sensational suggestion for a "hook" at the beginning before plowing into the body of my childhood, where I came from, and the miracle of where my destiny led me.

I thank Jack Mulholland, my "Photo Archivist" for the great pictures in the book, and to Norman Seeff, who provided the exquisite photo for the cover of this book.

I owe a special thanks to Diane Breedlove Eubanks and Peggy O'Neal Young who helped me find pictures of the girls back home in Mississippi.

And to my faithful "fairy" editor, CJ Schepers, for her dedication to my manuscript and all the extra research along the way that added such exquisite details, as well as to Jennifer Mola, my book designer, for creating the cover and a divine layout, including enhancing those well-aged photos with her brilliant touch.

And most of all, my deepest and heartfelt gratitude goes to Bill Macy, for our long, deeply fulfilling and happy marriage, and to Julian Barry, who picked up the pieces of my widow's broken heart and helped to make it strong and whole, sharing with me more love and happiness than any woman could ever hope for, and helping me learn to laugh again.

About the Author

Samantha Harper Macy is an actress, writer, poet, and teacher. She appeared in the Broadway, off-Broadway, San Francisco, and film versions of *Oh! Calcutta!* and in two films directed by Hal Ashby, *Bound for Glory* and *Lookin' to Get Out.* She was also a series regular on the hit late-night television comedy soap, *Mary Hartman, Mary Hartman*, guested often on TV shows for two decades, and taught acting in Los Angeles for seven years, coaching such stars as Jon Voight and Paul Michael Glaser. Her poetry includes a compilation of intimate poems entitled *Loving Men*, which was the genesis for this book. Her interest in metaphysics and esoteric knowledge within ancient and New Age traditions has led her to explorations of Science of Mind, Buddhism, the Kabbalah, and Western Mysticism. Those passions and her joy in celebrating her blessings have led her to author *Naked in Oh! Calcutta! and Other Stories: A Memoir.* She was happily married to actor Bill Macy for forty-nine years and is currently enjoying a second great love with a longtime and (who'd a thunk it?) eternal friend, Julian Barry, author and Academy Award nominee for the movie, *Lenny.*